KINGSPORT SPEEDWAY

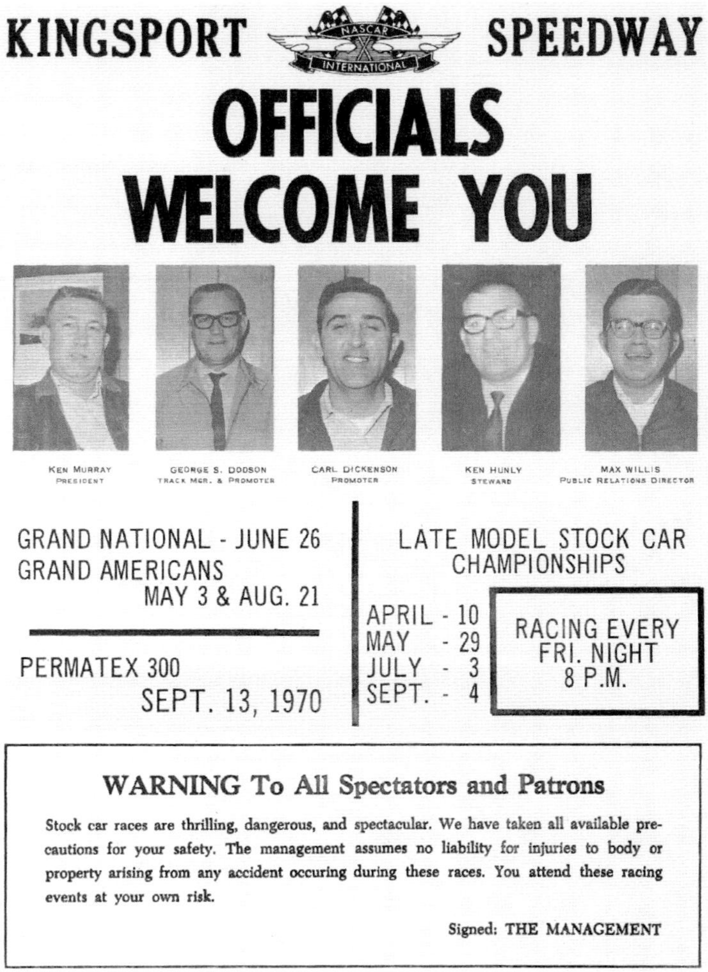

KINGSPORT SPEEDWAY

NASCAR INTERNATIONAL

OFFICIALS WELCOME YOU

Ken Murray President	George S. Dodson Track Mgr. & Promoter	Carl Dickenson Promoter	Ken Hunly Steward	Max Willis Public Relations Director

GRAND NATIONAL - JUNE 26
GRAND AMERICANS
MAY 3 & AUG. 21

PERMATEX 300
SEPT. 13, 1970

LATE MODEL STOCK CAR CHAMPIONSHIPS

APRIL - 10
MAY - 29
JULY - 3
SEPT. - 4

RACING EVERY FRI. NIGHT 8 P.M.

WARNING To All Spectators and Patrons

Stock car races are thrilling, dangerous, and spectacular. We have taken all available precautions for your safety. The management assumes no liability for injuries to body or property arising from any accident occuring during these races. You attend these racing events at your own risk.

Signed: THE MANAGEMENT

A page from a 1970 Kingsport Speedway program shows the men responsible for the track, including owner Ken Murray and original promoter George Dodson. The page also has information about upcoming events. There is a stern warning that auto racing can be dangerous, even for spectators, and that management assumes no liability for their safety. (Courtesy of Tony Morton.)

FRONT COVER: Hometown driver Gene Glover won Kingsport Speedway's first race and its first championship, and he became one of its biggest stars. Glover claimed the 1979 NASCAR Late Model Sportsman national title. (Photograph by Ray Taylor, courtesy of Robbie Henry.)

COVER BACKGROUND: The speedway complex has grown substantially over the years, as shown in this aerial view. (Photograph by Randall Perry.)

BACK COVER: A field of late-model stock cars cues up to race under the lights at the "Concrete Jungle." (Photograph by Randall Perry.)

KINGSPORT SPEEDWAY

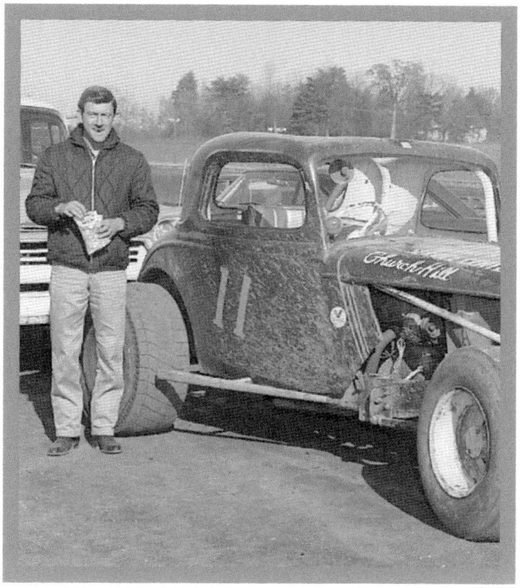

David M. McGee

ARCADIA PUBLISHING

ISBN 978-1-4671-1465-3

Published by Arcadia Publishing
Charleston, South Carolina

Printed in the United States of America

Library of Congress Control Number: 2015934979

For all general information, please contact Arcadia Publishing:
Telephone 843-853-2070
Fax 843-853-0044
E-mail sales@arcadiapublishing.com
For customer service and orders:
Toll-Free 1-888-313-2665

Visit us on the Internet at www.arcadiapublishing.com

This book is dedicated to all of the competitors, fans, and officials who have made and continue to make Kingsport Speedway one of the nation's most historically significant racing venues.

CONTENTS

ACKNOWLEDGMENTS

The author gratefully acknowledges the enthusiastic support of Kingsport Speedway promoter Karen Tunnell, owner Joe Loven, and track operators Keith Stiltner and Ervin Stiltner. Without their desire to help preserve this unique slice of American auto-racing history and heritage, information might have remained forever scattered on the wind.

Documenting 50 years is a massive undertaking when accurate records are scant. Saying "thank you" cannot begin to express my appreciation to Robert Walden, John A. Utsman, Randall Perry, Tony Morton, Kenny Hunley, Robbie Henry, Chris Haverly, Melvin Corum, Rusty and Beth Clendenin, Jeff Birchfield, and David Allio, whose recollections, photographs, and insight proved invaluable while preparing this work.

In addition, thanks also go to John Beach, Drew Hierwarter, Michael Moats, the Murray family, Mike O'Dell, and Ray Taylor for their photographs—as well as to some unidentified photographers whose images document moments in time.

Special thanks go to Debbie Helton for her support and encouragement and to fellow author and friend Joe Tennis, who always provided great advice.

My appreciation goes out to all of the drivers, track staff, fans, and others who shared memories and words of encouragement.

A thank-you goes to the folks at East Tennessee State University's Charles Sherrod Library for invaluable access to long-forgotten nuances buried on decades-old microfilm. And my undying gratitude goes to the former sportswriters of the *Kingsport Times News* and *Bristol Herald Courier*, who faithfully documented races—especially my friends Kenny Bruce, Bill Lane, and the late, great Denny Darnell.

Finally, a huge thank-you goes to everyone at Arcadia Publishing, especially Maggie Bullwinkel, for her support and guidance. This is our third project together and, I believe, some of our best work.

INTRODUCTION

Soon after opening in 1965, Kingsport Speedway gained the nickname the "Action Track." In the 1970s, promoters billed it as the "Track of Champions." Most recently, it goes by the nickname "Concrete Jungle." The track's proper name has also changed multiple times, including the following: Kingsport International Speedway, Raceland Kingsport, Kingsport Motor Speedway, New Kingsport Speedway, and Galaxy Kingsport Speedway. It reverted to its original moniker in 1996.

The changes in names typically signified changes in everything from ownership to promoters to track surfaces—and sometimes all three at once. Not unlike hundreds of other short tracks from coast to coast, Kingsport was converted from dirt to asphalt, then back to dirt. It became concrete in 1996. Remaining financially viable often meant finding new ways to attract fans.

When it opened as a high-banked, quarter-mile oval in 1965, a half-dozen other racetracks operated within an hour's drive, and an estimated 2,500 tracks served up speed in nearly every corner of the United States. Today, 50 years later, that number has diminished as tracks succumb to encroaching urbanization, higher land values, noise complaints, and, all too frequently, slumping support due primarily to a range of economic pressures. That Kingsport's speedway remains viable after experiencing its share of bumps earns the venerable track one more title: survivor.

Construction-company owner Ken Murray was enamored with auto racing and fancied the idea of building and operating a racetrack. So, in 1963, he purchased a hillside of shale and limestone a mile north of Kingsport's Stone Drive and began carving out his racetrack. After two years and $100,000 of construction, Murray described his track as "the highest-banked quarter-mile we know of." The facility had lights for night racing, paved entrance roads, ample parking, and a wooden grandstand seating 3,000.

In 1968, Murray invested another $450,000 to improve and expand nearly every aspect. The track surface was extended, and grandstands to accommodate 12,000 were installed. Those upgrades coincided with a name change to Kingsport International Speedway and sanction from the National Association of Stock Car Automobile Racing (NASCAR), an organization based in Daytona Beach, Florida, that was expanding from coast to coast.

The following year brought a new asphalt racing surface, more safety improvements, and additional upgrades as the track saw the first of three annual appearances by NASCAR's premier Grand National series. That series was rebranded Winston Cup in 1971 and made its final visit to Kingsport that May as part of a drastic reduction of races at smaller venues, required by new series sponsor R.J. Reynolds Tobacco. An October Cup race was canceled.

Despite that loss, Murray remained with NASCAR, and the track became a national showcase for its Late Model Sportsman cars. In the 1970s, East Tennessee drivers captured three national championships, and another half-dozen titles went to drivers who made regular visits to Kingsport's victory lane. This form of racing became so popular that NASCAR promoted those cars to their own national touring series in 1982. But the creation of what became known as the Busch Series again left smaller, local tracks like Kingsport behind. The track floundered after losing its signature class, but a dramatic change was on the horizon.

Jim "J.D." Stacy, a flamboyant former NASCAR premier series team owner and sponsor from Kentucky, left that segment of the sport after the 1983 season. Stacy began acquiring and leasing Southeastern short tracks, with plans to establish a circuit of high-profile, high-paying dirt-track races. In the spring of 1984, he completed a deal to lease Kingsport and established his company offices at the track. Red clay soon replaced Kingsport's worn-out macadam surface, kicking off a decade of mud-slinging action.

While Stacy's venture faded quickly, many other promoters tried steering the show, with varying degrees of success. During this time, Kingsport hosted several national dirt touring series races, attracting the biggest names from that segment of the sport. Murray grew weary of the enterprise after nearly 30 years and sold the track to Joe Loven, a Kingsport businessman and former NASCAR race team owner. After a couple of less-than-successful stabs at dirt racing, Loven turned to his primary business, Loven Ready-Mix Concrete, for a solution.

Kingsport became one of only a handful of concrete oval tracks in the nation, and its 1996 rebirth included a return to NASCAR sanction for its weekly racing programs. Some years were financially better than others, but Loven ultimately shut the gates after the 2002 season to focus on operating his Volunteer Speedway, a nearby dirt oval.

The saga might have ended there. Kingsport's speedway remained silent for seven long seasons, sparking widespread speculation that the property would ultimately be sold and converted into something else. That all changed in late 2009.

Kerry and Wink Bodenhamer, promoters of the United Auto Racing Association (UARA), had their season finale rained out and needed a neutral site to stage a single race in early November. They called longtime friend Loven, who agreed to host the event. Track officials spent a couple of weeks cleaning up and trimming brush. Despite cool temperatures and little advance publicity, the show attracted respectable numbers in terms of both fans and competitors. Based on that success, Bodenhamer and Loven agreed to schedule two races at Kingsport in 2010. It seemed the old track still had a pulse.

Among those in attendance was Robert Pressley, a former NASCAR premier series driver whose son Coleman raced with UARA. He had entered a number of business ventures since retiring from driving and decided to bring Kingsport all the way back. Pressley reopened the track in 2011, returned to NASCAR sanction, and offered a full complement of racing events and divisions. He promoted the track for three seasons before stepping aside to pursue other interests.

Virginia racers Ervin and Keith Stiltner quickly filled that void, anxious to build on the track's newfound momentum. They hired longtime race official Karen Tunnell to manage the operations at both Kingsport and Lonesome Pine Raceway in nearby Coeburn, Virginia. Their efforts sparked continued growth.

Throughout its considerable history, Kingsport has hosted dozens of nationally recognized champions, regardless of track surface or era. Of NASCAR's 50 all-time greatest drivers, 20 have raced—and many won—at Kingsport. Among the drivers, crew chiefs, and car owners enshrined by the International Motorsports Hall of Fame in Talladega, Alabama, more than 20 competed at Kingsport at some time in their careers. Among the first six classes inducted into the NASCAR Hall of Fame in Charlotte, North Carolina, 11 turned laps or owned cars that competed at Kingsport. And more than 25 inductees into the National Dirt Late Model Hall of Fame in Florence, Kentucky, competed—and often won—at Kingsport.

Track of Champions? More like Track of Legends.

1

The Early Years

Auto racing was a wildfire sweeping across East Tennessee in the summer of 1965.

Bristol showcased its NASCAR oval and a new drag strip; NASCAR's Grand National series raced in nearby Maryville; and racetracks dotted the countryside from Chinquapin to Chattanooga. Against that backdrop, Kenneth Murray opened his steeply banked, quarter-mile dirt oval on June 12, 1965. More than 3,000 fans came out to watch 15 race cars, and they loved the action.

Every week, fans filled the wooden grandstands to watch a gaggle of modified coupes—prewar machines with wide tires, primitive steering, and unmuffled engines—race for a $300 top prize. The cars were fast and difficult to drive; many slammed into or soared over the guardrails encircling the track. "We've had more than 25,000 in attendance," Murray claimed that August after just eight races.

Earning much of the early acclaim were hometown hero Gene Glover, former NASCAR Grand National and convertible series regulars Bill Morton and Ken "Bear" Hunley, future NASCAR driver John A. Utsman, and Paul Gose. Glover was crowned track champion in 1965 and 1966.

Cars and competition evolved quickly, as fuel injection replaced carburetors and most cars sported large overhead wings to help drivers deftly power-slide through the turns. "Fuel injection was expensive. When Kingsport went to fuel injection, that was the end of the modifieds," Utsman recalled.

The 1967 season was brutal. The cars of Glover and Hunley were seriously damaged after flying out of the track, and the speedway suffered its lone on-track fatality. Kingsport driver Adel Shaheen had slowed after finishing fifth in an August heat race when his tires became tangled with another machine. When Shaheen's car flipped, his seat belts failed, and he was thrown onto the track and struck by another car.

Glover suffered a blown engine during the season's final race and lost a heated battle with Bill Morton and Georgian Buck Simmons for the 1967 title. Morton scored enough points to surpass Glover, while the 21-year-old Simmons won both 50-lap features and finished third in points.

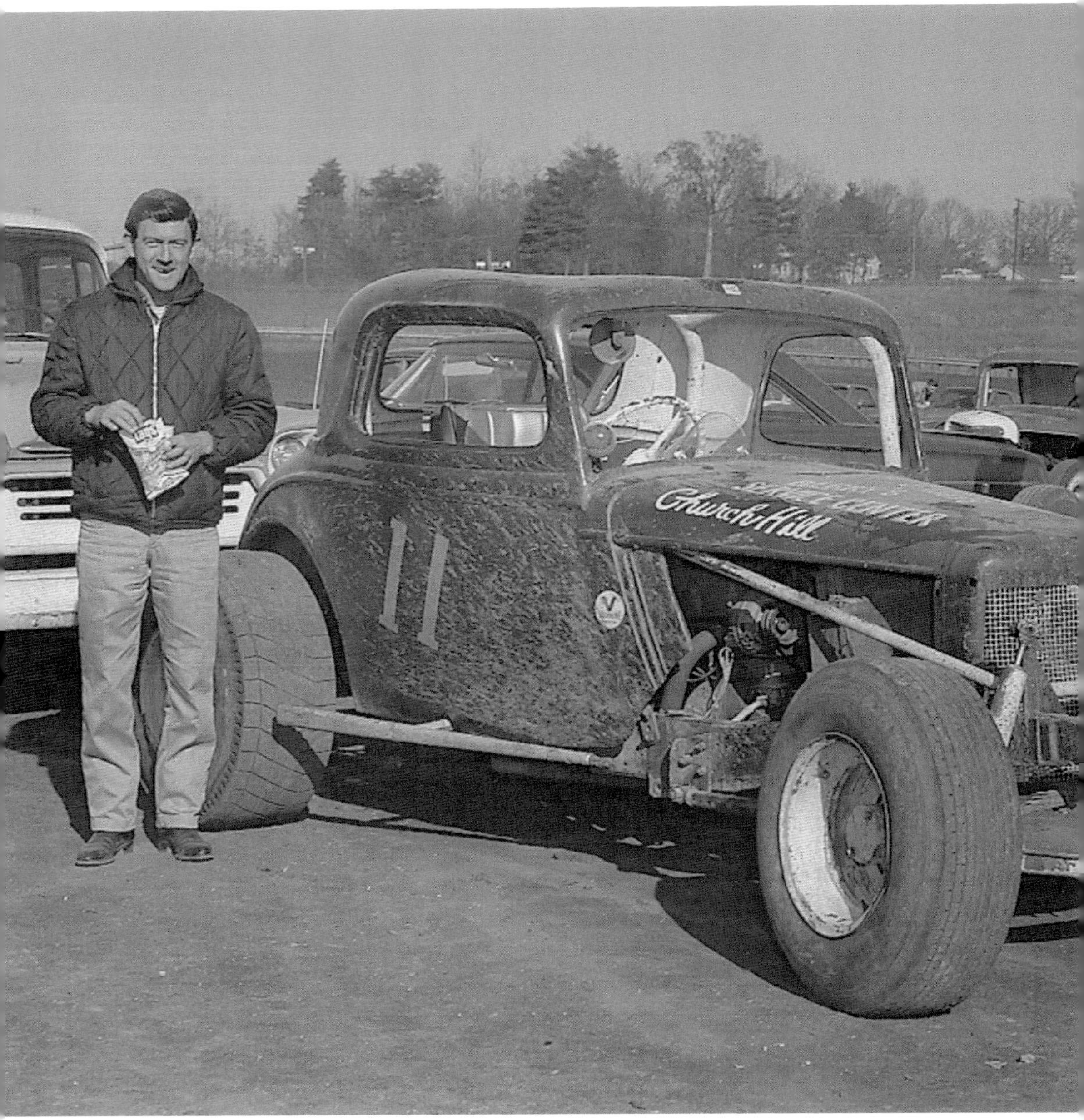

Gene Glover of Kingsport, Tennessee, poses beside his modified coupe. He won consecutive Kingsport Speedway championships in 1965 and 1966. The home-built car won more than a dozen 50-lap feature races in that two-year span. Despite a midseason crash in 1967, Glover still led that season's points entering the final race. A blown engine prevented Glover from contending for a third straight title. But he came back to claim the 1968 track and NASCAR Tennessee state Modified championships over 1967 track champion Bill Morton. (Photograph by Ray Taylor, courtesy of Robbie Henry.)

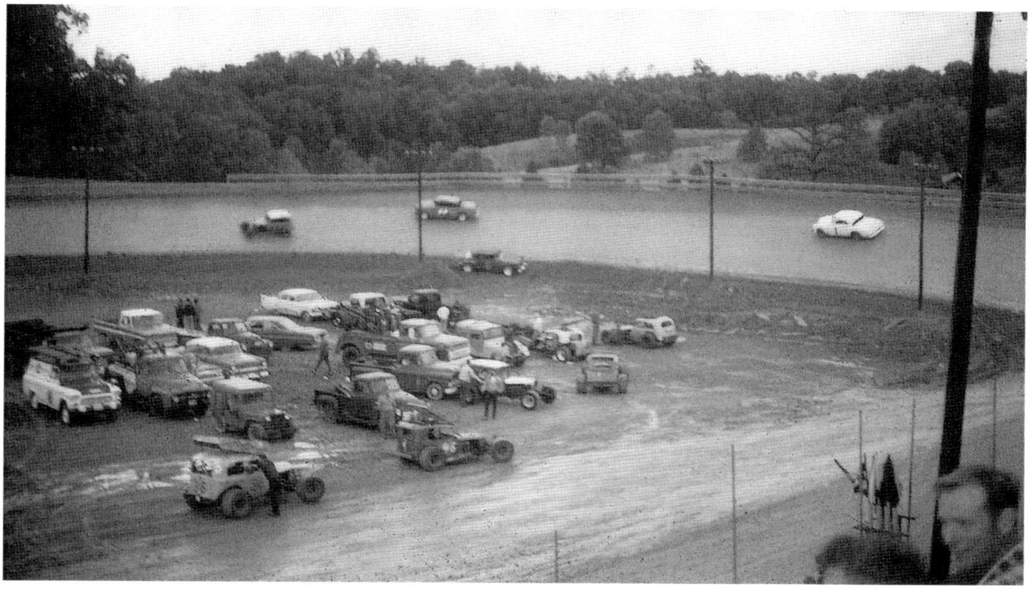

A modified coupe shares turn two of Kingsport Speedway with hobby stock cars during a prerace practice session. On pit road, two other modified drivers wait for their chance to practice. The track's original configuration was a quarter-mile dirt oval with banked turns. Those early races attracted between 20 and 40 competitors and thousands of racing fans from across Northeast Tennessee and Southwest Virginia. (Courtesy of Tony Morton.)

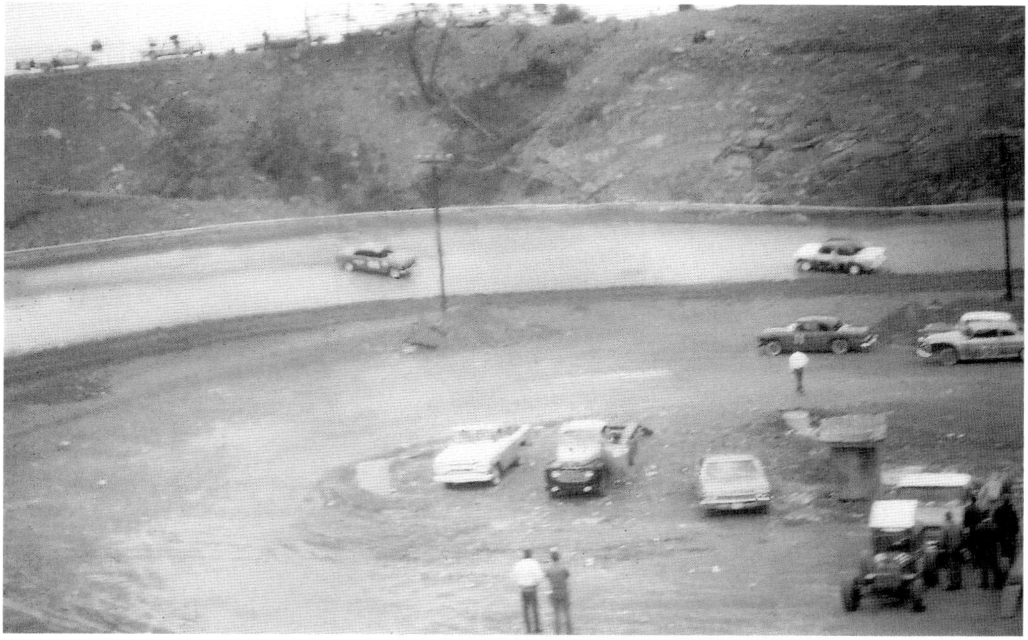

A hobby stock car driven by Rudy Arnold spins out at the entrance to turn three, while an unidentified approaching driver slams on the brakes to avoid being collected. The bulky hobby cars provided a less-expensive way for drivers to compete and hone their skills. (Courtesy of Tony Morton.)

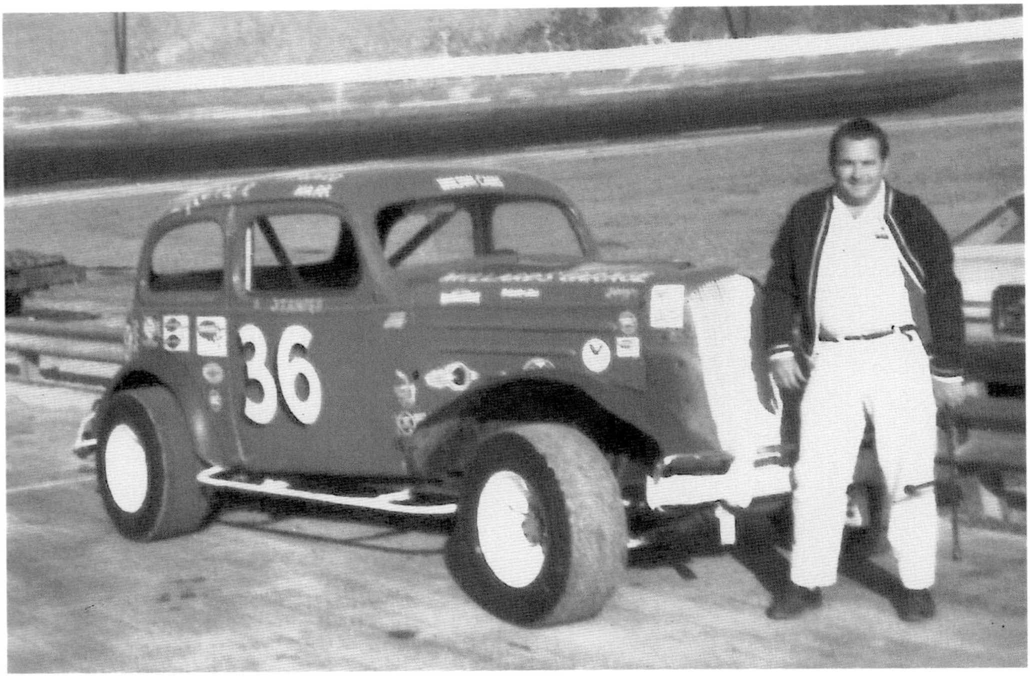

Veteran East Tennessee racer Millard Harr drove his 1936 Chevrolet coupe (No. 36) to a track-qualifying record in Kingsport's Cadet division in 1965 that stood for three years. He finished fourth in the 1967 points standings and was awarded the Best Appearing Car trophy, then continued racing after the track was paved. (Courtesy of Rusty and Beth Clendenin.)

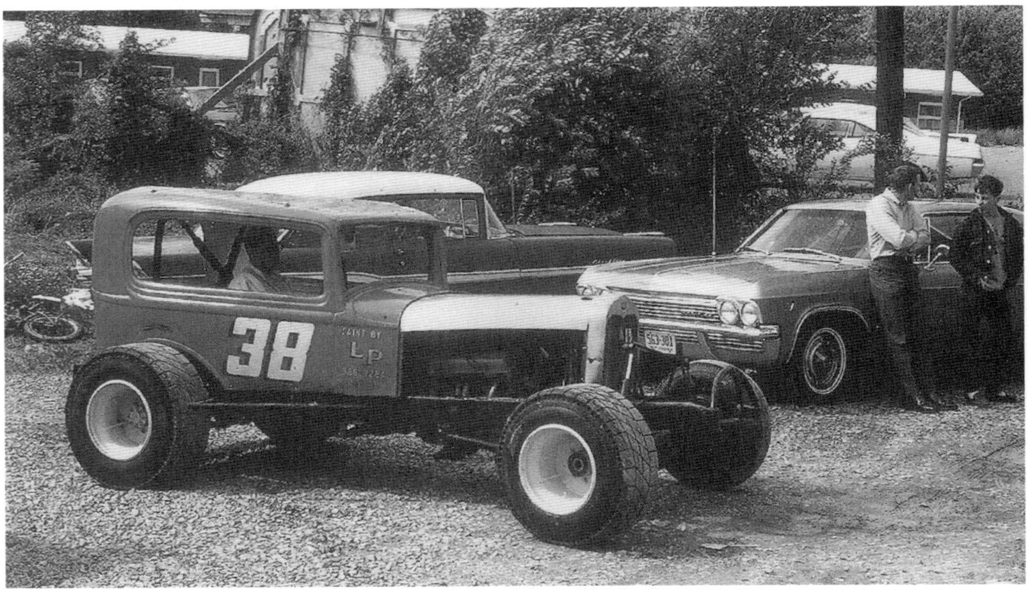

This beautiful red-and-yellow modified was driven by J.D. McMurray of Kingsport. Cars of that era had no power steering, lots of horsepower, and were relatively lightweight, which made them incredibly hard to drive. Drivers sat in the car's center and were protected only by a rudimentary roll bar, seat belt, and helmet. (Courtesy of Tony Morton.)

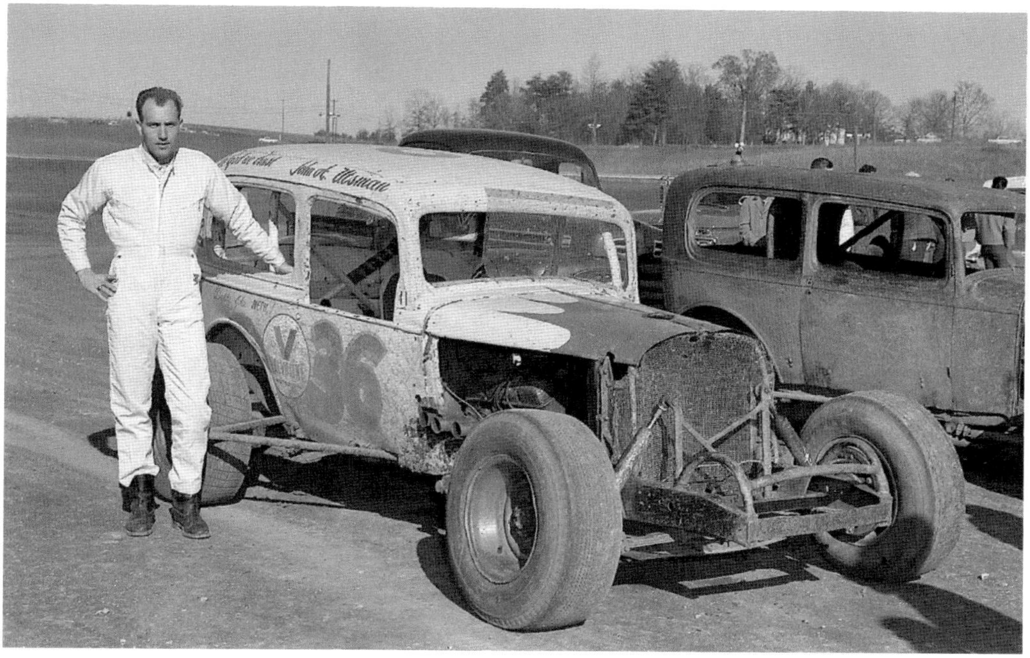

John A. Utsman of Bluff City, Tennessee, enjoyed considerable success at Kingsport Speedway through four decades of racing. Utsman, whose entire family was involved in the sport, began driving in 1960. He was the fastest qualifier on Kingsport's opening night, won regularly in this yellow modified coupe, and set the track qualifying record on numerous occasions. (Photograph by Ray Taylor, courtesy of Robbie Henry.)

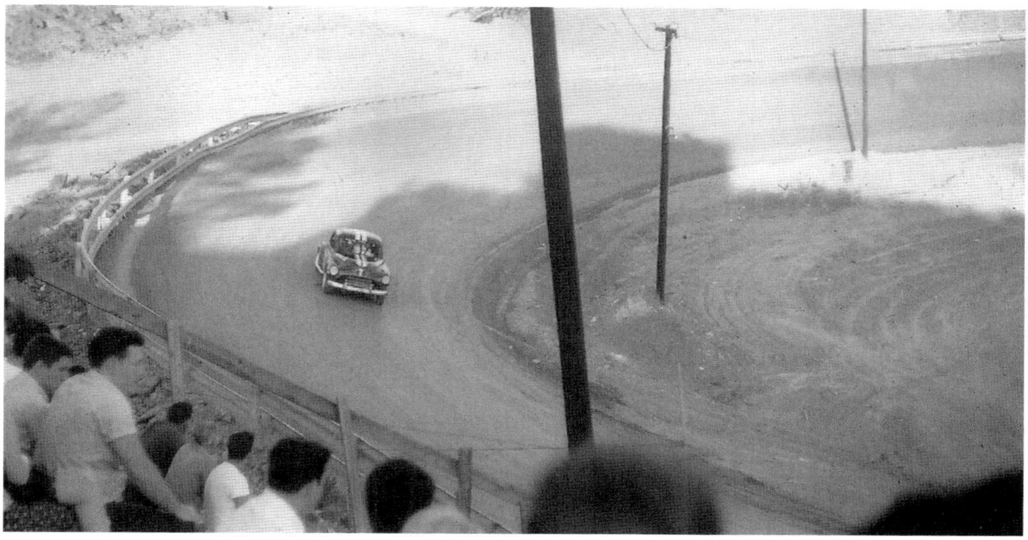

Jim Agee, also known as the "Bounty Hunter," steers his six-cylinder 1952 Chevrolet through turn four at Kingsport Speedway as a large crowd looks on in 1967. Agee, who lived in Kingsport, captured three consecutive Hobby class titles from 1966 to 1968. In the background is evidence of Ken Murray's work to expand the track from a quarter mile to three-eighths of a mile. (Courtesy of Tony Morton.)

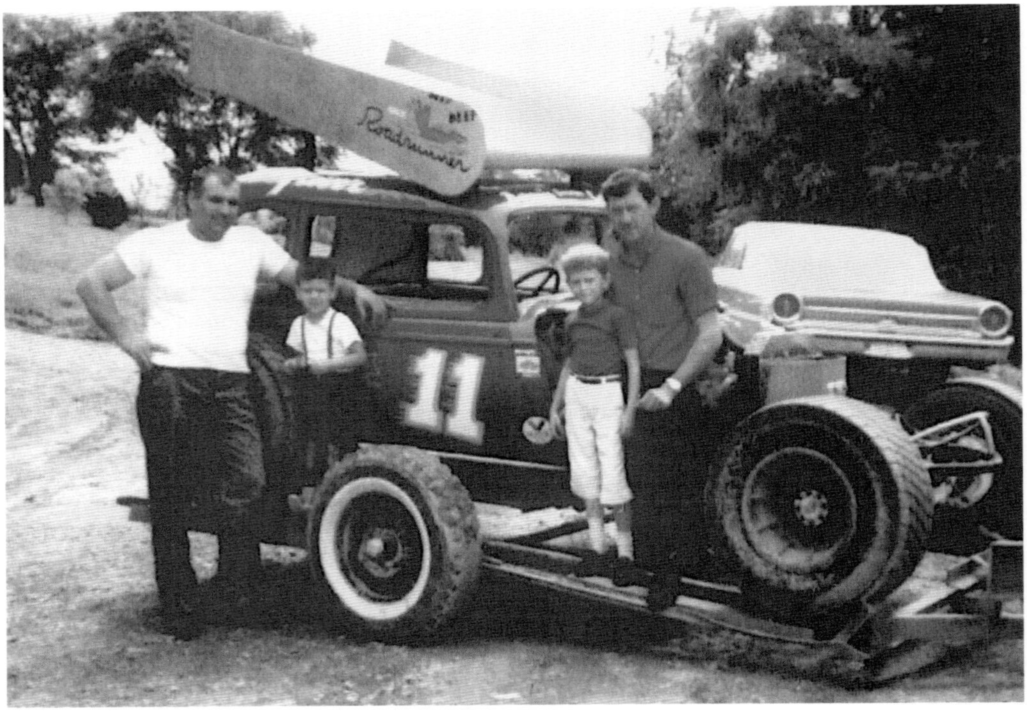

Legendary Kingsport competitors and teammates pose beside the No. 11 modified of Gene Glover. At left are Ken "Bear" Hunley and his son Kenny. On the right are Glover and his son Tony. Hunley is regarded as one of the most innovative racers of his era, winning four straight national titles as a crew chief. Glover was among the most successful, with a national driving championship and hundreds of race wins. Both sons now work for NASCAR after lengthy careers as crew members. (Courtesy of Tony Morton.)

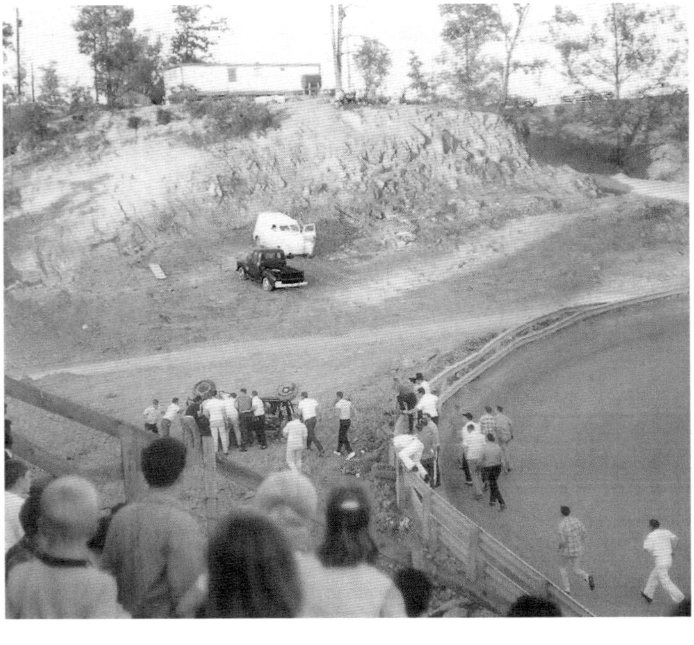

Crew members and officials rush to check on Gene Glover after his modified coupe sailed over the turn four guardrail and out of the racetrack during the 1967 season. Glover was uninjured and back in competition that night. His teammate, Ken Hunley, suffered a similar crash a few weeks later, sailing an estimated 100 feet through the air and crashing outside the third turn. (Courtesy of Tony Morton.)

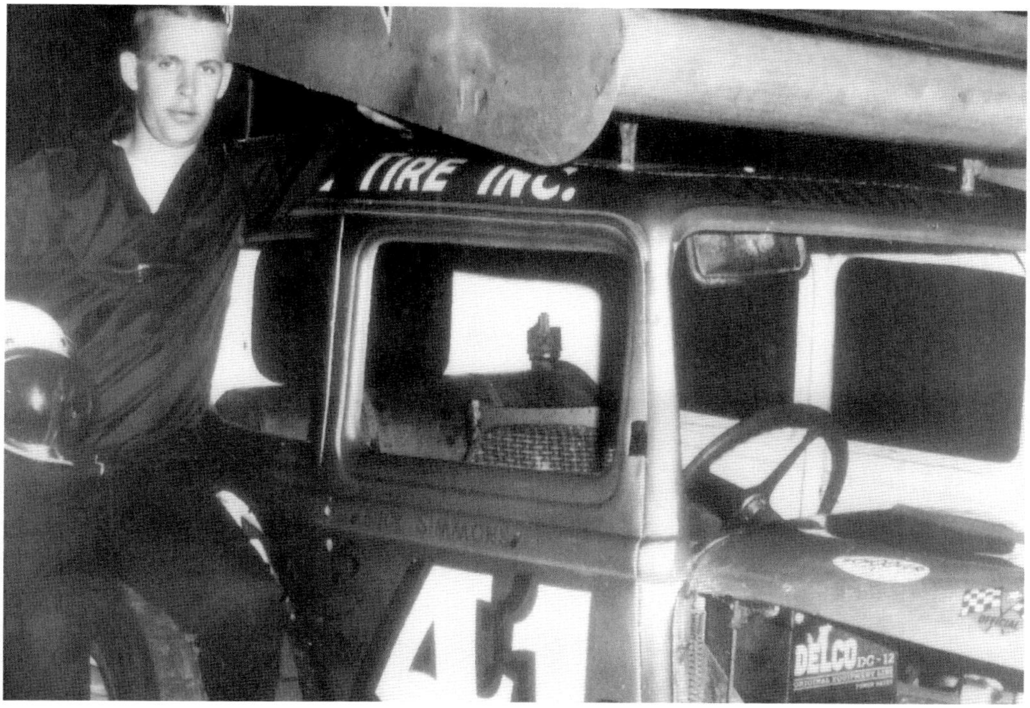

Youthful Chuck Leroy "Buck" Simmons (above) won 10 Kingsport Speedway feature races during regular weekly treks from Georgia in 1967. Promoters billed the youthful Simmons as a teenager, but he actually turned 21 in July 1967. He began racing at age 14 and amassed more than 1,000 feature victories during his legendary career. Below, a large crowd looks on as Simmons slings his winged modified into Kingsport Speedway's first turn during a qualifying lap. (Above, courtesy of Melvin Corum; below, courtesy of Tony Morton.)

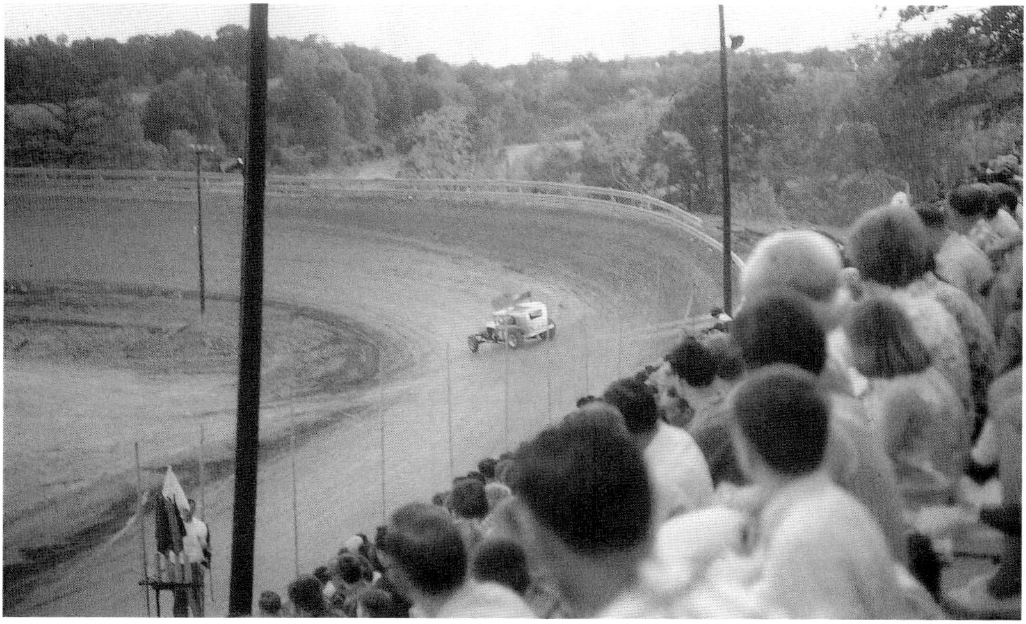

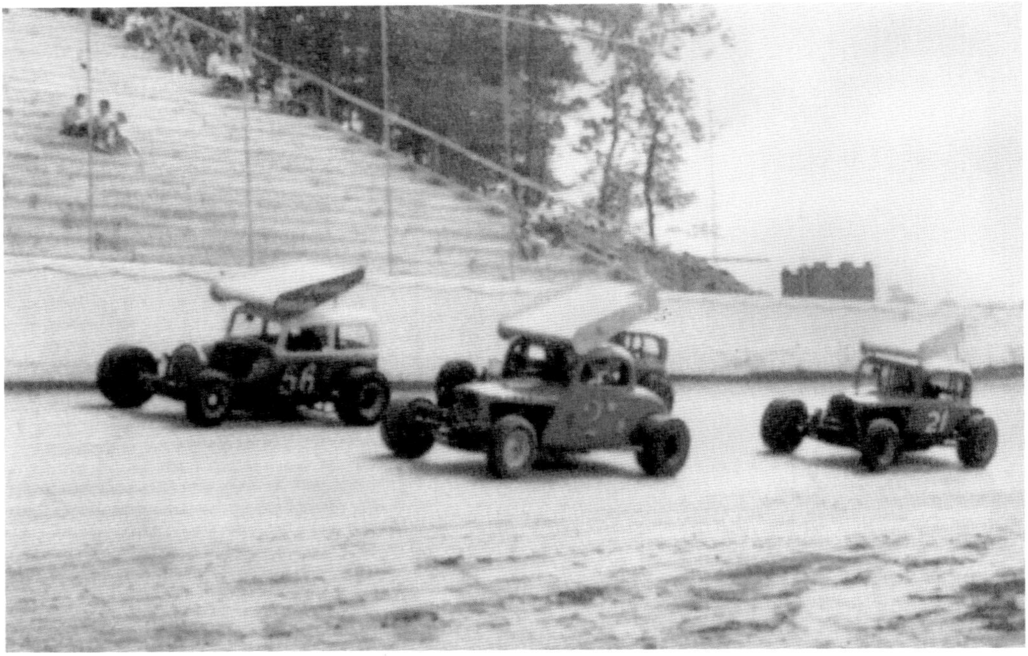

The field forms up for a modified heat race at Kingsport Speedway in 1968, the final year for weekly modified action. Pictured here are Junior Fickle (No. 2), Bill Morton (No. 56), Herb "Tootle" Estes (No. 21), and Gene Glover (No. 11). Glover defeated Morton for the season title. In the background are the new concrete bleachers and concrete retaining wall that were part of a substantial track-improvement program. (Courtesy of Tony Morton.)

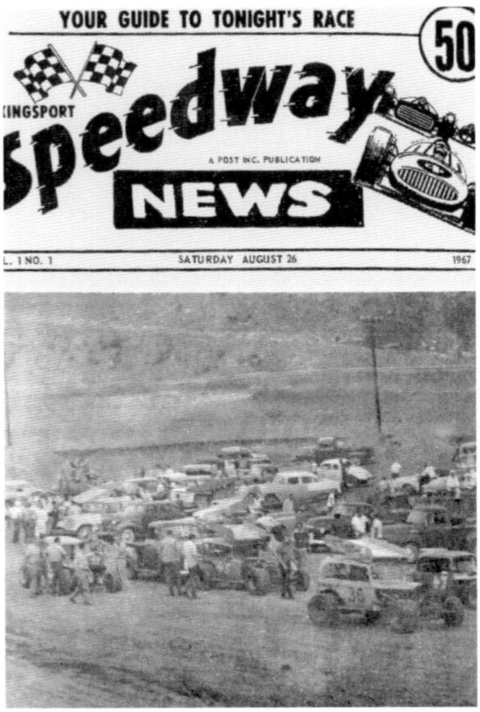

This is the cover of the track's first souvenir program/newsletter. *Kingsport Speedway News* premiered near the end of the season in August 1967. The first issue includes a story about Gene Glover winning a furious duel with Buck Simmons to take the 50-lap feature race, a photograph of Ken Hunley's damaged car after a serious crash, a story about driver Junior "Slim" Kinsler, and points standings. (Courtesy of Tony Morton.)

2

Kingsport's Golden Era

Flush with early success, Kingsport Speedway owner Ken Murray wanted to raise his track's profile, and his template was the nearby Bristol Speedway. With its NASCAR sanction and massive facing concrete grandstands filled with crowds of 18,000 for premier series races, Bristol provided Murray's inspiration.

Between late 1967 and spring 1969, Murray invested $450,000 to create concrete grandstands along the front stretch and backstretch, expanded and ultimately paved the racing surface, and made other improvements. He received NASCAR sanction in January 1968. The ensuing 14-year stretch was truly Kingsport Speedway's golden era.

In June 1969, a crowd of 8,500 came out on a Thursday night to see Richard Petty, David Pearson, and other Grand National stars run the Kingsport 250. Bobby Isaac won the pole and led early, but his engine expired, and Petty drove a Ford to his 95th career victory. Petty dominated in 1970, qualifying fastest in a Plymouth and leading most of the 297 laps, in a race that attracted 6,200 fans. "It was a little third of a mile with rough asphalt," Petty recalled years later. "We had some tire problems but we also won there."

Petty experienced those problems in 1971, and Bobby Isaac dominated the 300-lap race. Run for the first time on a Sunday afternoon, the race attracted more than 8,000, according to media reports. An October race was canceled, and the series never returned. "We had to keep up and things had to change, so places like Kingsport got pushed to the side. The little guys got cut out and some of the racing like we used to do got cut out," Petty said.

But NASCAR's Late Model Sportsman cars took center stage, and Kingsport races consistently attracted the nation's best drivers. "Kingsport was as tough as any place in the country, and I ran at them all," five-time national champion Jack Ingram said. "You had all the guys who traveled and the locals were all good." Among them was John A. Utsman, who said, "Kingsport, when everybody ran over there, had to be the best racing that's ever been—anywhere. I'm just thankful I got to be a part of it."

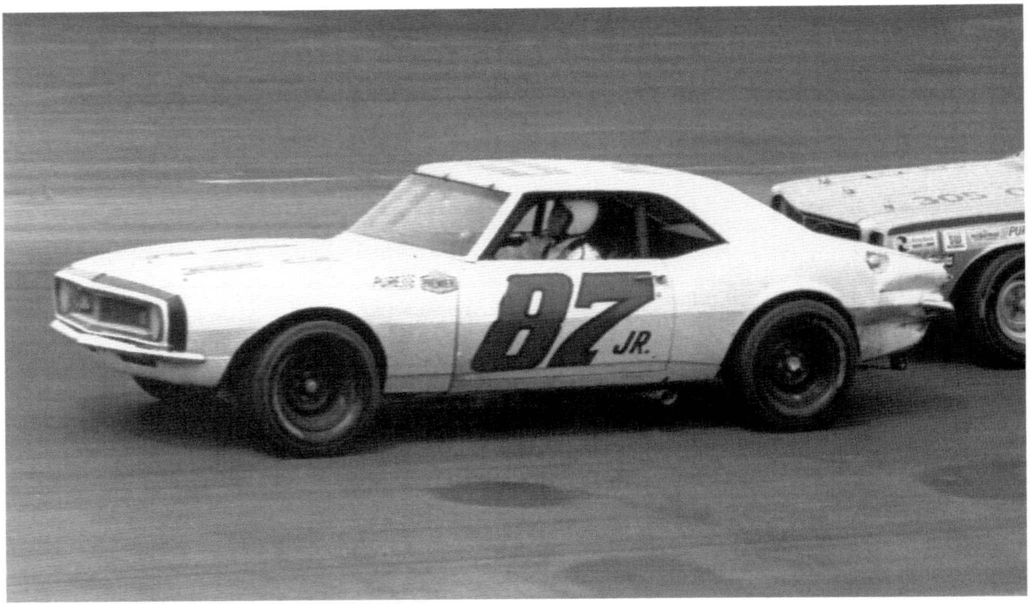

The first NASCAR race ever held at Kingsport was the Model City 100 for the new NASCAR Grand Touring Series, which featured "pony" cars like Camaros, Mustangs, and Javelins. The race was an oval version of the Trans-Am Series. It was run on dirt and won by former Grand National champion Buck Baker (No. 87) in his Camaro. This photograph was taken a few weeks later at Bristol Motor Speedway. (Photograph by John Beach.)

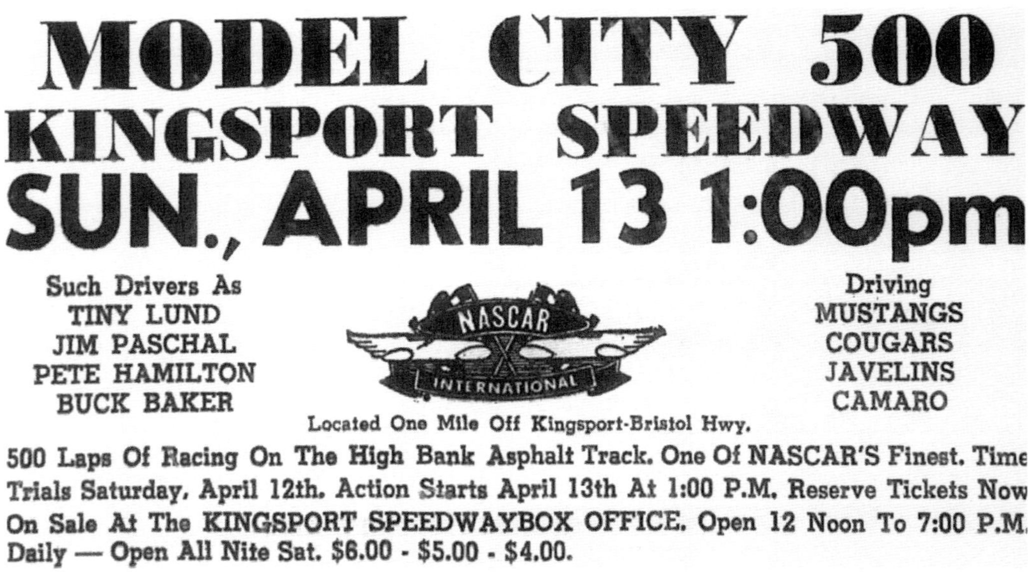

A 1969 newspaper advertisement promotes the Model City 500, a torture test of 500 grueling laps around Kingsport's brand-new paved surface. Despite stars like Tiny Lund, Pete Hamilton, and Buck Baker in the race, crew member Russell Nelson drove the last 325 laps to win for driver T.C. Hunt, who became ill during the contest. (Author's collection.)

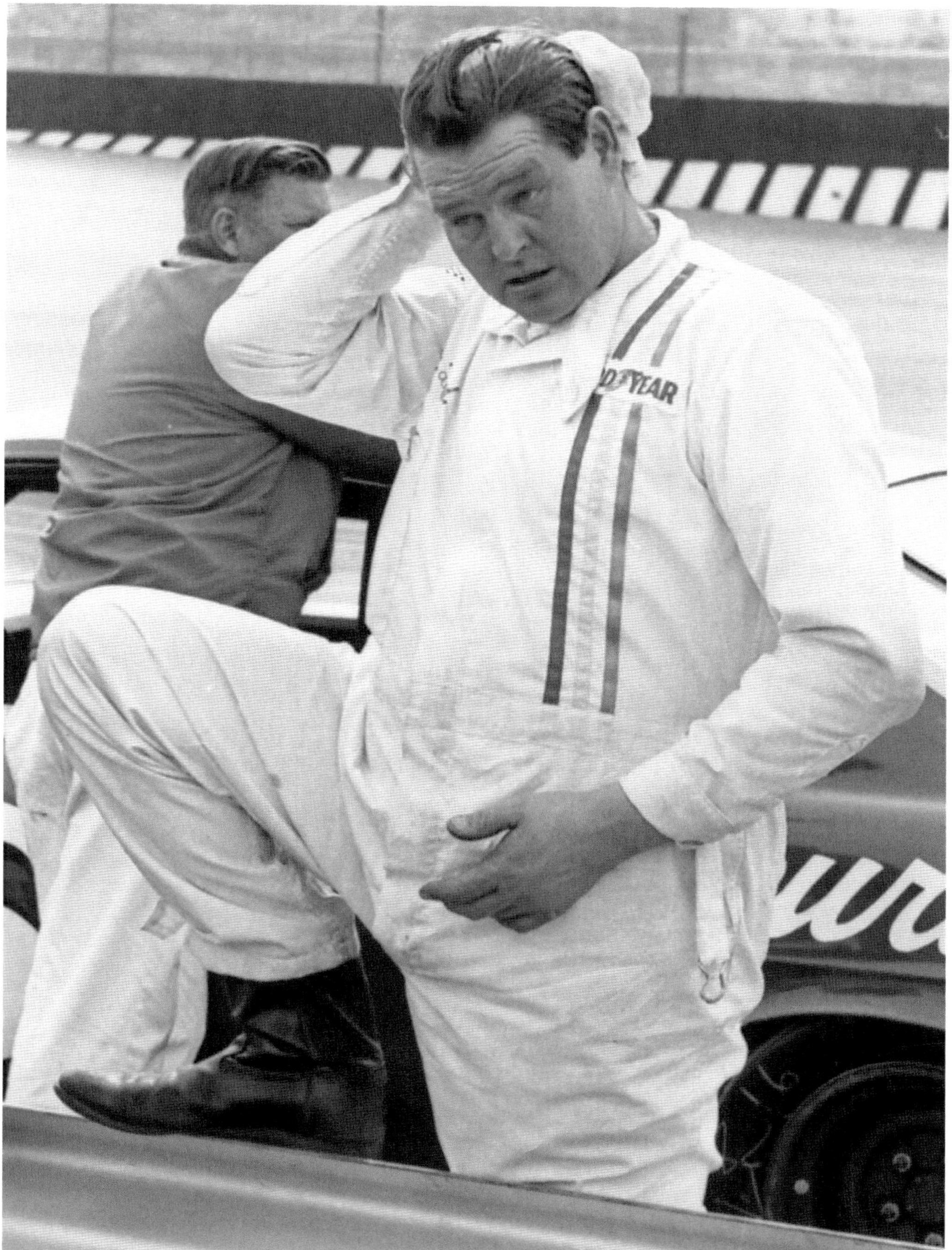

Dwayne "Tiny" Lund qualified Bud Moore's Mercury Cougar on the pole for the 1969 Model City 500, Kingsport's first NASCAR race run on asphalt, on April 13. Lund withdrew the previous year because of poor track conditions, but he placed third in 1969. He went to victory lane at Kingsport a year later in his own Camaro. This photograph was taken at Bristol Motor Speedway. (Photograph by John Beach.)

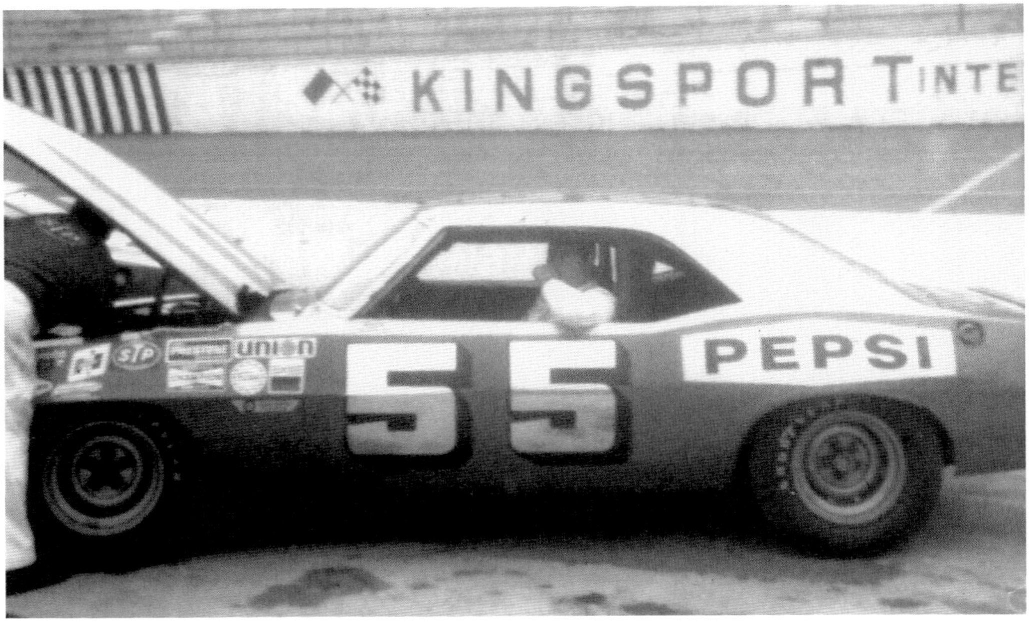

Tiny Lund sits in his Camaro during a 1970 practice session at Kingsport. The former Daytona 500 winner claimed that spring's Model City 300 as part of a series record 10 consecutive victories in the Ronnie Hopkins–prepared Chevrolet. Lund would post 19 wins and claim his second series championship later that season. (Courtesy of Rusty and Beth Clendenin.)

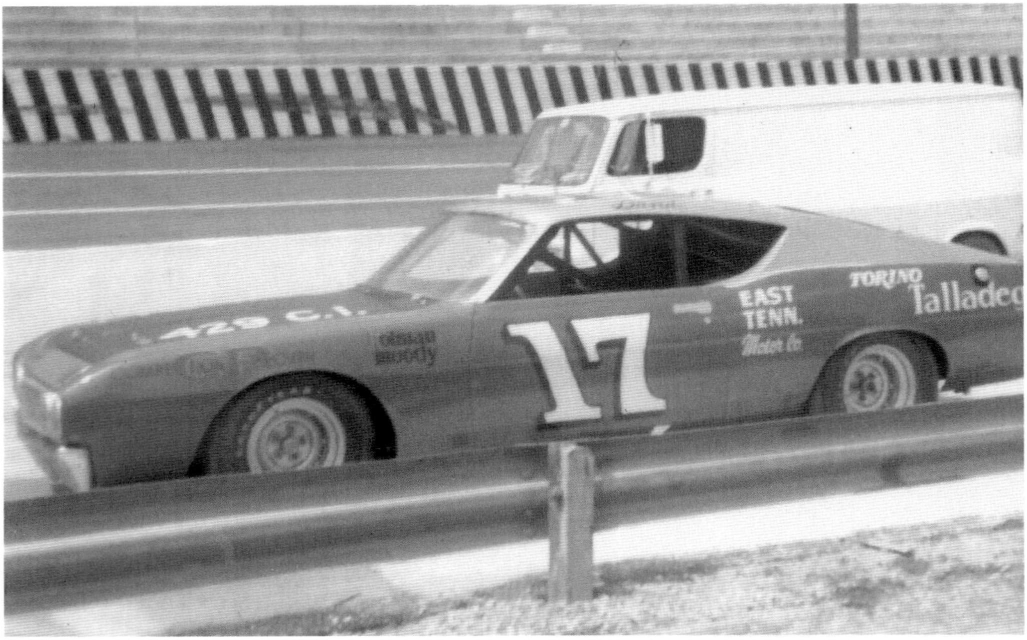

The Ford Torino Talladega of 1968 national champion David Pearson sits on pit road at Kingsport in June 1969. Pearson finished third in his only Kingsport appearance, two laps off the pace of winner Richard Petty. Pearson later claimed the 1969 Grand National title. (Courtesy of Rusty and Beth Clendenin.)

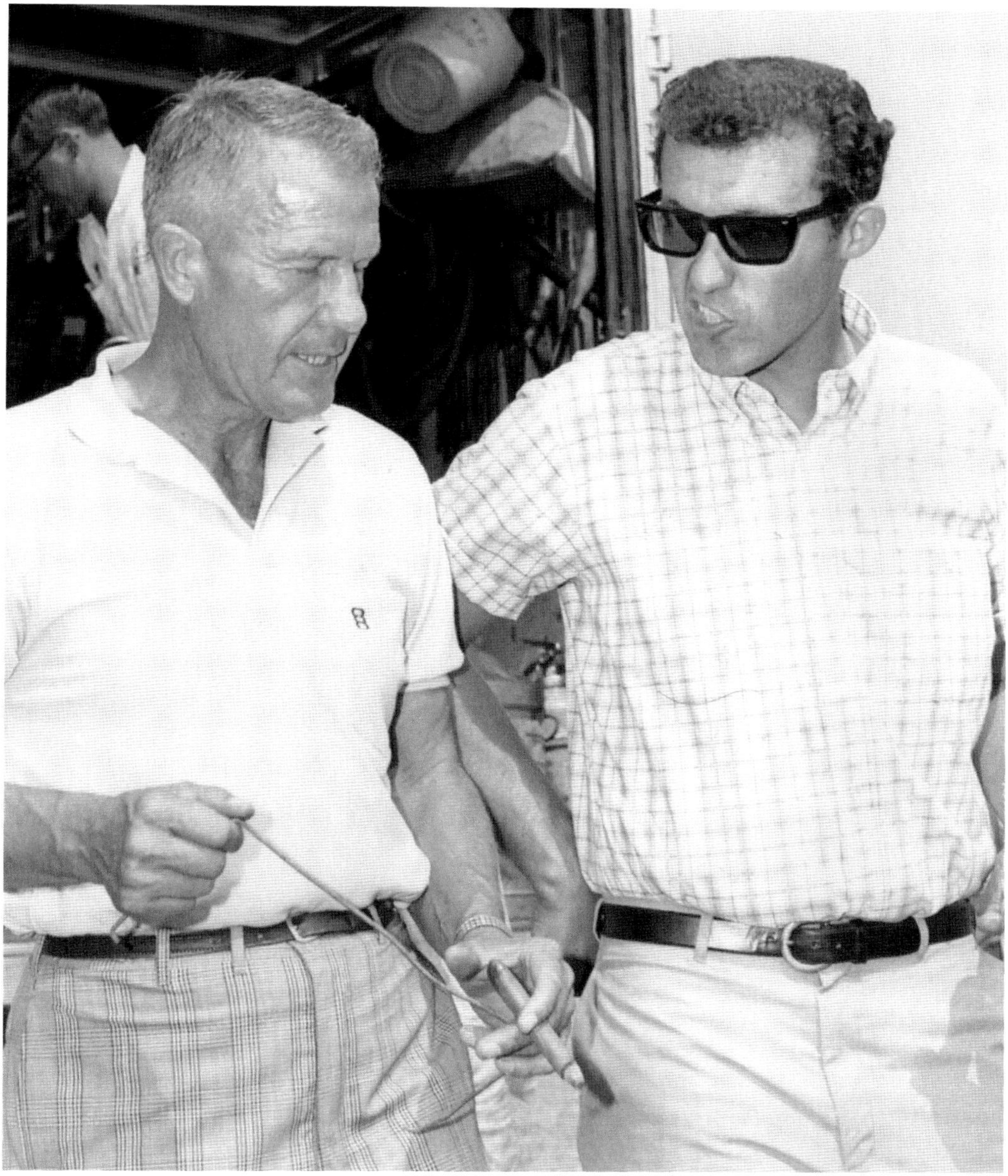

Racing royalty came to Kingsport in 1969, when the track hosted the Kingsport 250 on Thursday, June 19. Richard Petty (right) won Kingsport's first Grand National race in his only year with Ford. Here, he confers with his father, Lee Petty. Known as "the King," Richard Petty scored his 95th career Grand National win after pole-sitter Bobby Isaac blew an engine late in the race. A crowd of 8,500 saw John Sears, David Pearson, Neil Castles, and G.C. Spencer round out the top five finishers. Pearson also led laps that night in the 23-car field. (Photograph by John Beach.)

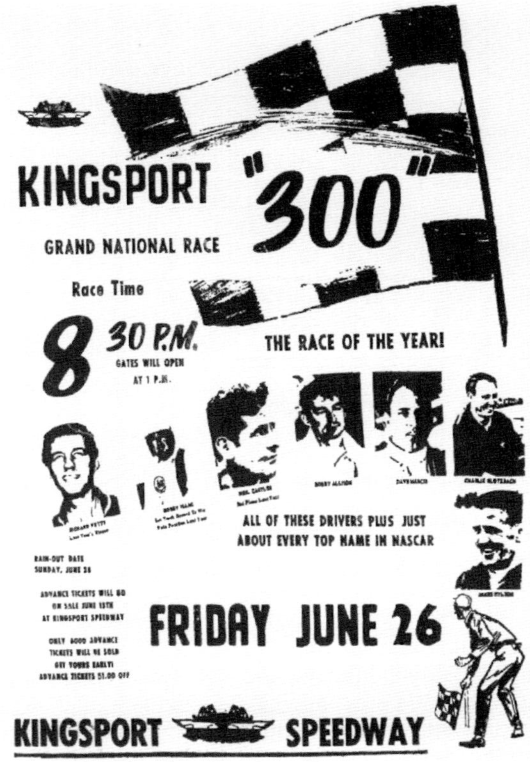

NASCAR's Grand National stars returned in June 1970 for the Kingsport 300. Ironically, the race was only 297 laps, or roughly 100 miles on the tight short track. This newspaper advertisement touts the return of Richard Petty and Bobby Isaac, who established the track qualifying record during the 1969 event. (Author's collection.)

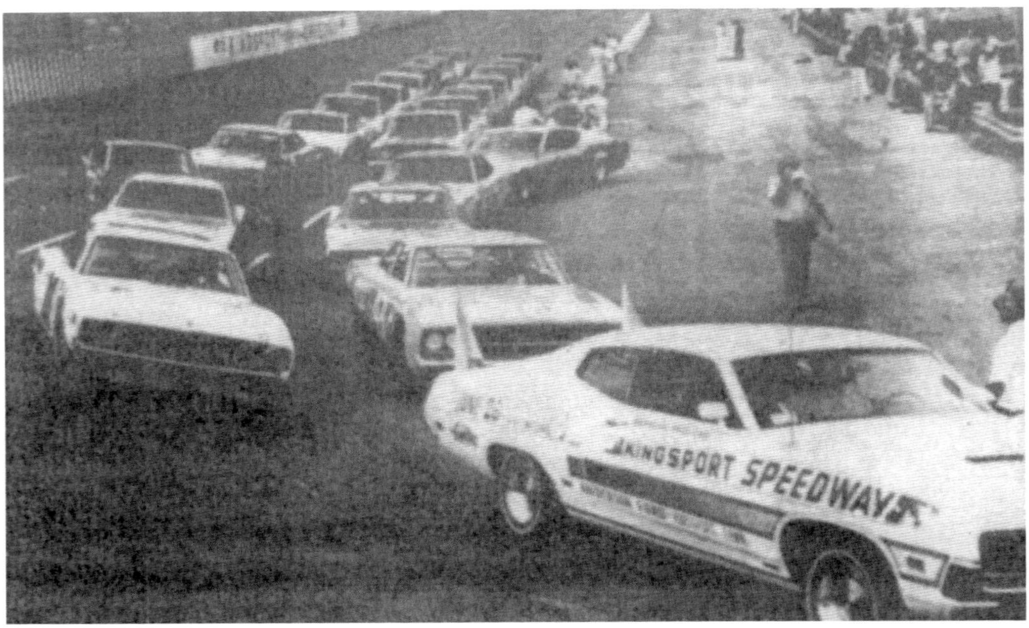

The field for the 1970 Kingsport 300 NASCAR Grand National race assembles behind the Kingsport Speedway Ford Torino pace car. Richard Petty won after starting on the pole. Neil Castles started his Dodge on the front row and finished fifth after 297 laps. (Author's collection.)

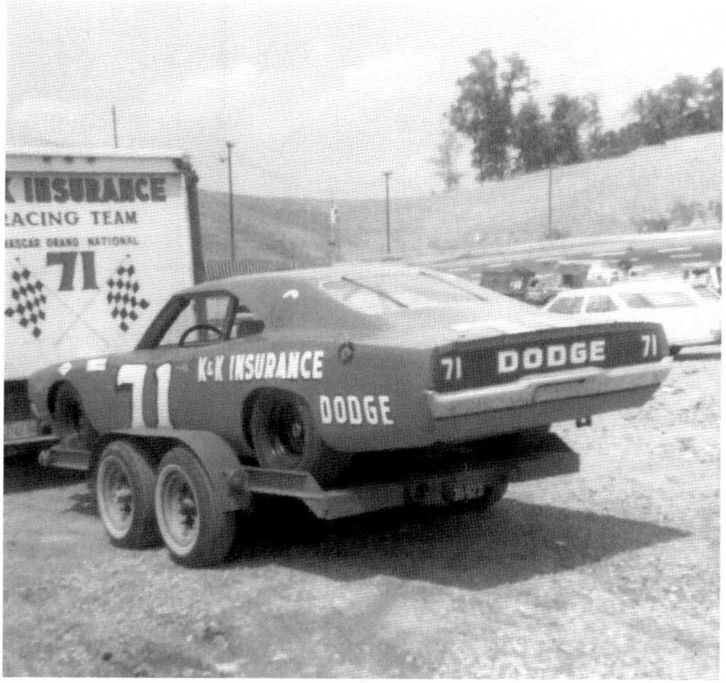

The vaunted K&K Dodge arrived on an open trailer for the 1969 NASCAR premier series race at Kingsport. Driver Bobby Isaac established the track qualifying record that day at 90.112 miles per hour, but he suffered a blown engine in the race. Isaac won the 1970 NASCAR Grand National championship and dominated the 1971 Kingsport race, leading all but six laps. (Courtesy of Rusty and Beth Clendenin.)

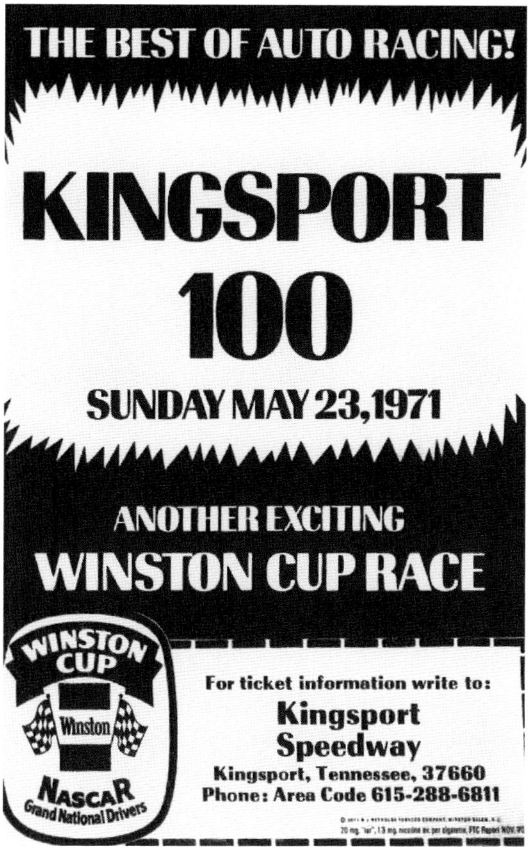

NASCAR's premier series was rebranded Winston Cup in 1971. The May 23 Kingsport 300 race was incorrectly advertised as the Kingsport 100 by the series sponsor. The race was held on a Sunday afternoon, rather than a weeknight, and attracted a crowd of 8,000 but marked its last appearance in Kingsport. The series was scheduled to return to Kingsport in October 1971, but that race was canceled. (Author's collection.)

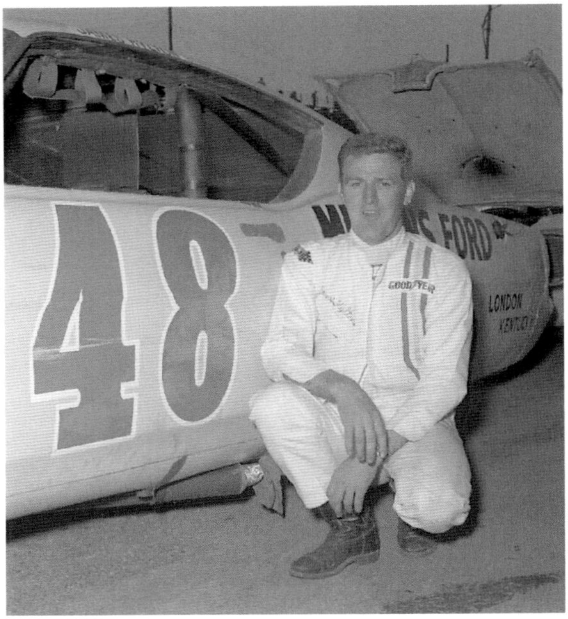

James Hylton (No. 48) finished second to Richard Petty in Kingsport's 1970 Grand National race and third in the 1971 Kingsport 300. Hylton was among the sport's top independent drivers in that era, finishing in the top three in points six times between 1966 and 1972. This photograph was taken at Smoky Mountain Raceway. (Photograph by Ray Taylor, courtesy of Robbie Henry.)

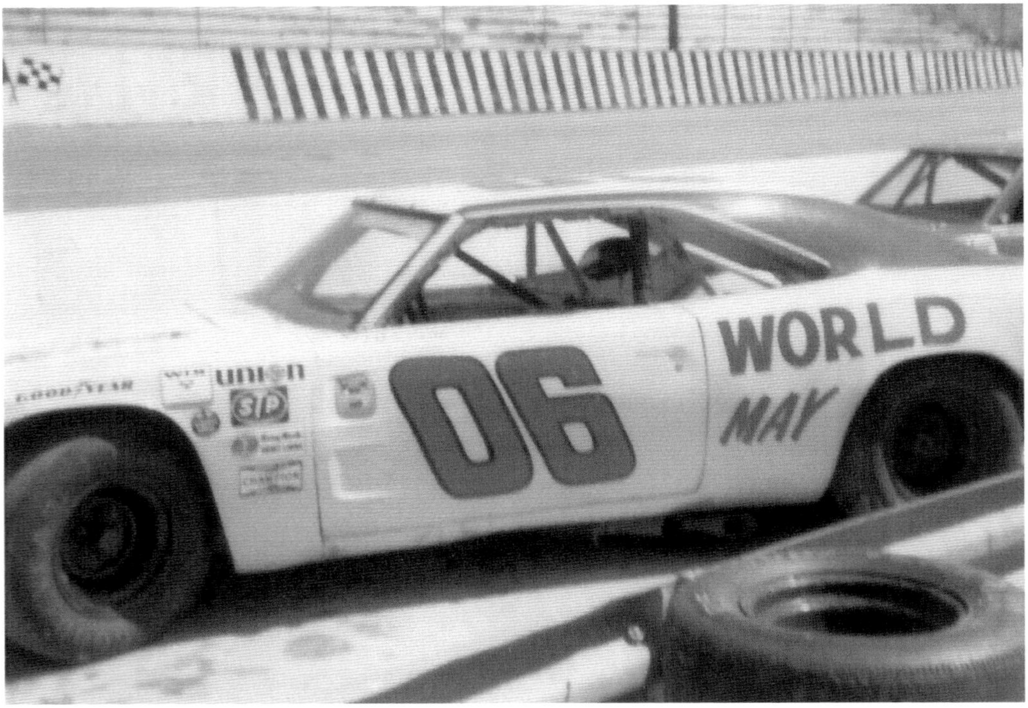

Neil Castles's Dodge Charger promoted the World 600 race on its fenders while on pit road at Kingsport prior to the 1971 Kingsport 300. Castles fell out with brake problems that year after posting consecutive top-five finishes in Kingsport's first two Grand National races. He charged from last to finish fourth in 1969 and returned to qualify second and finish fifth in 1970. Both years, he posted top-five finishes in the NASCAR season points. (Courtesy of Rusty and Beth Clendenin.)

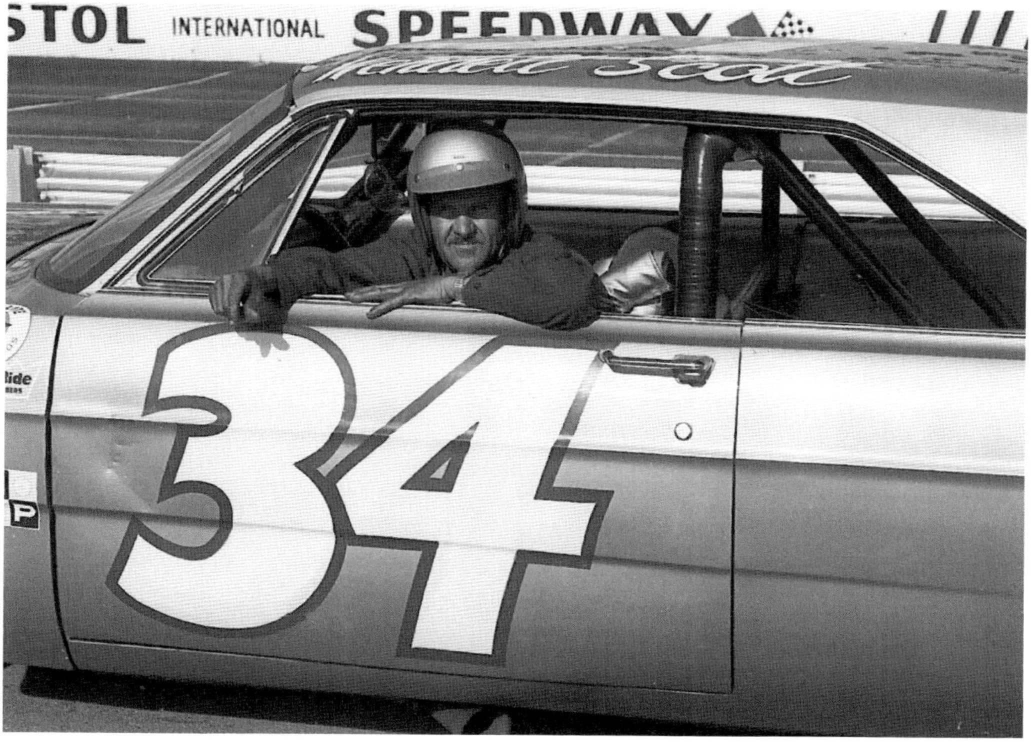

Wendell Scott, seen here at Bristol, registered top-10 finishes in all three Kingsport premier series races, finishing tenth, sixth, and sixth from 1969 to 1971. The Danville, Virginia, native was widely respected for getting the most out of his cars and was a 2015 inductee into the NASCAR Hall of Fame. (Photograph by John Beach.)

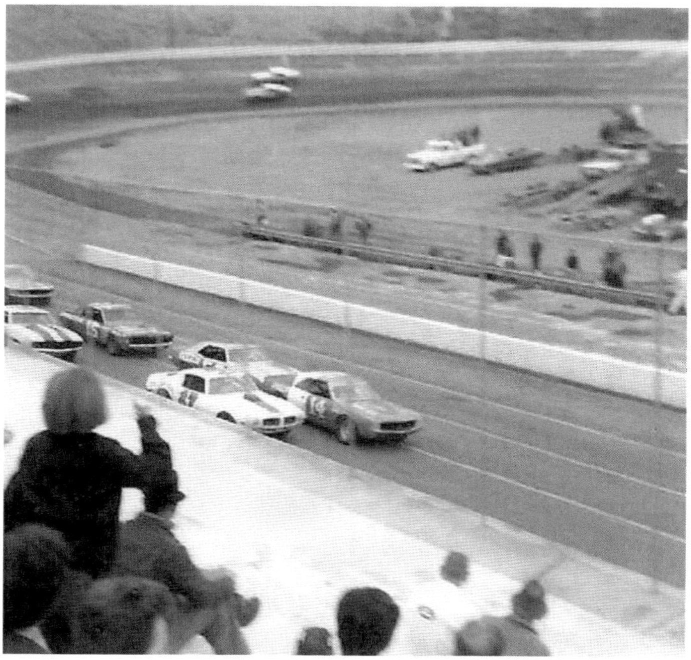

Jim Paschal (No. 14) battles door-to-door with Buck Baker (No. 87) in the Kingsport 300 Grand American series race on September 5, 1970. Automaker American Motors bought full-page magazine advertisements touting Paschal's Kingsport win in his Javelin. Wayne Andrews finished second and Baker third. Fast qualifier Tiny Lund (No. 55) was idled by a broken fuel pump. (Photograph by Chris Haverly.)

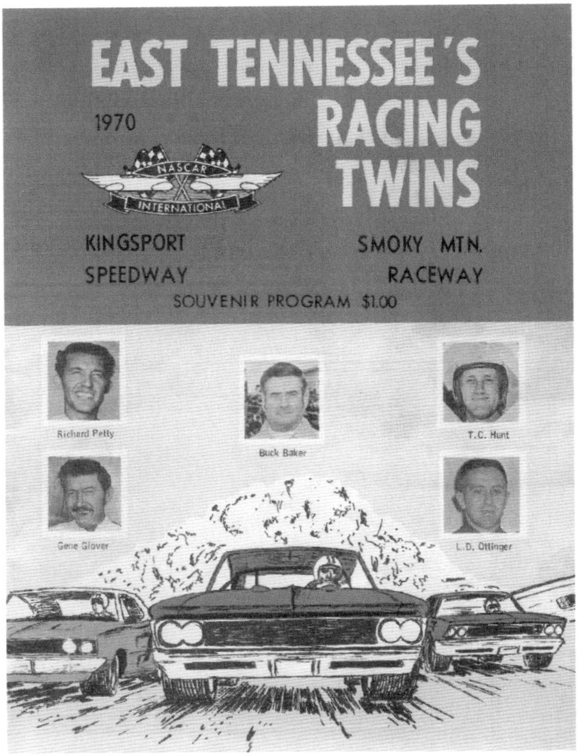

For 1970, Kingsport Speedway worked with Smoky Mountain Raceway in Maryville, Tennessee, to promote each other's races, as shown on the cover of this souvenir program. The tracks are separated by about 100 miles, and both promoted Grand National series races at that time. (Courtesy of Tony Morton.)

GRAND NATIONAL EAST

Apr.	19—South Boston, Va. (.357 Mi Pvd)	100	M	*8,600
May	10—Myrtle Beach, S. C. (½ Mi Pvd)	100	M	*8,600
May	13—Nashville, Tenn. (.596 Mi Pvd)	100	M	*8,600
May	14—Maryville, Tenn. (.520 Mi Pvd)	100	M	*8,600
May	18—Asheville, N. C. (1/3 Mi Pvd)	200	L	*8,600
May	21—Ona, W. Va. (7/16 Mi Pvd)	500	L	*17,525
July	11—Malta, N. Y. (.362 Mi Pvd)	250	L	*8,600
July	13—Islip, N. Y. (1/5 Mi Pvd)	250	L	*8,600
July	27—Columbia, S. C. (.510 Mi Pvd)	200	L	*8,600
July	28—Hickory, N. C. (.363 Mi Pvd)	276	L	*8,600
July	29—Greenville, S. C. (½ Mi Pvd)	100	M	*8,600
July	30—Kingsport, Tenn. (.337 Mi Pvd)	300	L	*8,600
Aug.	11—Winston-Salem, N. C. (¼ Mi Pvd)	250	L	*8,600
Aug.	13—Maryville, Tenn. (.520 Mi Pvd)	200	L	*8,600
Sept.	6—Beltsville, Md. (.537 Mi Pvd)	100	M	*8,600
Oct.	29—Kingsport, Tenn. (.337 Mi Pvd)	300	L	*8,600
Nov.	12—Jacksonville, Fla. (½ Mi Pvd)	100	M	*8,600

NOTE: Some changes in above schedule may be necessary because of postponed Winston Cup Grand National events.

This 1972 NASCAR schedule shows two Kingsport races for a newly established Grand National East series, but neither race happened. The short-lived series was designed to bring premier series–style racing back to smaller tracks cut out by a reduced schedule. The series suffered from low attendance and participation, and it lasted just two seasons. (Author's collection.)

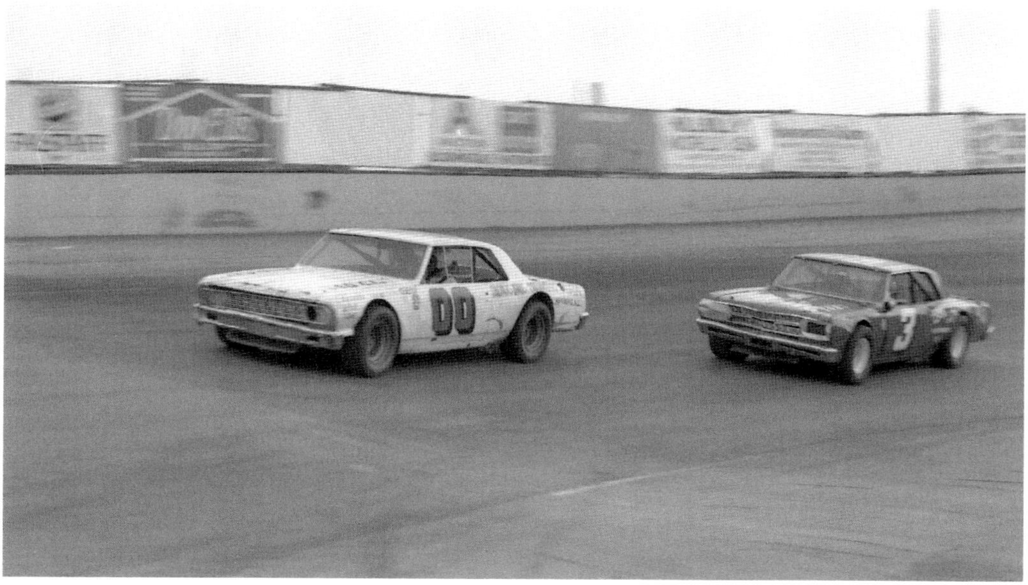

Sam Ard (No. 00) races with Brad Teague (No. 3) in NASCAR Late Model Sportsman action. Ard, a South Carolina native, raced regularly at Kingsport. He went on to win two NASCAR Busch Series national championships in the 1980s. Teague, from Johnson City, Tennessee, was runner-up in the 1981 Sportsman national standings and won several races at Kingsport. (Courtesy of Murray family collection.)

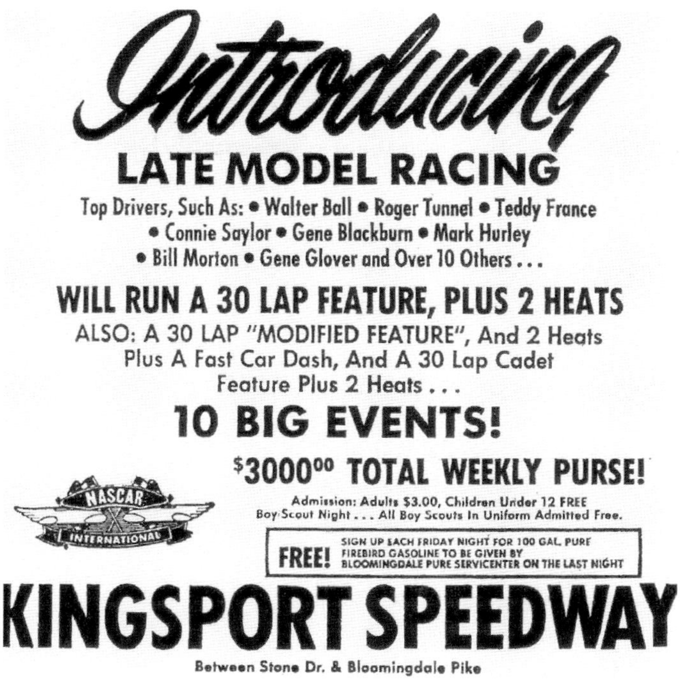

A 1968 newspaper advertisement announces Kingsport's new NASCAR sanction and its new Late Model Sportsman class. The track ran modifieds for one more season, but built its reputation on the newer, more recognizable 1960s cars. Ironically, Gene Glover and Bill Morton continued to be the leaders in both divisions. Glover won the 1968 Modified title over Morton, while Morton captured the track's first Late Model championship. (Courtesy of Tony Morton.)

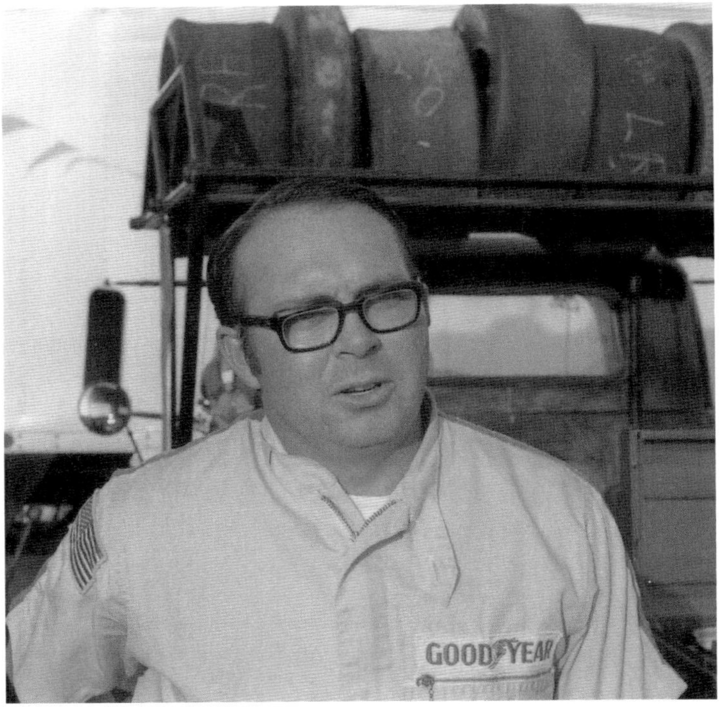

Hank Maxwell of Newport, Tennessee, dominated early Late Model Sportsman racing action at Kingsport, winning the 1971 track title and finishing second or third in points in four other seasons in the late 1960s and early 1970s. At one point, Maxwell won 14 consecutive races at Kingsport. He won the 1971, 1972, and 1973 Tennessee state NASCAR championships. (Courtesy of Murray family collection.)

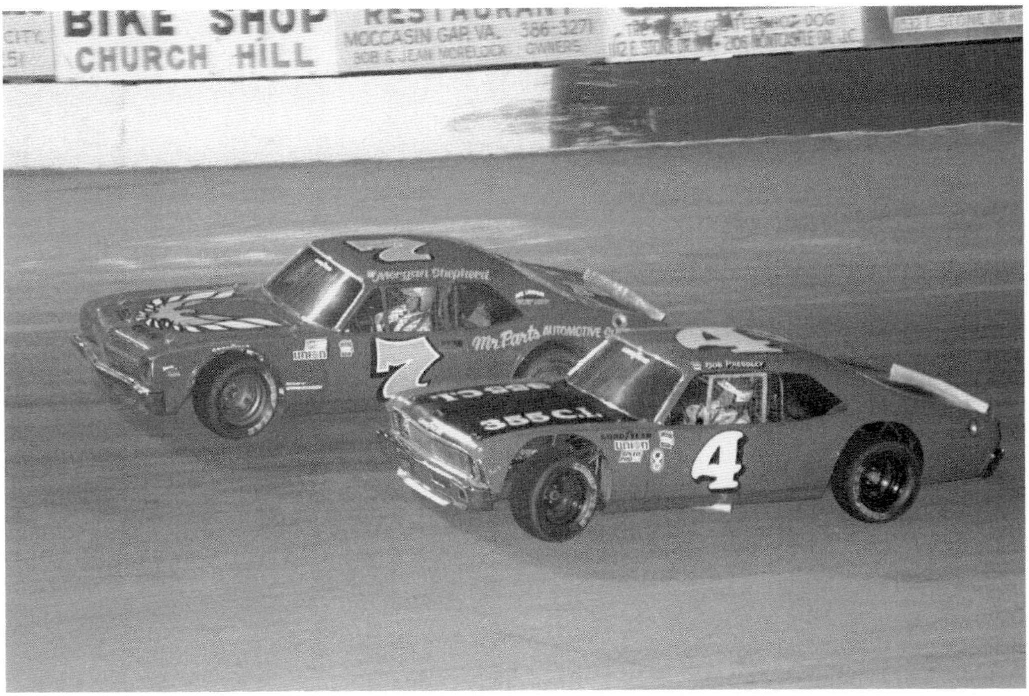

NASCAR Late Model Sportsman stars Morgan Shepherd (No. 7) and Bob Pressley (No. 4) race side by side in weekly action at Kingsport. These North Carolina drivers made regular visits to Kingsport and victory lane. Both were among the track's most successful drivers in the 1970s. (Photograph by David Allio.)

Butch Lindley holds the trophy for winning the Miller 150 NASCAR Winston Late Model Sportsman double points feature at Kingsport International Speedway in May 1978. Lindley was one of the nation's most successful drivers, but his career was cut short by a catastrophic accident. Kingsport hosted several races to benefit Lindley and his family. (Photograph by David Allio.)

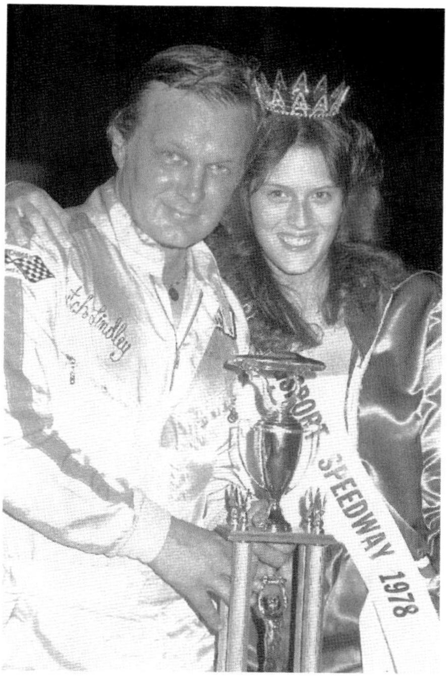

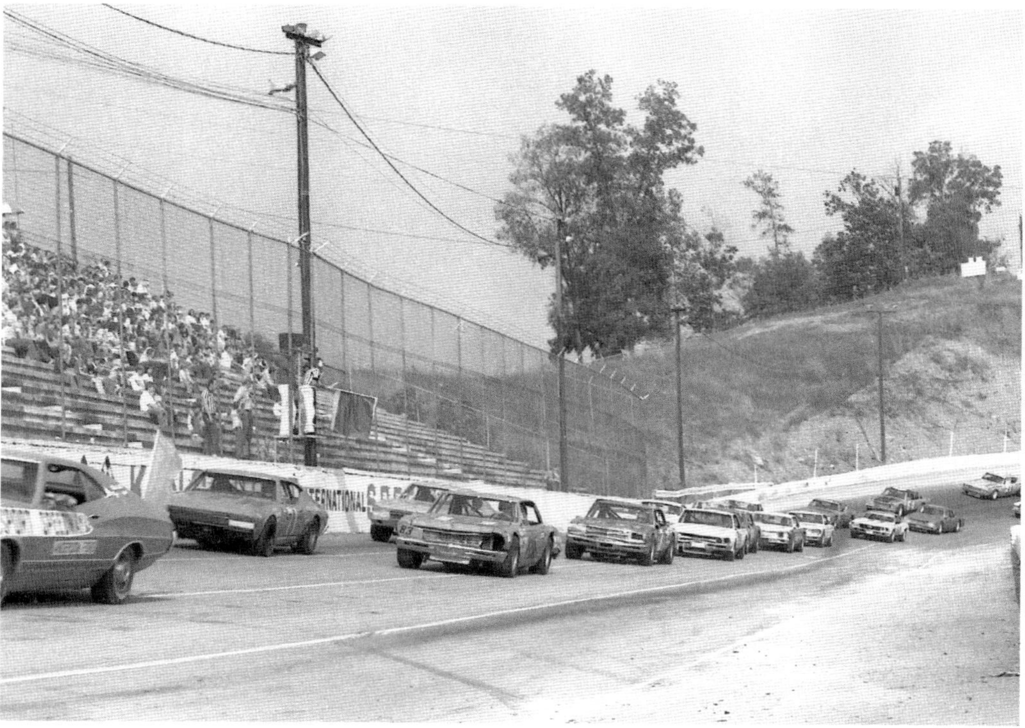

The field for the 1973 Permatex 300 follows the Kingsport Speedway pace car, prior to the green flag. Lonnie Rush (No. 83) qualified on the pole and shared the front row with Morgan Shepherd (No. 71), while Brad Teague (No. 3) qualified third. Shepherd went on to capture the victory. (Courtesy of Murray family collection.)

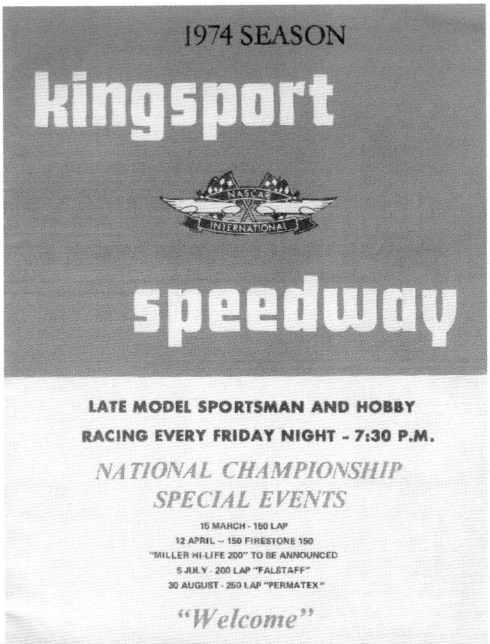

This 1974 souvenir program shows Kingsport's emphasis on the NASCAR Late Model Sportsman series, including a number of special events that offered national championship points and generous payouts. The races typically attracted the nation's best drivers. (Courtesy of Tony Morton.)

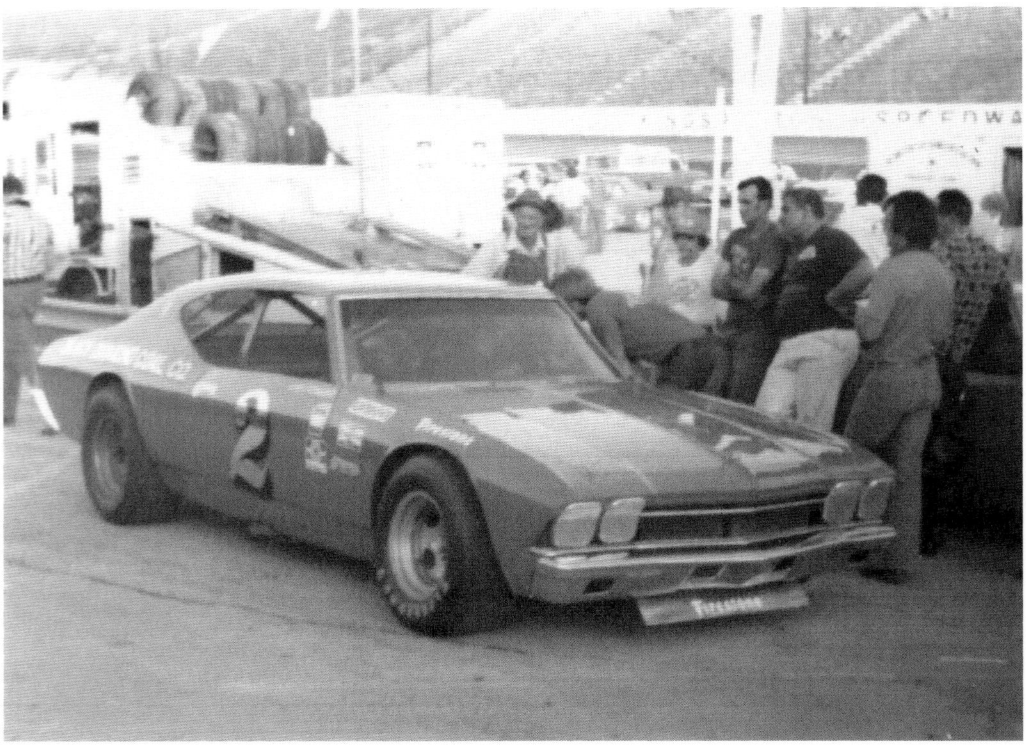

L.D. Ottinger (No. 2) waits to roll onto the track at Kingsport. Ottinger, of Newport, Tennessee, used success at the local level as a springboard to two Sportsman national championships in Chevrolets prepared by Ken "Bear" Hunley and owned by Kennie "Coal Miner" Childers. (Courtesy of Rusty and Beth Clendenin.)

Jerry Cook of Lockport, New York, captured six NASCAR Modified national championships in the 1970s. The open-wheel Modified touring series raced four times at Kingsport in the 1970s, attracting a number of notable eastern racers, including Cook and archrival Richie Evans. (Courtesy of Murray family collection.)

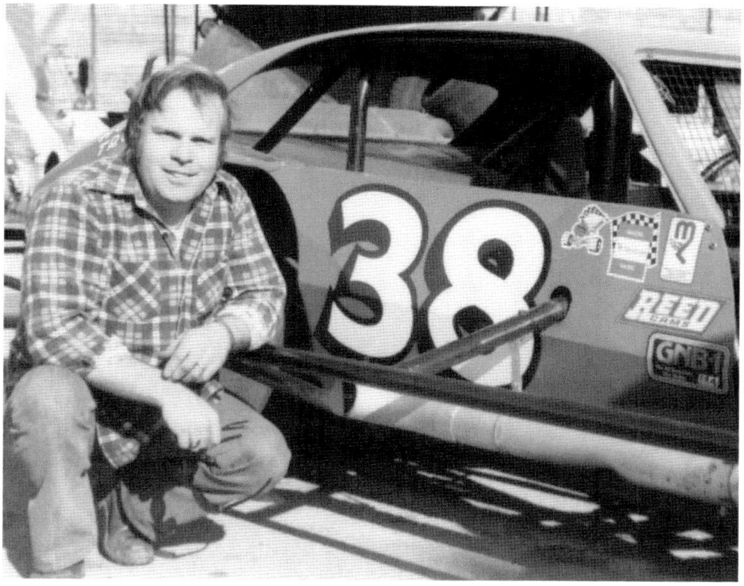

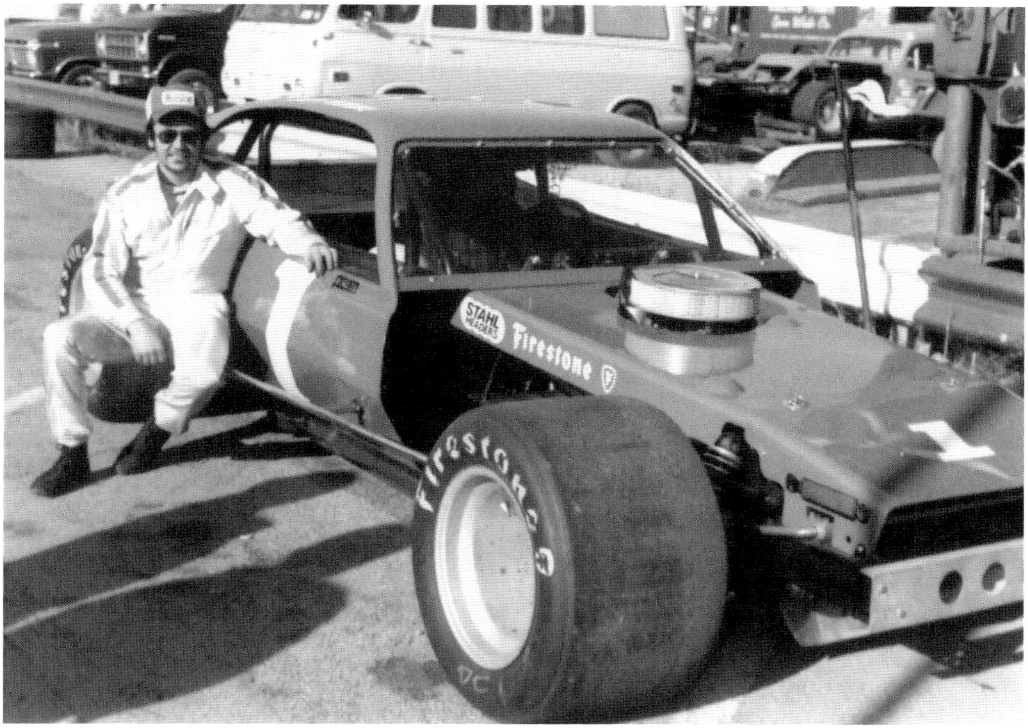

Geoff Bodine of Chemung, New York, won the first 250-lap NASCAR Modified series race run at Kingsport Speedway in November 1976. The race was part of a doubleheader with the Late Model Sportsman cars. Bodine wheeled a "Big Red Machine" No. 1 Ford owned by Dick Armstrong to victory. He went on to star in NASCAR's premier series. (Courtesy of Murray family collection.)

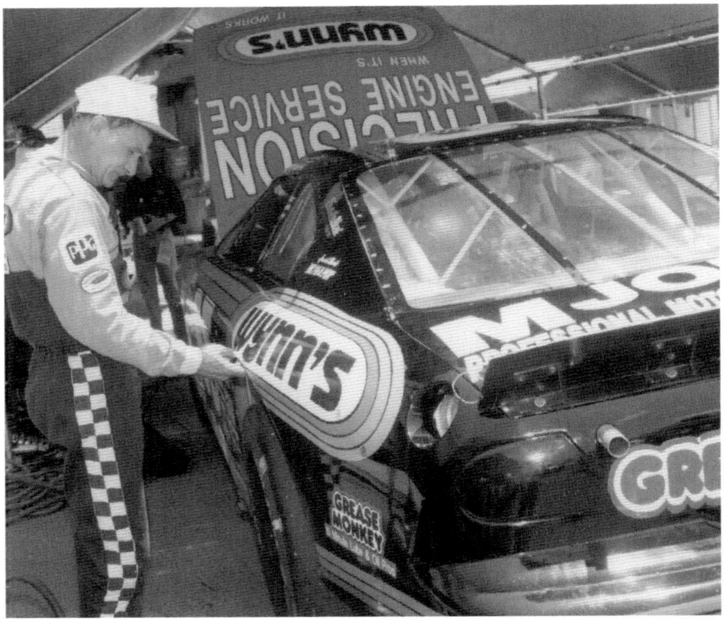

Will Hobgood won the Fairway Ford 125 for the Goody's Dash series machines in April 1997 at Kingsport. The Dash series was a longtime NASCAR series that primarily ran on short tracks. Hobgood, seen here at Bristol, outran his son Jake for the series victory. It was the first time a father and son finished first and second in that series. (Photograph by the author.)

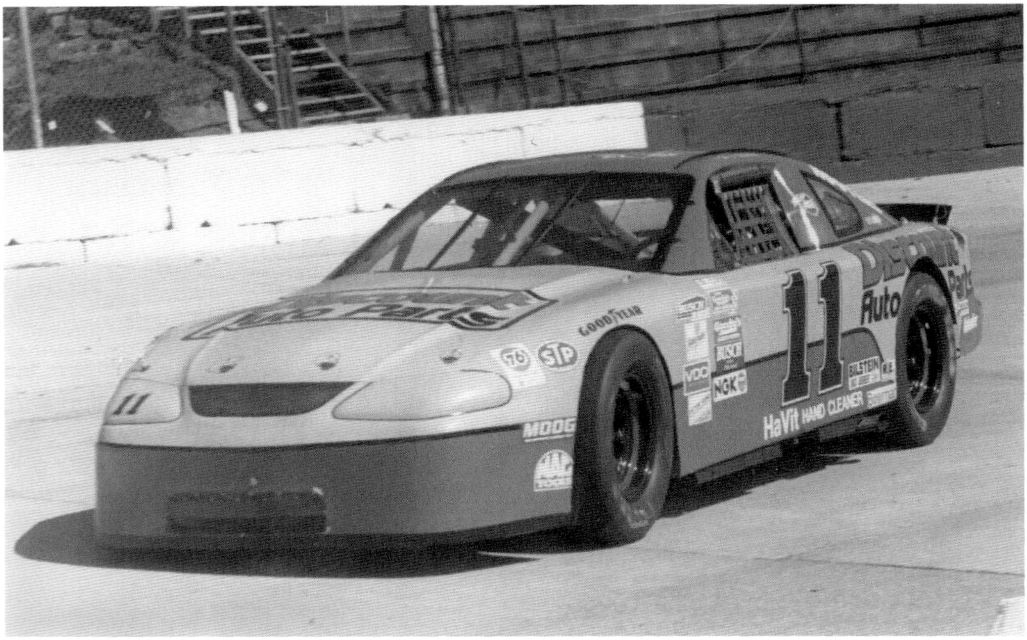

Kingsport's 1997 Dash series race held a bitter ending for Pat Patterson (No. 11), whose Ford Mustang led much of the race but hit the wall with just four laps remaining, knocking Patterson from contention. He finished 12th. Patterson is best known as a broadcaster on Performance Racing Network, Sirius, and ESPN Radio. (Photograph by the author.)

3

KINGS OF KINGSPORT

Unlike some tracks that faded into relative obscurity or ultimately closed after losing NASCAR premier series races, Kingsport Speedway found new life and its greatest identity hosting the stars of NASCAR's Late Model Sportsman division. Throughout the 1970s and up to 1981, drivers could accumulate points toward track, state, and national championships at every sanctioned track that hosted the cars.

NASCAR also had an extensive schedule of national championship races, and Kingsport typically hosted three or four each season. When paired with Smoky Mountain Raceway in Maryville, Tennessee, and later Lonesome Pine Raceway in Virginia, racers could drive a reasonable distance and earn points two nights each week.

With the track's central geographic location, drivers actively seeking a national title—including champions Jack Ingram and Butch Lindley—visited Kingsport regularly. So, too, did the likes of Dale Earnhardt, Tommy Ellis, Harry Gant, Jimmy Hensley, Dave Marcis, Bob Pressley, and Morgan Shepherd. "There was a gang there every Friday night. I loved Kingsport and I won a lot of races there," Hensley recalled. "It was a big deal because you had so many guys there capable of winning races. The driver combination we had back then at all those tracks was great and the fan support was great."

But none of those travelers was guaranteed a win, and they knew it. That is because fans had plenty of local heroes to cheer for, including national champions Gene Glover and L.D. Ottinger, along with Larry Utsman, John A. Utsman, Brad Teague, Connie Saylor, Hank Maxwell, Paul Lewis, and a couple dozen more. "It was brutal," Larry Utsman said of competing at Kingsport. "When I started in 1974, you had numerous people from the Winston Cup ranks; people who were superstars. You had national champions and track champions there every Friday night. If you finished in the top five you were doing really good and we were very fortunate."

Kingsport honored track champions during most years of operation, but the drivers featured in this chapter were clearly the kings during this significant segment of its history.

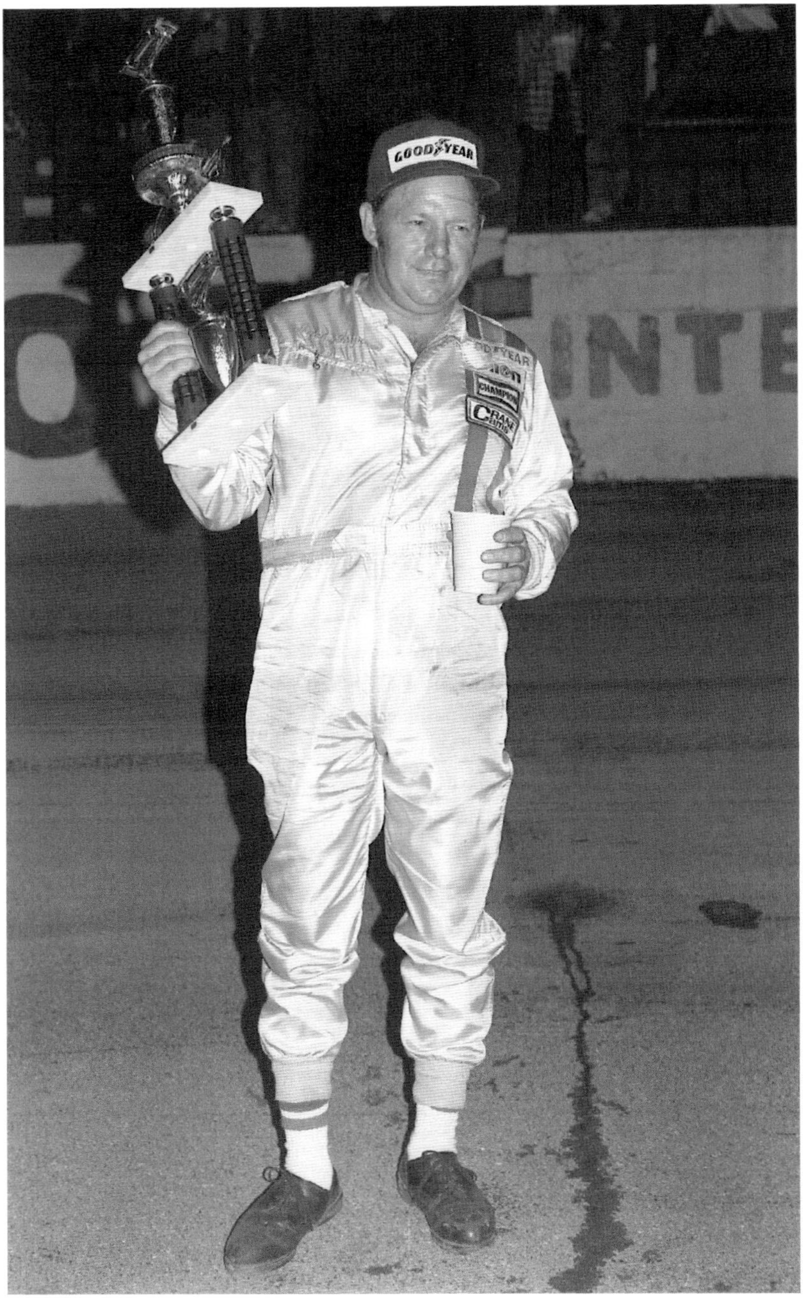

Fans could count on two things in the 1970s and early 1980s: Jack Ingram competed regularly at Kingsport Speedway when he was not running a championship event elsewhere; and he would hoist more than his share of trophies. Ingram, from nearby Asheville, North Carolina, won three NASCAR Late Model Sportsman national championships and two titles in the Busch Series. Along the way, he won more than a half-dozen national points races at Kingsport. In fact, Ingram drove a 1955 Chevrolet to victory in Kingsport's first Late Model Sportsman race on pavement, in April 1969. (Photograph by Mike O'Dell.)

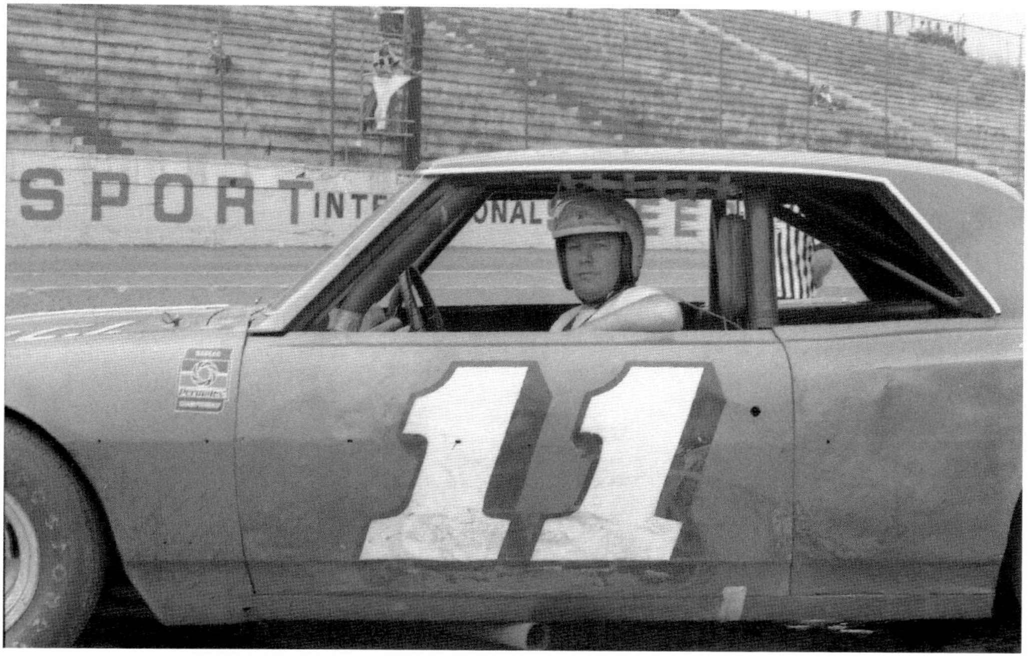

Jack Ingram put together three consecutive Late Model Sportsman series championships between 1972 and 1974. Fielding a pair of matching 1964 Chevelles, Ingram raced three or four nights most weeks, including regular visits to Kingsport. In 1972, he won 15 of 82 races started and got a national win at Kingsport. (Courtesy of Murray family collection.)

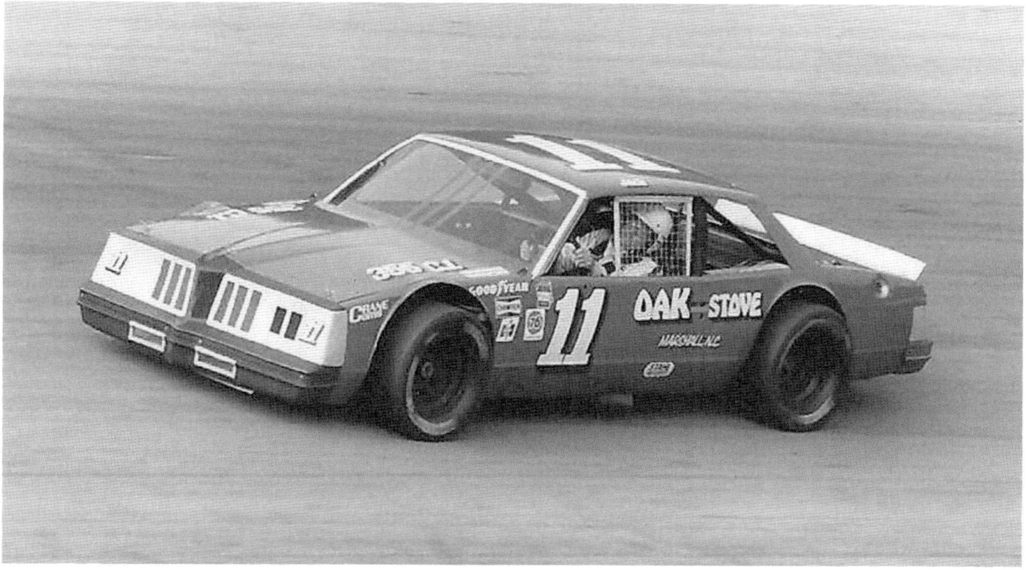

Jack Ingram and his copper-colored No. 11 Pontiac earned consecutive Kingsport Speedway track championships in 1980 and 1981, the final two years of Late Model Sportsman races before the cars evolved into the Busch Series. Ingram scored national wins at Kingsport both years, finished fourth in the national standings, and won the Tennessee state title each season. (Photograph by Chris Haverly.)

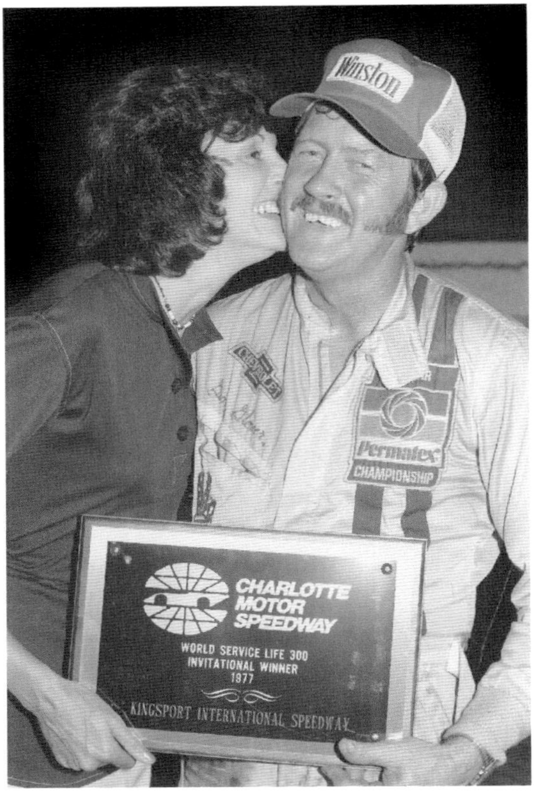

Reba Glover gives husband Gene a kiss following the second annual Jim Hayes Memorial 200 NASCAR Winston Late Model Sportsman race in 1978. The race was a qualifier to compete at a special event at Charlotte Motor Speedway. Glover left behind dirt modified racing when Kingsport was paved and became a national contender and the 1979 national champion. (Photograph by David Allio.)

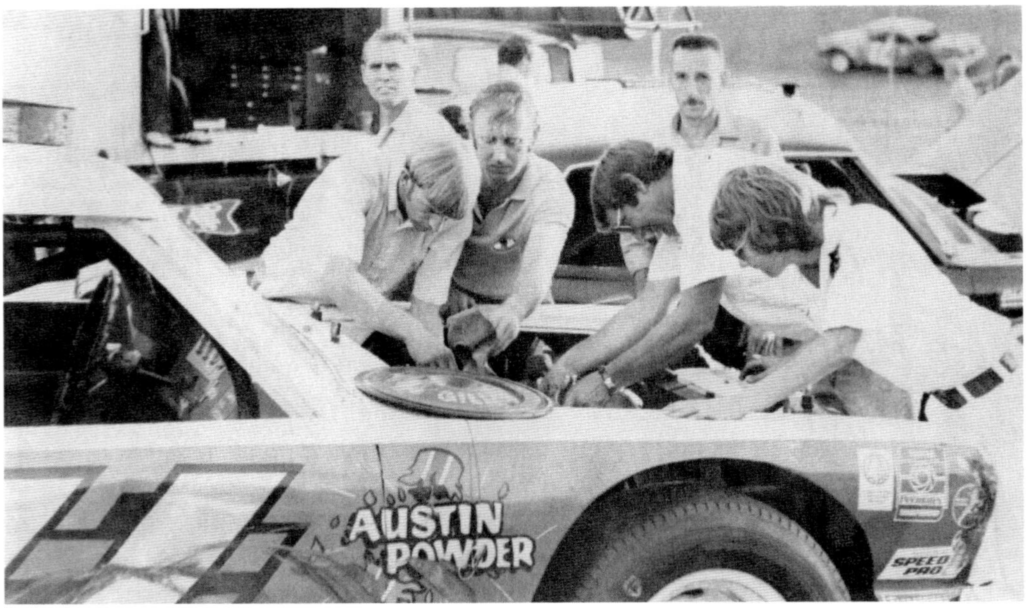

Gene Glover's crew members shown here are, from left to right, Jerry Gillis, Larry Price, Bobby Gillis, and Gene's son Tony Glover. They are diving into the top of the engine of an early Chevelle at Kingsport. Gene Glover made his first appearance in the national points in 1973, finishing in the top 20. (Courtesy of Murray family collection.)

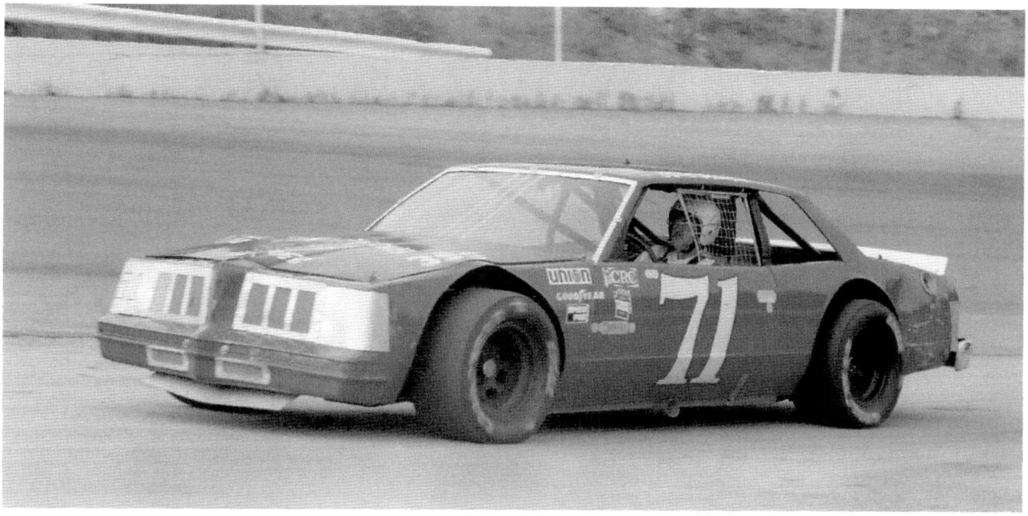

Gene Glover adopted the red No. 71 scheme made popular in the Winston Cup Series and won the 1979 NASCAR Late Model Sportsman national title. In a remarkable string from 1978 to 1980, Glover finished third, first, and third in the national standings. He won three of forty-two national races during his title season, including a dominant victory that October at Kingsport. (Photograph by Chris Haverly.)

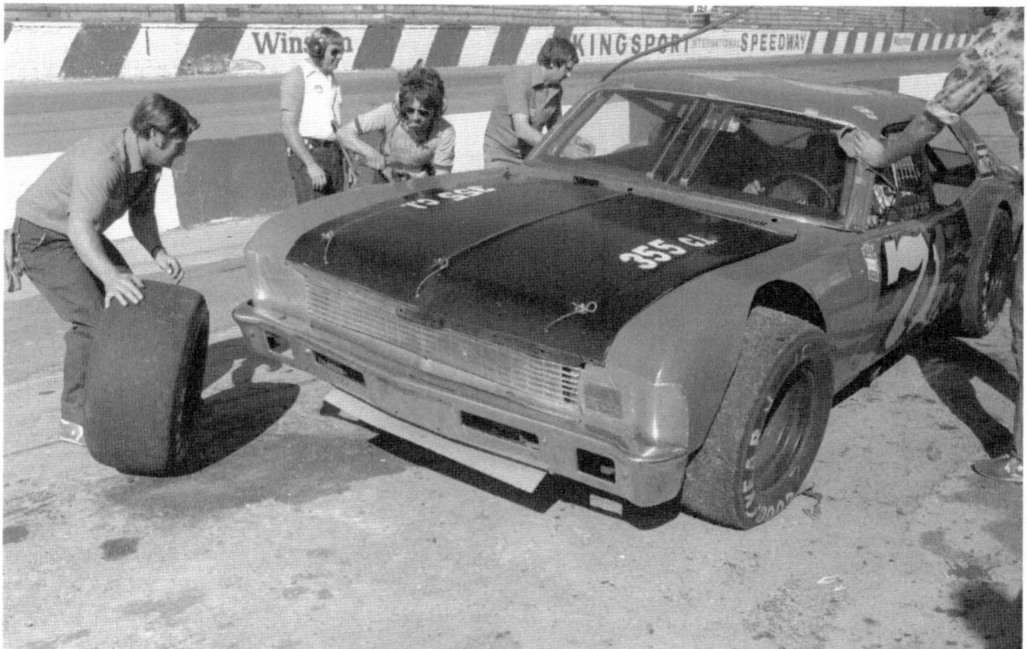

Gene Glover's crew makes a tire change in the third annual Winston Twin 250s NASCAR Winston Late Model Sportsman national championship at Kingsport International Speedway in 1978. Glover's son Tony later enjoyed a successful career as a NASCAR premier series crew chief, with 14 victories, including three Daytona 500 wins with Morgan-McClure Motorsports, a team based in nearby Abingdon, Virginia. (Photograph by David Allio.)

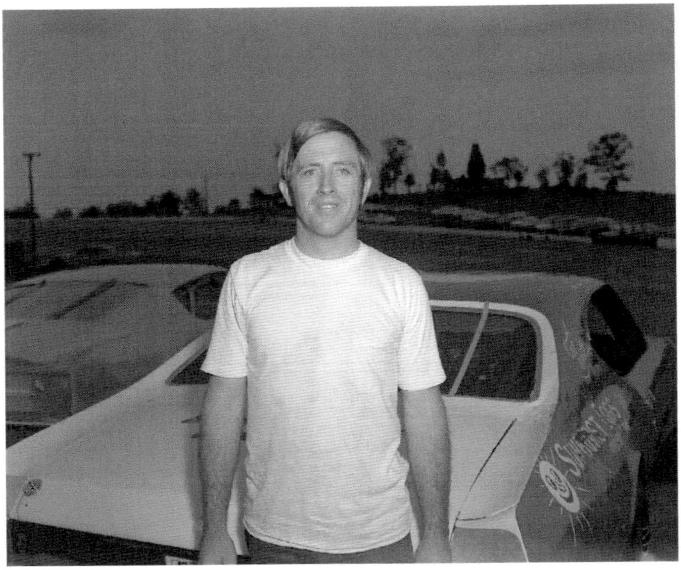

Lloyd "L.D." Ottinger had plenty of reasons to smile during a hugely successful NASCAR career. Ottinger, from Newport, Tennessee, won two Late Model Sportsman national titles driving for Kennie Childers and three races in the Busch Series, which succeeded it. Ottinger often raced at Kingsport and won three track championships—in 1970, 1973, and 1983. (Photograph by Ray Taylor, courtesy of Robbie Henry.)

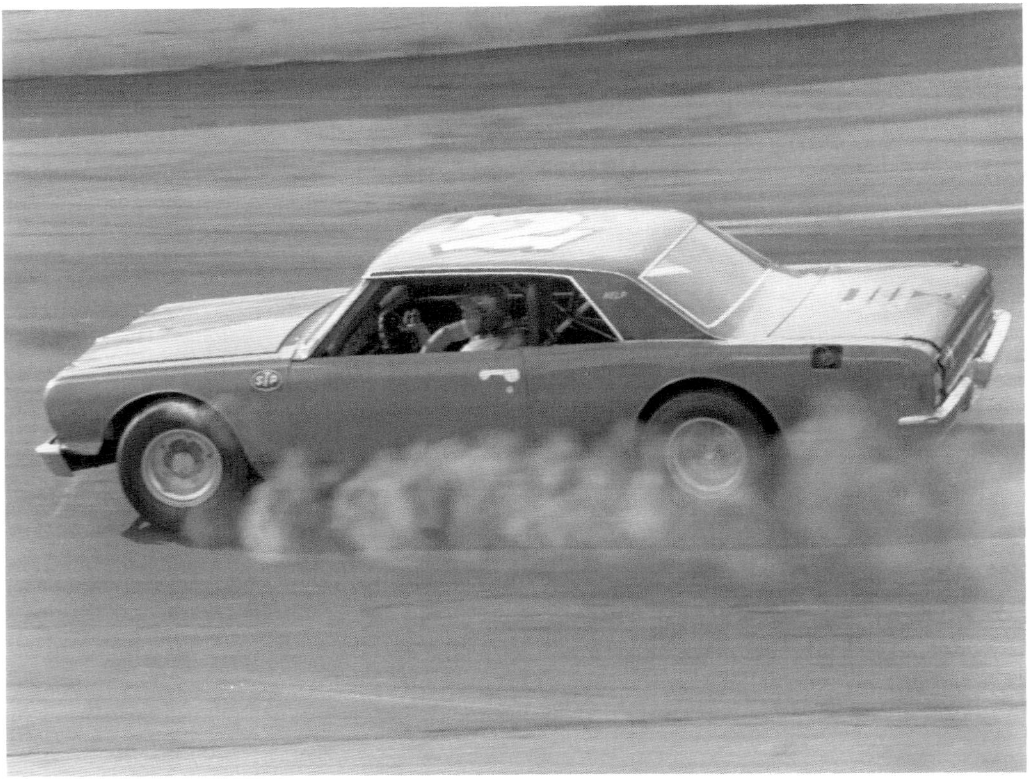

Smoke trails from beneath the Chevelle raced by L.D. Ottinger. His rise to national prominence coincided with winning the 1970 Kingsport points title. Ottinger finished seventh nationally after winning the Tennessee title. That began a string of top-10 finishes, numerous victories, and two national titles. (Courtesy of Murray family collection.)

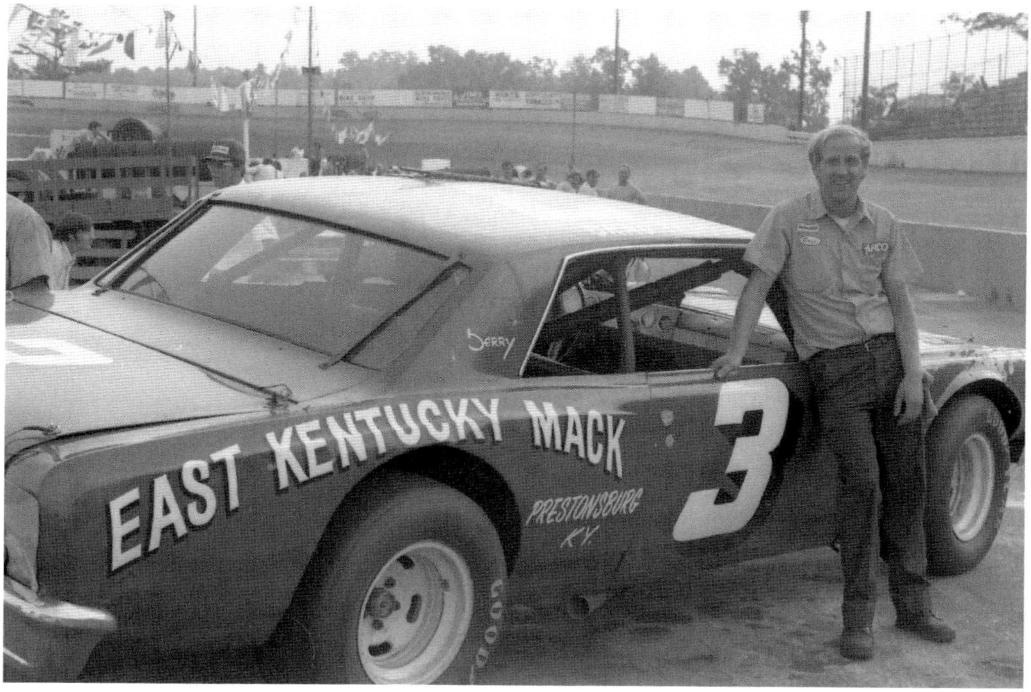

Brad Teague poses beside the No. 3 Chevelle that provided his first experience in NASCAR's Late Model Sportsman class. Teague won championships at Lonesome Pine International Raceway in Coeburn, Virginia, narrowly missed out on three Kingsport track titles, and was a national points contender. (Courtesy of Murray family collection.)

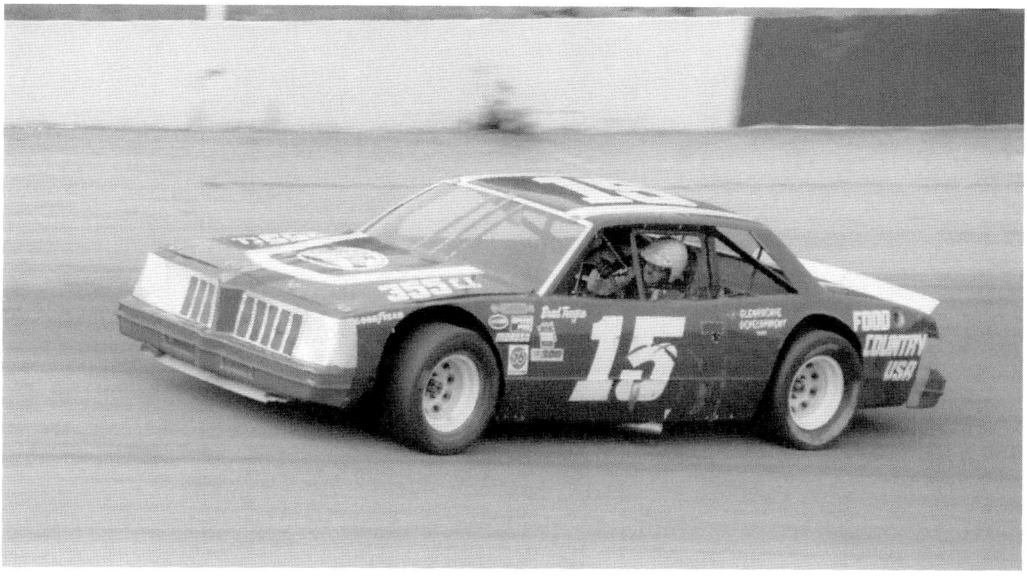

Driving for Henderson Motorsports, Brad Teague made a furious run for the 1981 Late Model Sportsman championship. With just a single car, his team finished second behind Tommy Ellis. Teague went on to have a notable career racing in all three of NASCAR's top touring series. (Photograph by Chris Haverly.)

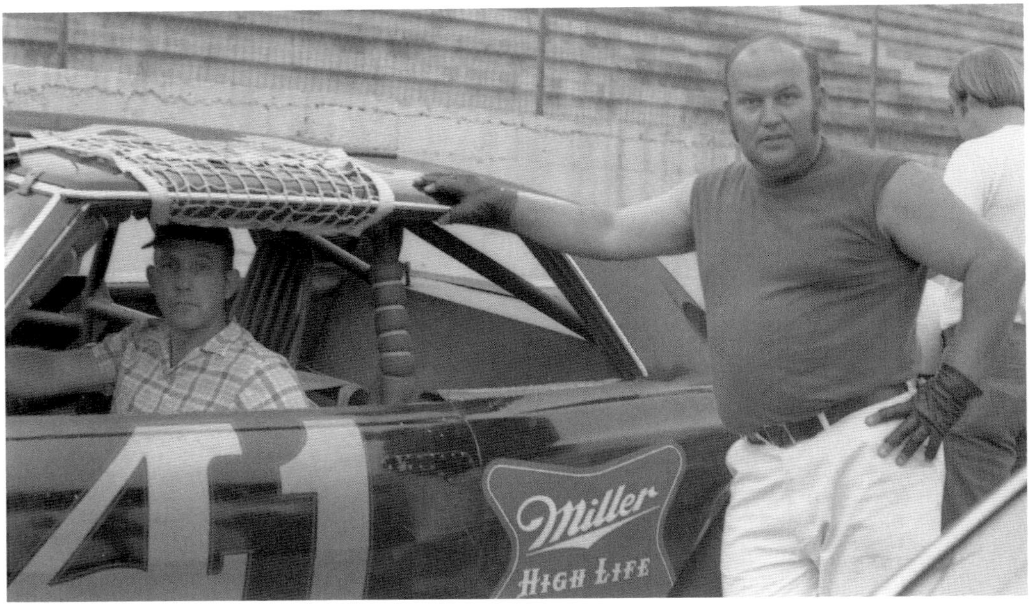

Former NASCAR premier series regular Bill Morton (right) was always a factor during Kingsport's first dirt era. He sometimes ran some Late Model Sportsman races on pavement in the No. 41 Chevelle owned by Bud Rambo. That car was regularly driven by Larry Foster. (Courtesy of Murray family collection.)

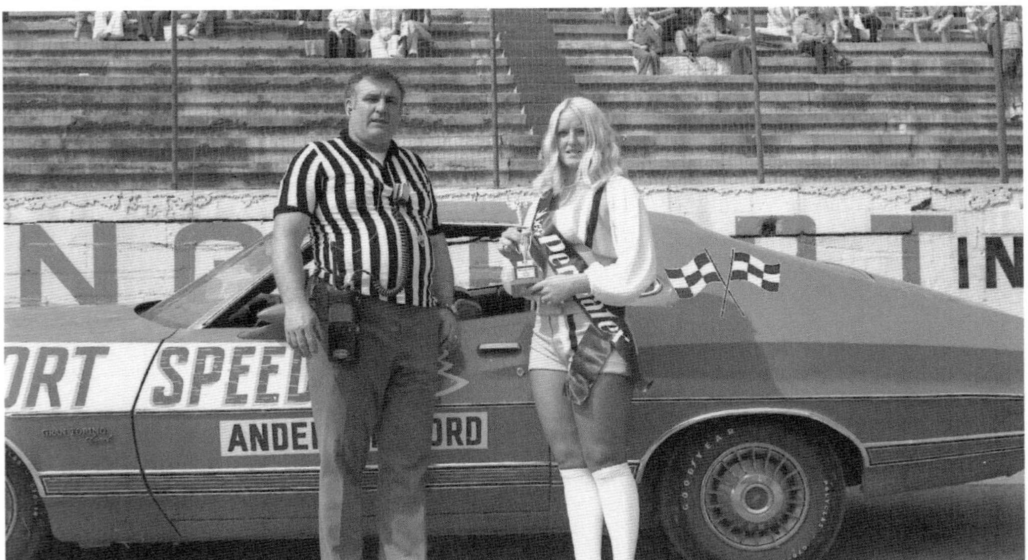

Driver, car builder, crew chief, and innovator Ken "Bear" Hunley had a couple of stints serving as a Kingsport Speedway track official. Here, he poses with Miss Permatex, Connie Christian, and the 1973 speedway pace car. Hunley later became a highly successful NASCAR Late Model Sportsman crew chief, tuning L.D. Ottinger to two national championships and then winning two more with Butch Lindley. He was also involved with Gene Glover's 1979 national title. (Courtesy of Murray family collection.)

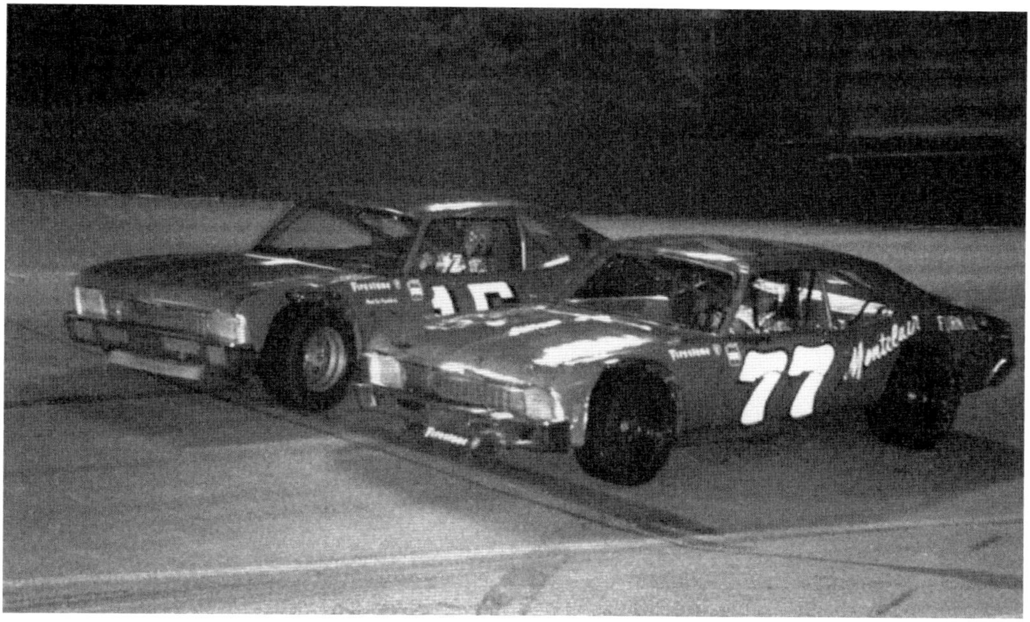

Among the most dominant, yet most popular, drivers in the NASCAR Late Model Sportsman era were Harry Gant (No. 77) and Butch Lindley (No. 16), shown racing door-to-door at Kingsport International Speedway. Both claimed multiple major wins at Kingsport in the 1970s, and Gant went on to become a star in NASCAR's premier series. (Photograph by David Allio.)

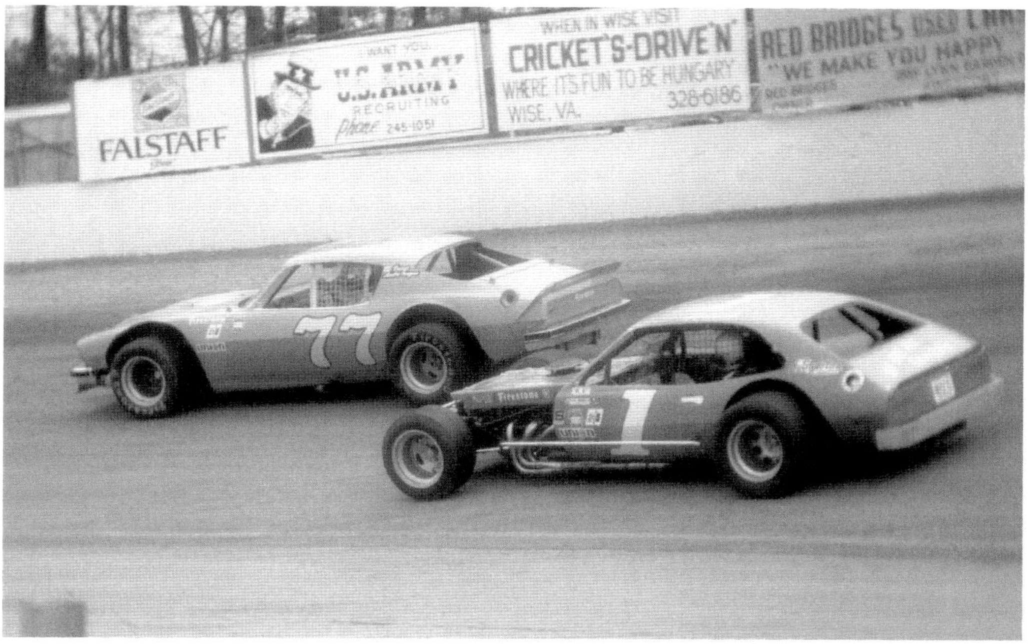

Harry Gant (No. 77) in his Chevrolet Camaro leads Geoff Bodine (No. 1), driving a Ford Pinto, in the first Winston 500 NASCAR Modified national championship race at Kingsport in November 1976. Gant qualified on the pole, but he blew an engine. Bodine claimed the victory, his 32nd of that season. (Photograph by David Allio.)

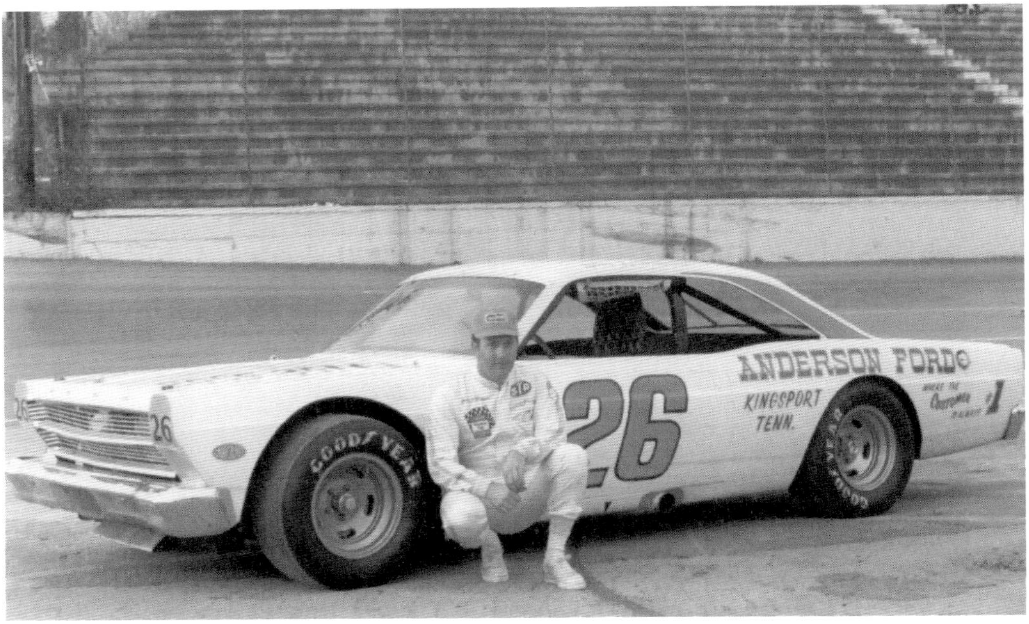

John A. Utsman was known as "the people's choice" for his success in homebuilt Fords and his congenial personality. Utsman won the 1972 Kingsport title and numerous races, and he placed well in the track and national points standings for more than a decade. He went on to race in NASCAR's premier series before returning to dirt racing. (Courtesy of John A. Utsman.)

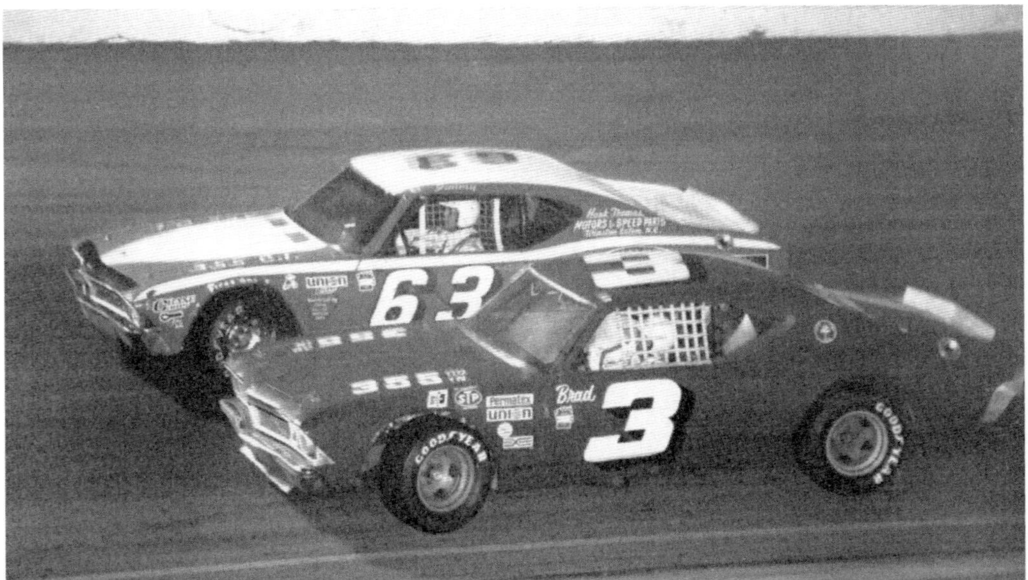

Jimmy Hensley (No. 63) races Brad Teague (No. 3) in 1976 action at Kingsport. Hensley, the "Virginia Gentleman," made an eight-hour round-trip each week to claim four consecutive Kingsport track titles and several national championship victories in machines owned by Hubert Hensley. These two had quite a rivalry, finishing first and second in Kingsport points in 1974, 1975, and 1976. (Photograph by David Allio.)

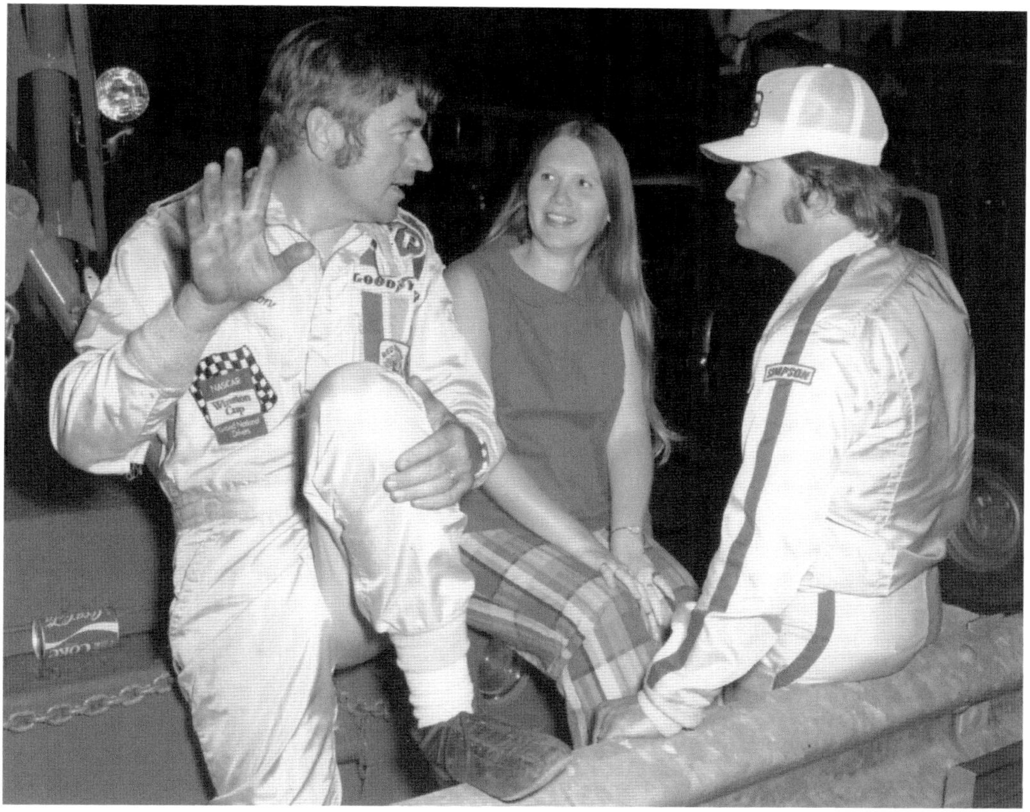

NASCAR Hall of Fame driver Bobby Allison (left) talks with Larry Utsman and his wife, Jeanie, in the pits at Kingsport Speedway. Utsman, of Bluff City, Tennessee, earned two Kingsport Late Model Sportsman track championships in 1977 and 1979 and wins in both weekly and national points races. Allison occasionally competed in Kingsport Late Model Sportsman events. (Courtesy of Larry Utsman.)

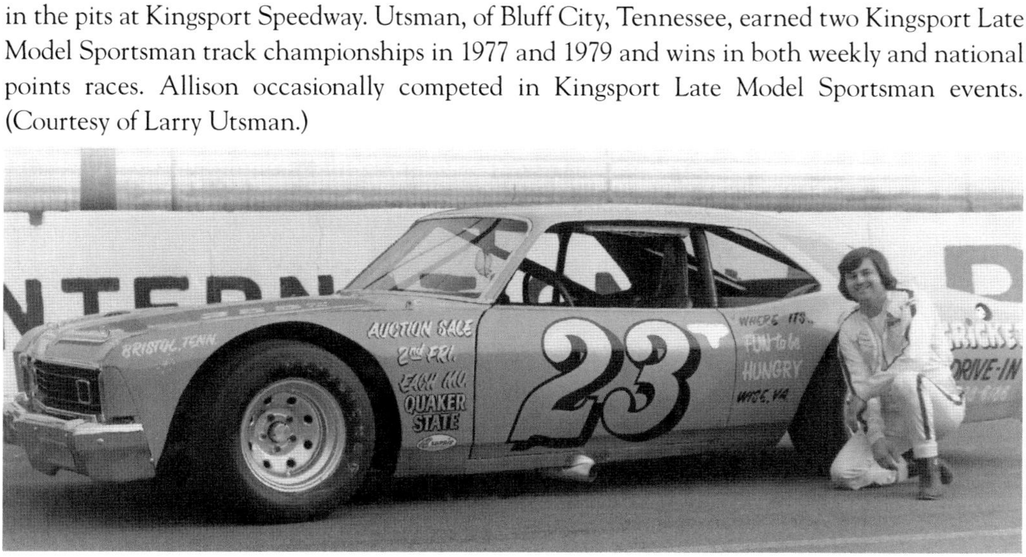

After a successful career in the hobby class, Larry Utsman was a contender at both Kingsport and Lonesome Pine International Raceway with this Nova. A cousin of the racing Utsman family, Larry more than held his own against John A., Layman, and other family members and the rest of the competition. (Courtesy of Larry Utsman.)

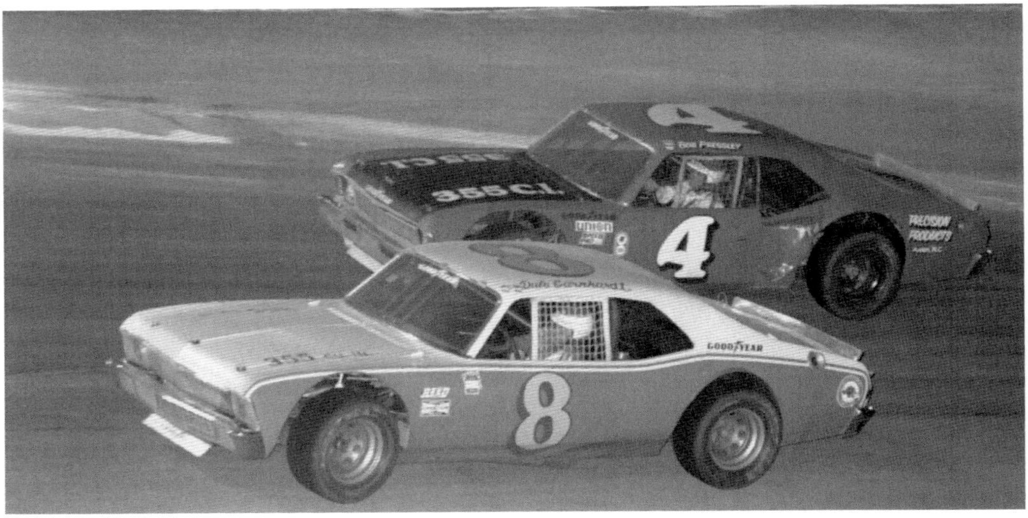

Dale Earnhardt (No. 8) races Bob Pressley (No. 4) in the NASCAR 150 Winston Late Model Sportsman double points feature at Kingsport International Speedway in March 1978. Pressley was a well-respected star at the time, while young Earnhardt had but four premier series starts and was trying to eke out a living in racing. A year later, Earnhardt won a Winston Cup race at Bristol, went on to be the rookie of the year, and eventually enjoyed a hall-of-fame NASCAR career. (Photograph by David Allio.)

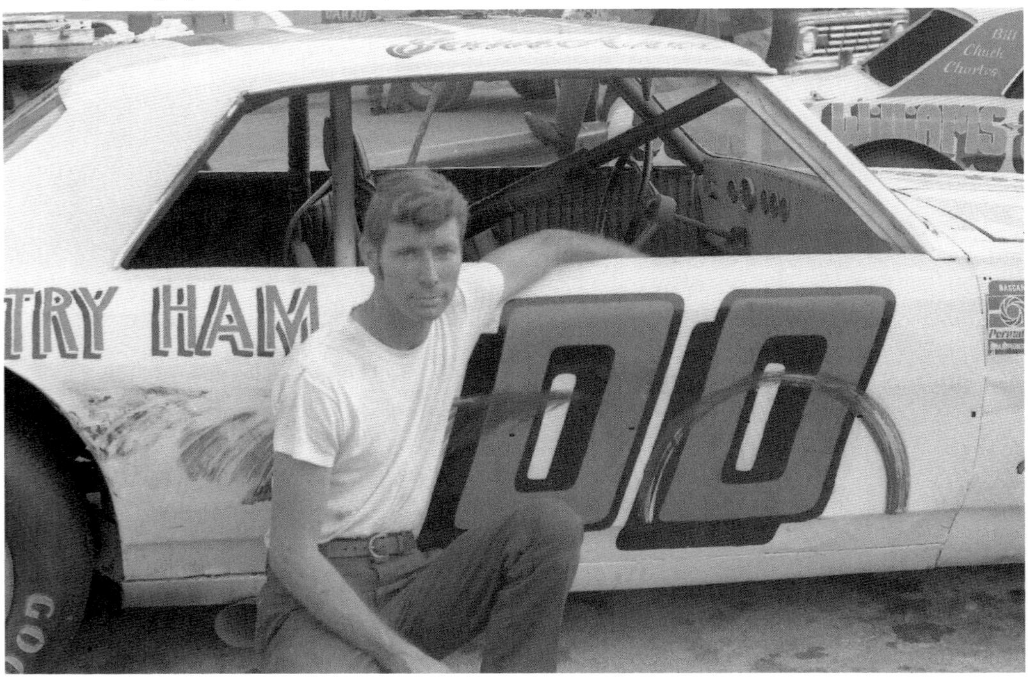

Sam Ard (No. 00) battled Jack Ingram every week for the national Late Model Sportsman title, which meant regular visits to Kingsport Speedway. Ard wound up second to Ingram in 1973, but he later won two Busch Series championships. Ard is widely regarded as one of the sport's greatest driving talents. (Courtesy of Murray family collection.)

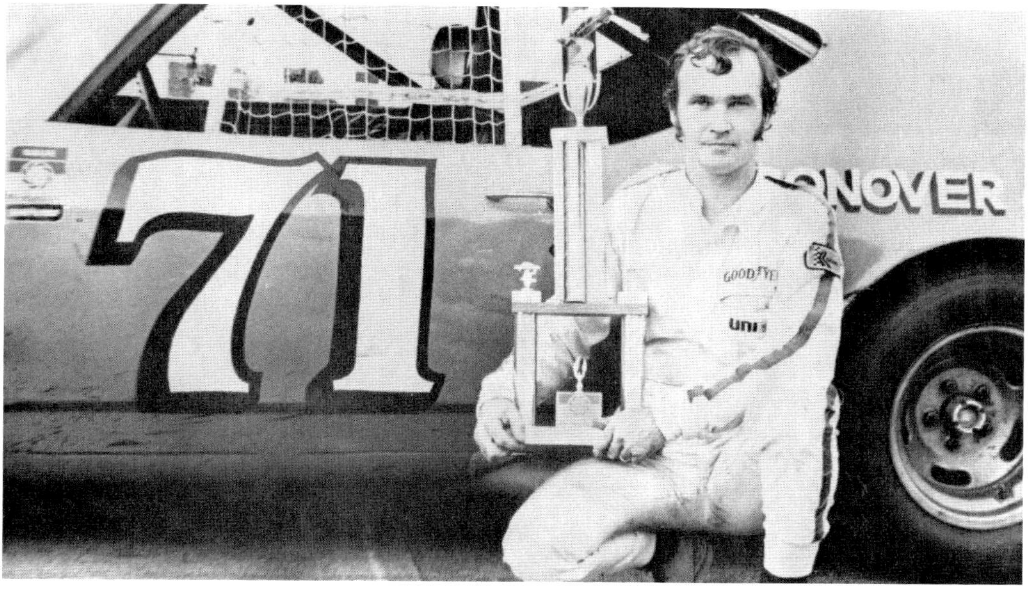

Morgan Shepherd shows off the trophy for winning the 1973 Permatex 300 NASCAR Late Model Sportsman race at Kingsport Speedway. Shepherd was a regular factor in the Sportsman national races, finishing second in national points during that 1973 season, despite driving for 17 different car owners. He won the 1980 series title and raced for decades in NASCAR's premier series. (Author's collection.)

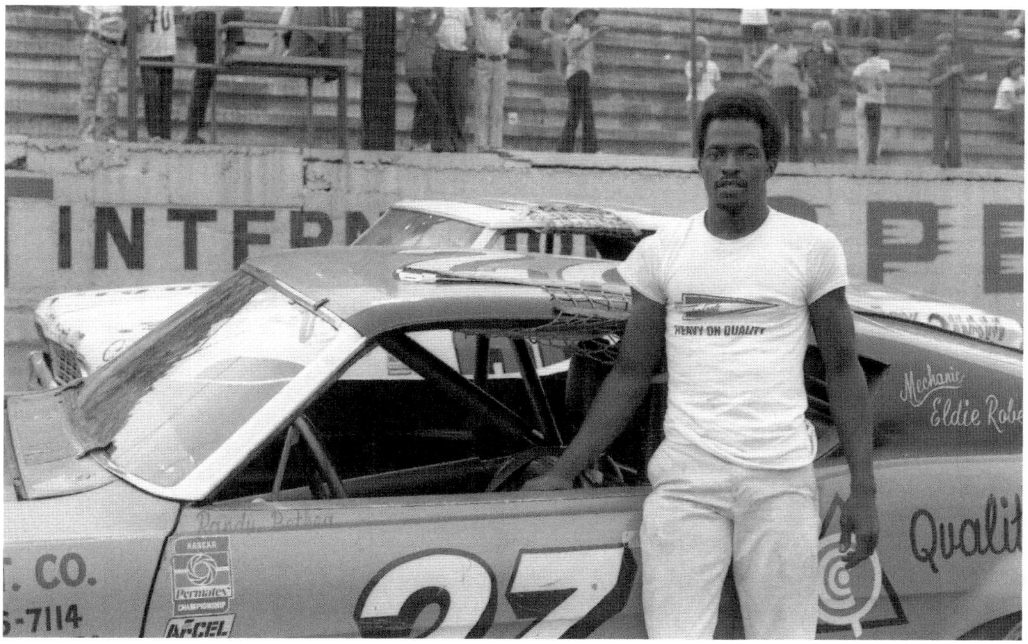

Randy Bethea was a popular driver in the Late Model series. He began racing in the hobby division, winning the 1970 NASCAR Tennessee championship. In the Sportsman class, the Newport, Tennessee, driver often wheeled this Ford to finishes among the leaders. (Courtesy of Murray family collection.)

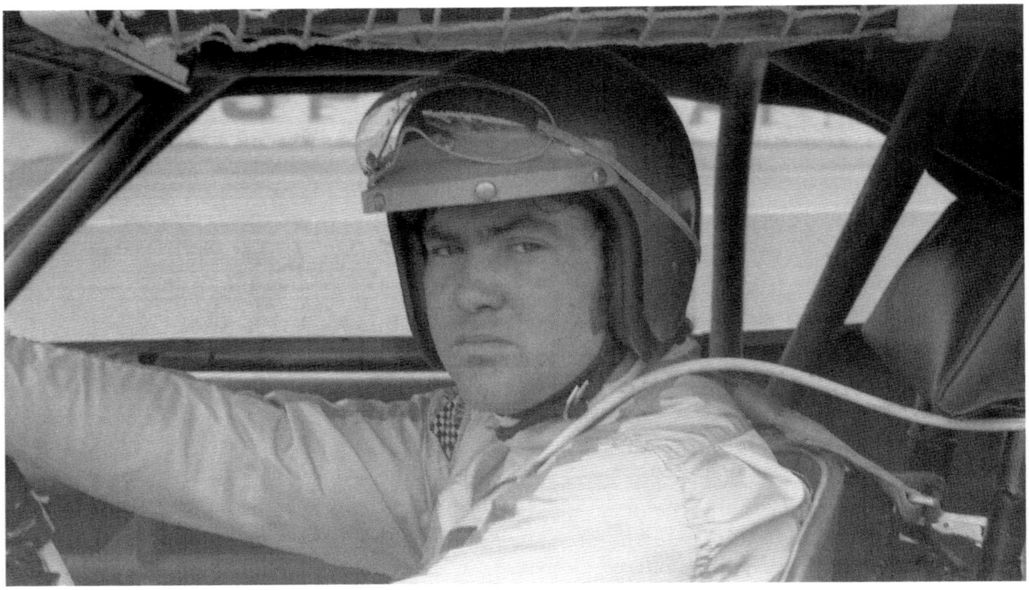

Young Grant Adcox of Chattanooga, Tennessee, was a rising star in the 1970s when he raced Late Model Sportsman cars at Kingsport. He finished fifth in the 1972 national points before moving to NASCAR's premier series. His greatest success came in the Automobile Racing Club of America series, where he won eight races and four poles on superspeedways like Daytona and Talladega. (Courtesy of Murray family collection.)

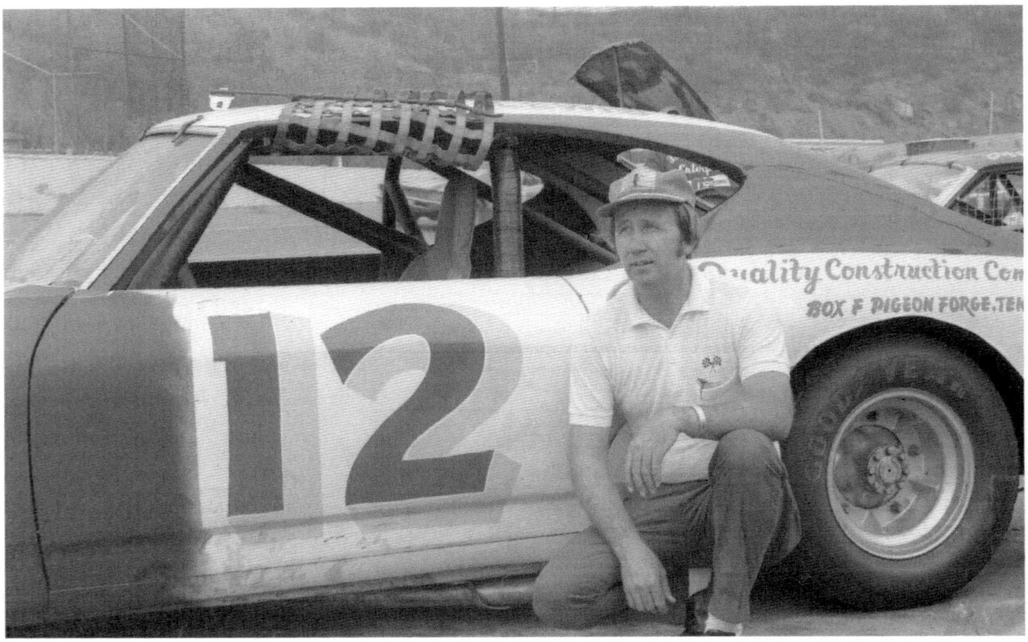

Paul Lewis of Johnson City, Tennessee, was a former winner in the NASCAR Grand National series in the 1960s who enjoyed a second career in the Late Model Sportsman cars. Lewis estimates that he won about 20 Sportsman races, primarily driving Chevelles for the Brackins brothers of Sevierville, Tennessee. (Courtesy of Murray family collection.)

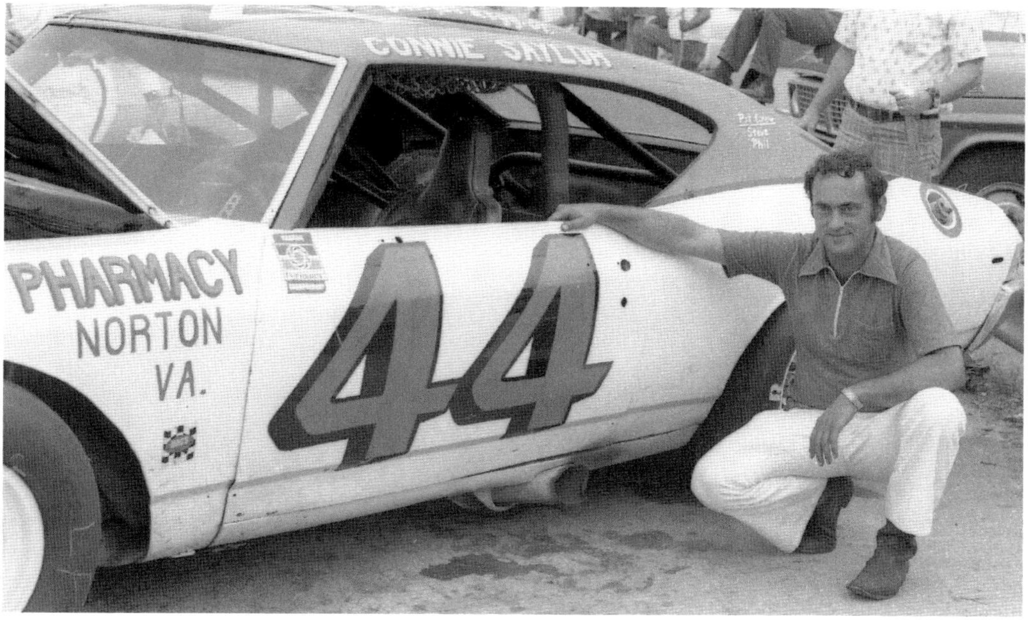

Connie Saylor was always competitive in the NASCAR Late Model Sportsman series at Kingsport and Lonesome Pine, as evidenced by a string of top-10 points finishes. He later raced sporadically in NASCAR's premier series in the 1970s and 1980s and won a 1984 Daytona 500 consolation race that included J.D. McDuffie and Ramo Stott. (Courtesy of Murray family collection.)

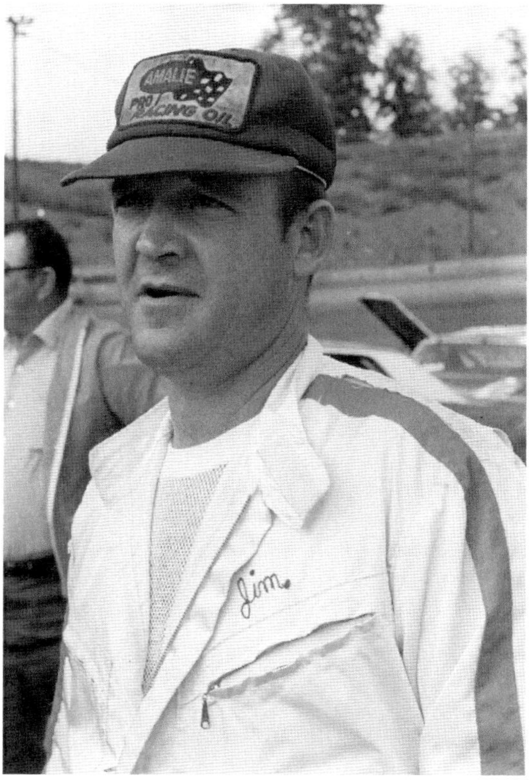

Jim Hayes of Jonesborough, Tennessee, was a national champion motorcycle racer who was also a competitive and popular regular at Kingsport. In the early 1970s, he raced a Plymouth "kit car" prepared by Petty Engineering. Hayes died suddenly during heart surgery in 1976. For many years, Kingsport held a Jim Hayes Memorial race. (Courtesy of Tony Morton.)

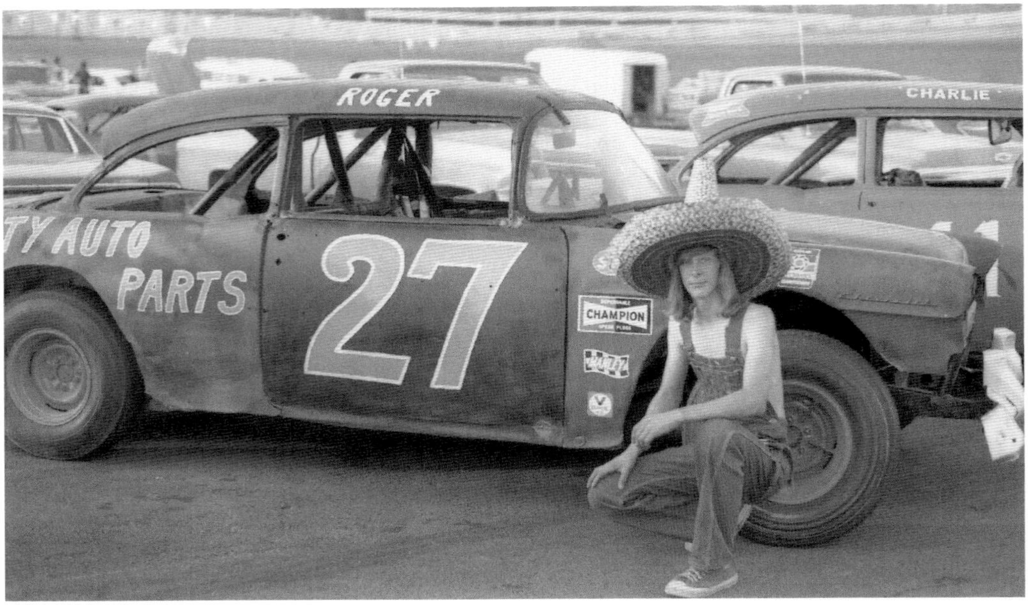

Longtime Kingsport Speedway competitors who rose through the ranks are Roger Clendenin (above) and Jeff Berry (below). Clendenin raced on Kingsport's track when it was dirt and asphalt, winning three amateur class championships and one Late Model title. Berry also enjoyed considerable success at different levels, advancing from the amateur class to the Late Model division. In these photographs from the early 1970s, both racers display the latest in hats and hairstyles. (Both, courtesy of Murray family collection.)

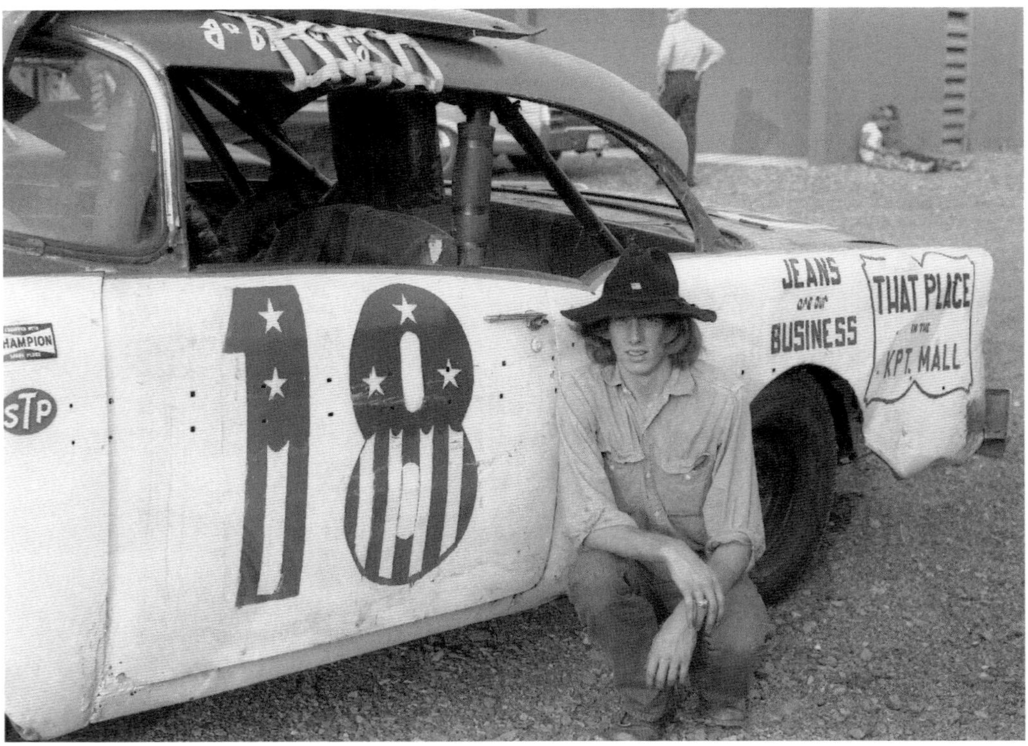

4

Down and Dirty

Throughout the first half of Kingsport Speedway's "golden era," the track flourished despite competing for fans and drivers with Appalachian Speedway, a well-built dirt oval track operating less than two miles away. Appalachian, built by business rivals of Kingsport owner Ken Murray, held its grand opening the same night in April 1969 that Kingsport hosted its first NASCAR race on pavement.

The two tracks went head-to-head for years before Appalachian's owners gave up in 1975, following a string of consecutive rainouts. With the closure of the Sportsman Speedway in Johnson City that same year, a local newspaper columnist pronounced dirt racing "dead" in the Tri-Cities region.

Imagine the shock waves in 1984 when new Kingsport promoter J.D. Stacy began tearing out the asphalt surface and replacing it with dirt. The transition included a name change to Raceland Kingsport, a purported $500,000 in renovations, and the erection of corporate offices for Stacy's Raceland Motorsports, an organization designed to promote dirt racing at his Southeastern racetracks. "J.D. Stacy bought Cordelle, Georgia, and Kingsport and put together what was going to be the biggest weekly racing program that has ever been and pay $2,000 to win. That, today, is good money. When they put that together at Kingsport, that became my total focus," hall-of-fame driver Scott Bloomquist said of that season. "My goal was to win every race. I didn't get the car done in time for the first one but we won every race but one. The one I did not win was when NDRA [National Dirt Racing Association] came to town."

While Raceland was short-lived, the red clay stayed down for more than a decade and further enhanced Kingsport's reputation as home to championship-winning drivers like Bloomquist and, later, Jimmy Owens, who scored his first-ever victory there. Other promoters enjoyed varying degrees of success, but competing with faster, higher-profile dirt tracks proved challenging. Most tracks raced on the more lucrative Saturday nights, while Kingsport primarily raced on Fridays. That often meant starting later, to accommodate work schedules and travel time. This too often spelled smaller crowds.

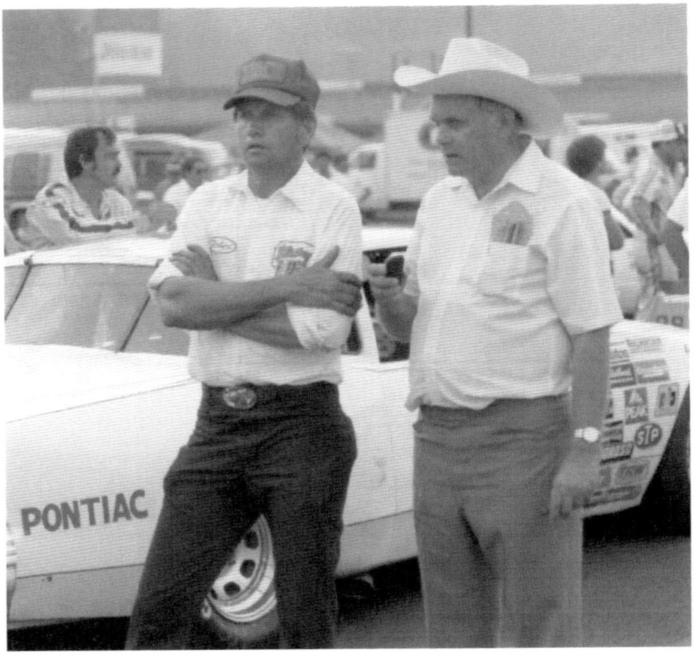

From 1976 to 1983, James "J.D." Stacy (right) was a NASCAR premier series team owner and sponsor, fielding cars for Neil Bonnett, Dale Earnhardt, Tim Richmond, and Morgan Shepherd, among others. However, the flamboyant Kentuckian changed directions in 1984, investing in racetracks in Georgia, South Carolina, and Kingsport, Tennessee, aiming to establish a prominent dirt racing series. (Photograph by the author.)

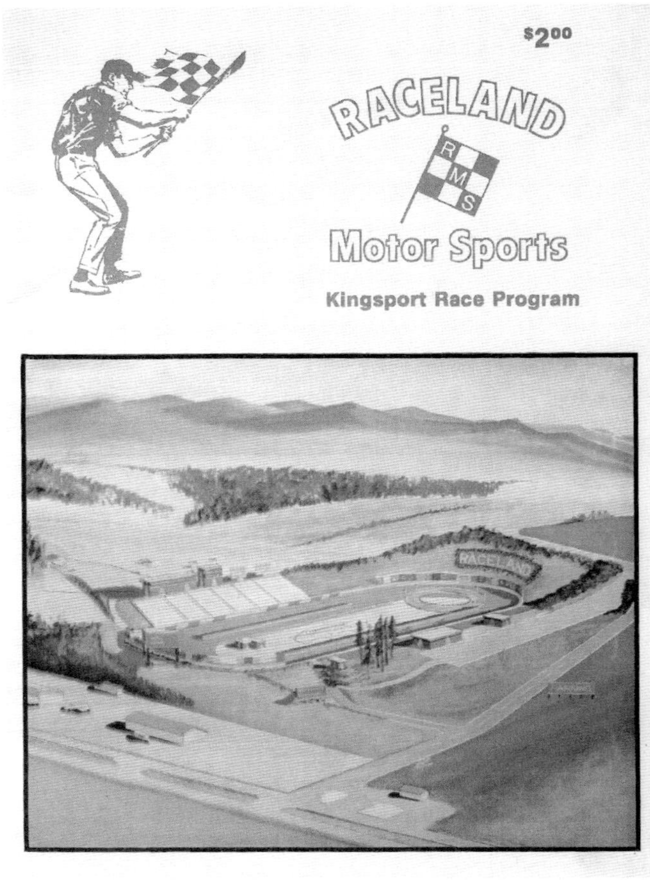

This 1984 souvenir program cover shows an artist's concept for Raceland, Stacy's name for the new venture. He painted walls and buildings the same shades of blue and yellow that adorned Winston Cup cars he sponsored, and he overhauled the facility. The biggest change was ripping up the asphalt and returning Kingsport to its red clay roots. The Raceland Corporation opened an office next to the track, but its tenure was short-lived. (Author's collection.)

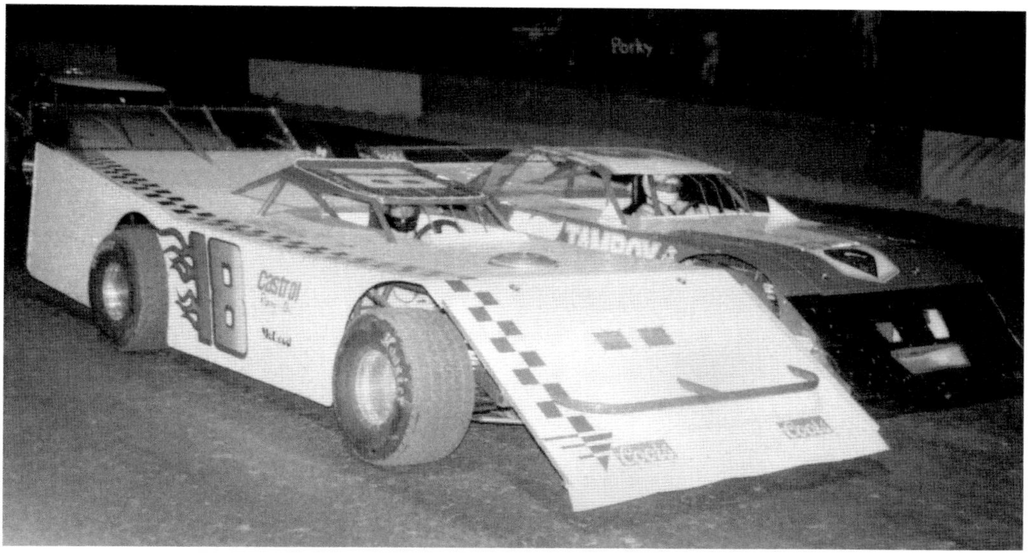

Kingsport's transition to dirt coincided perfectly with youthful Californian Scott Bloomquist's move to East Tennessee. Bloomquist (No. 18) and Rodney Combs (No. 5) were among the top names competing for Raceland Kingsport's weekly $2,500 top prize. Bloomquist claimed the 1984 Kingsport title, winning 22 of 24 races. (Photograph by Mike O'Dell.)

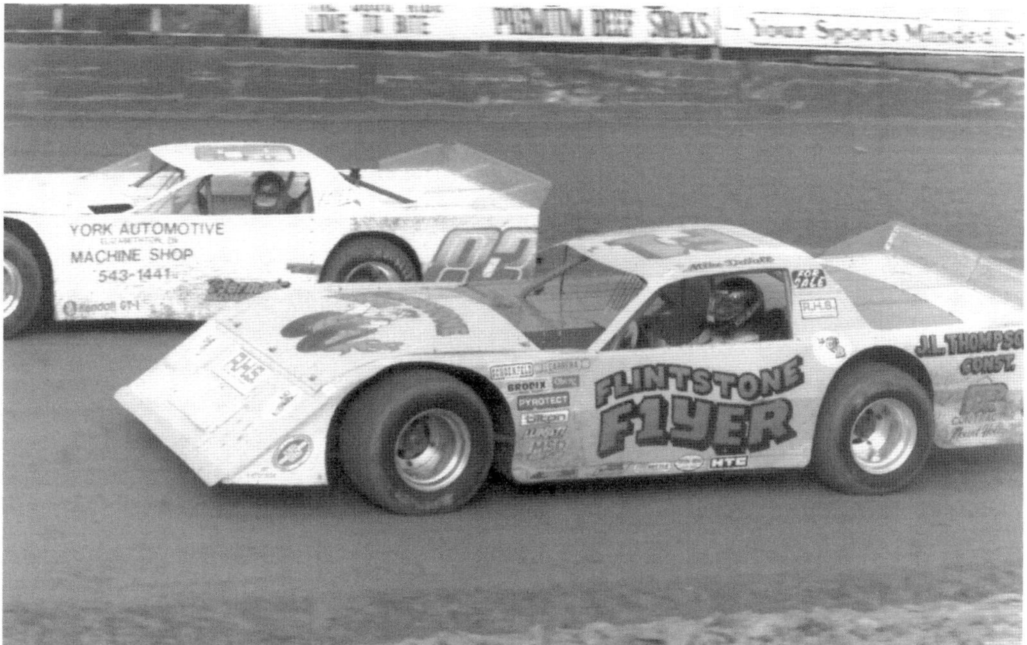

Mike Duvall wheeled his *Flintstone Flyer* to victory in the August 1984 Ram Tough 50 at Kingsport. It marked the first appearance of the Kingsport-based National Dirt Racing Association at its hometown track. Duvall was the 1982 series champion and finished second in 1984. He was later named to the National Dirt Late Model Hall of Fame. (Courtesy of Bradley Poulson and Michael Moats.)

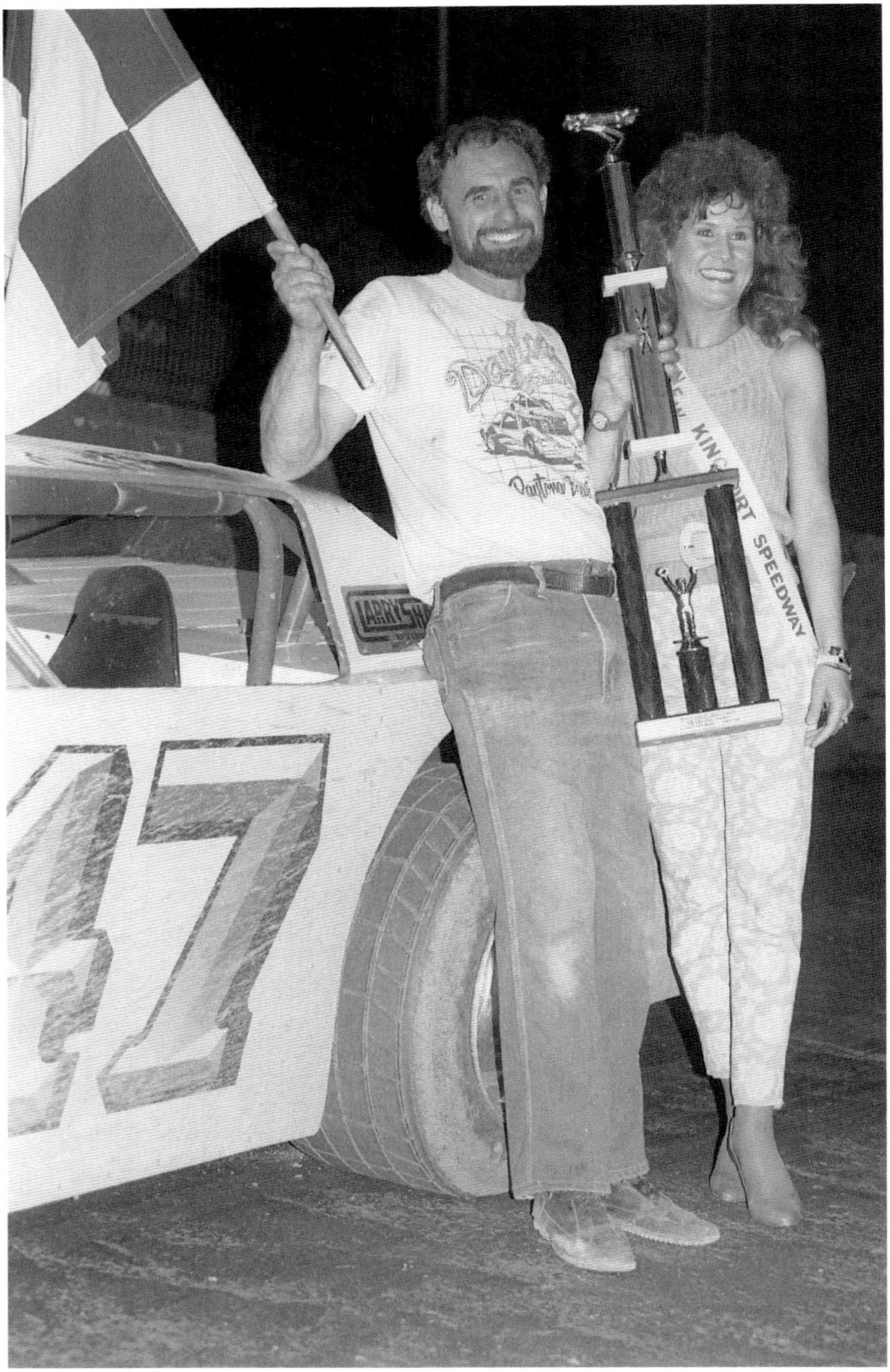

Howard "Buzz" Collins (No. 47) earned more than 400 feature race wins during his career, including many at Kingsport Speedway. After dominating the six-cylinder class, Collins jumped into late models. This photograph is from one of his many victories. (Photograph by Mike O'Dell.)

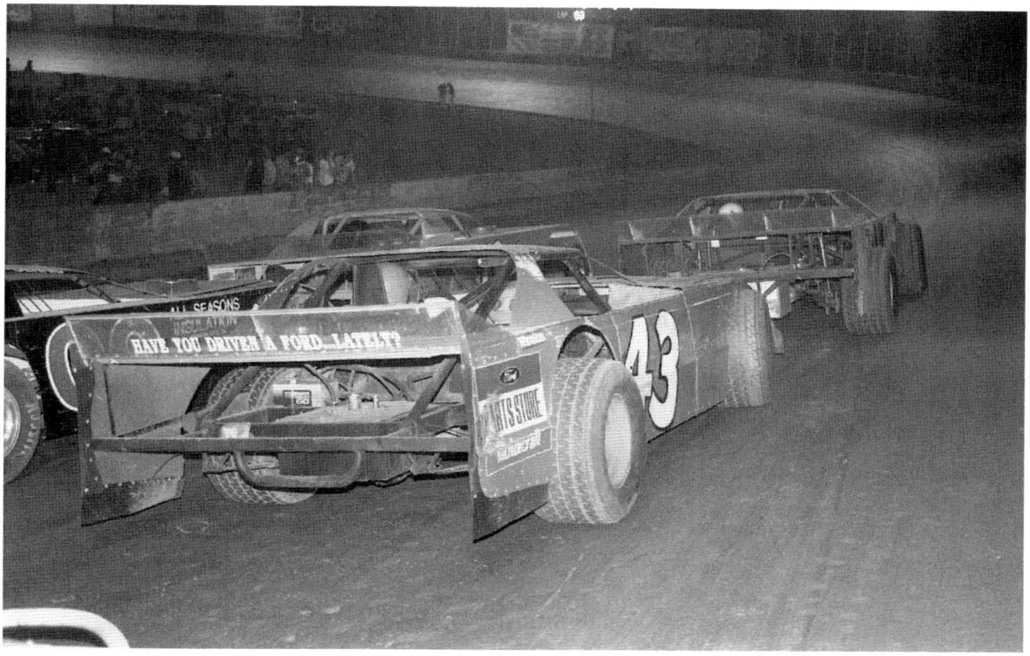

The field is lined up on the front straightaway at Kingsport Speedway, ready to sling some mud on a Friday night. Brogie Broyles (No. 43) was a prolific winner at Kingsport and other area dirt tracks for a number of seasons. (Photograph by Mike O'Dell.)

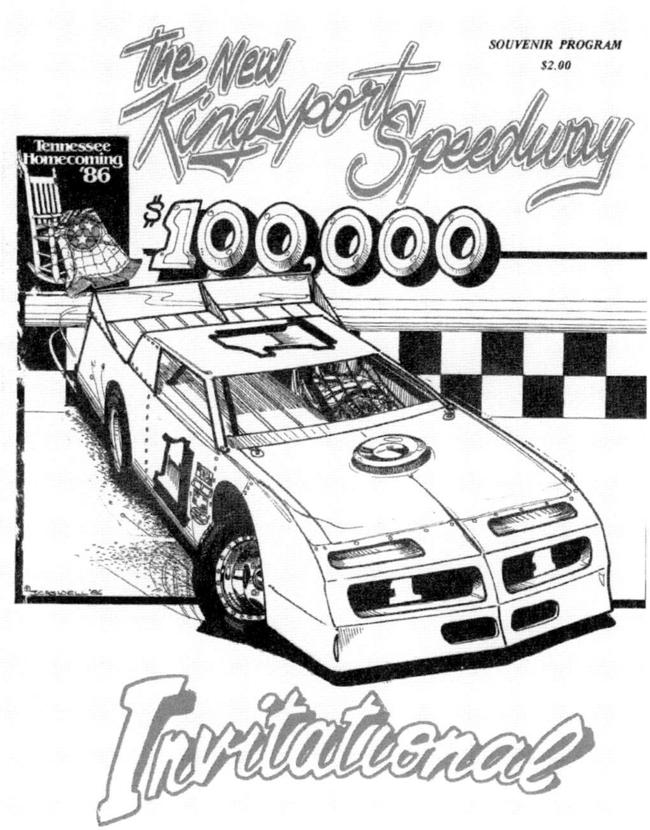

For three seasons (1985–1987), Kingsport hosted a fall Late Model invitational race with a generous payout. The 1986 event, represented here by the souvenir program cover artwork, went to Jack Pennington. Fellow Georgian Buck Simmons won in 1985, and Tennessean Jeff Purvis captured the 1987 race. (Courtesy of Tony Morton.)

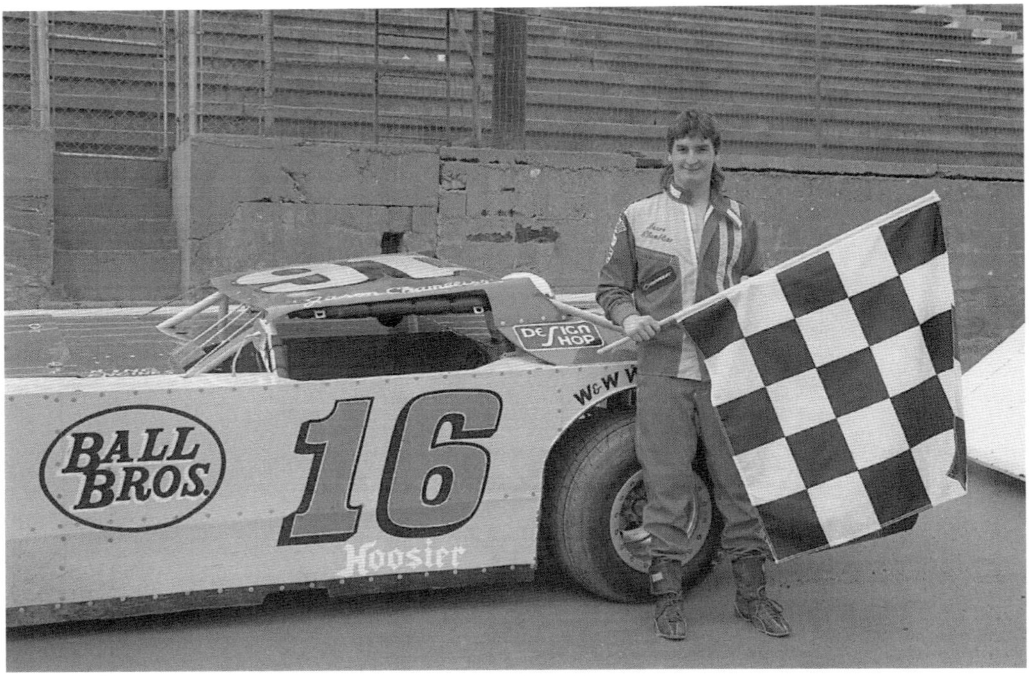

"Racin'" Jason Chambliss proudly holds the checkered flag late in the 1989 season, when he captured the Kingsport Speedway Late Model championship a few months after graduating from Sullivan Central High School. (Photograph by the author.)

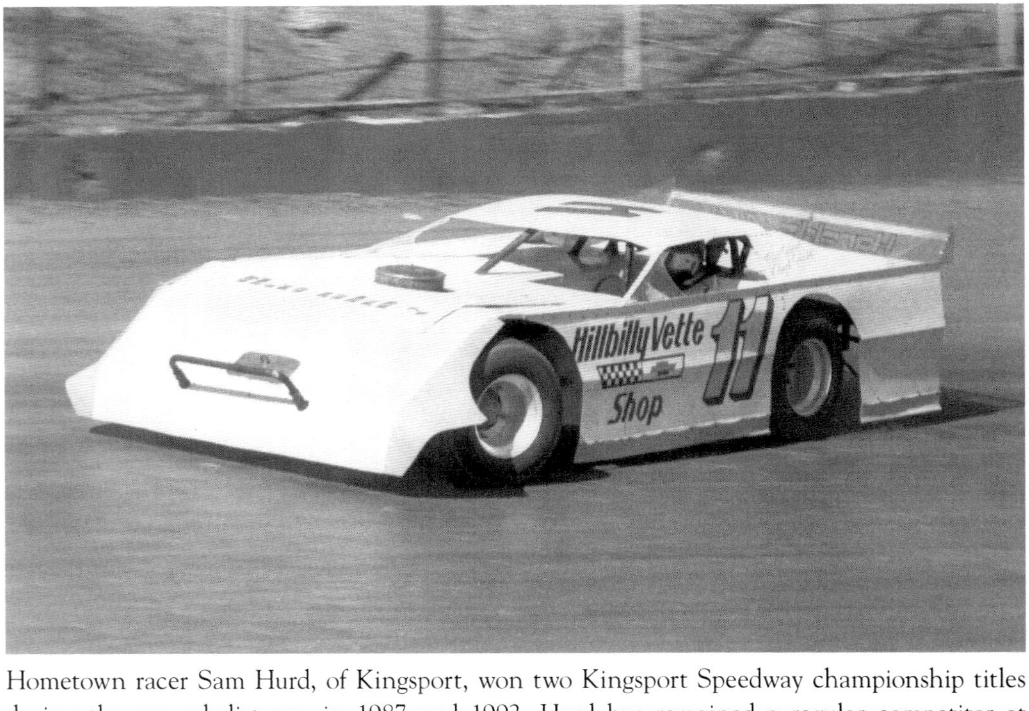

Hometown racer Sam Hurd, of Kingsport, won two Kingsport Speedway championship titles during the second dirt era, in 1987 and 1992. Hurd has remained a regular competitor at Kingsport decades later. (Photograph by the author.)

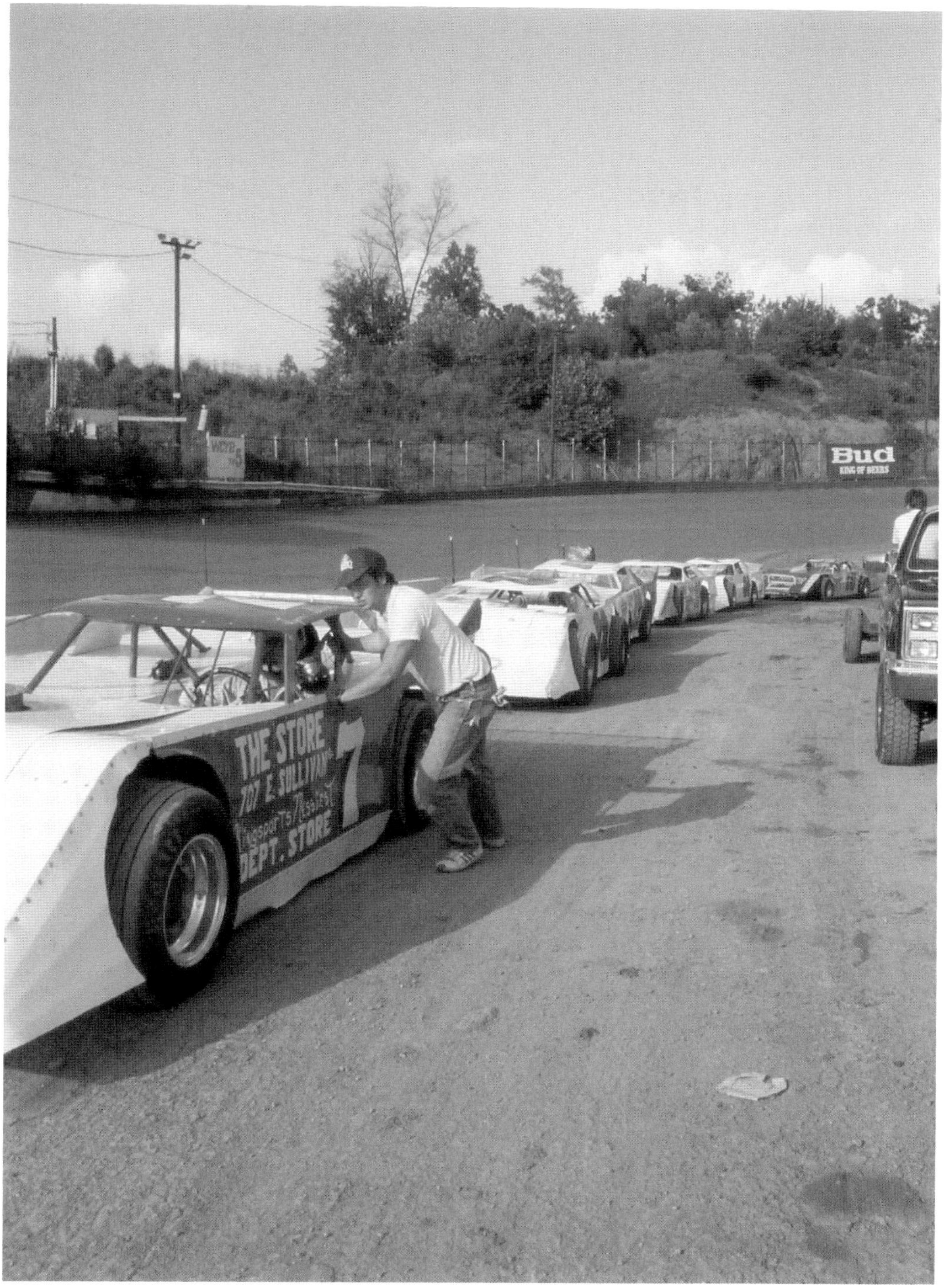

A full field of dirt Late Model stock cars is lined up on pit road and prepared to practice and qualify—including the machine of Lynn Shankle (No. 7). Whether the surface was dirt, asphalt, or concrete, Late Model cars have been the feature class at Kingsport since the late 1960s. (Photograph by the author.)

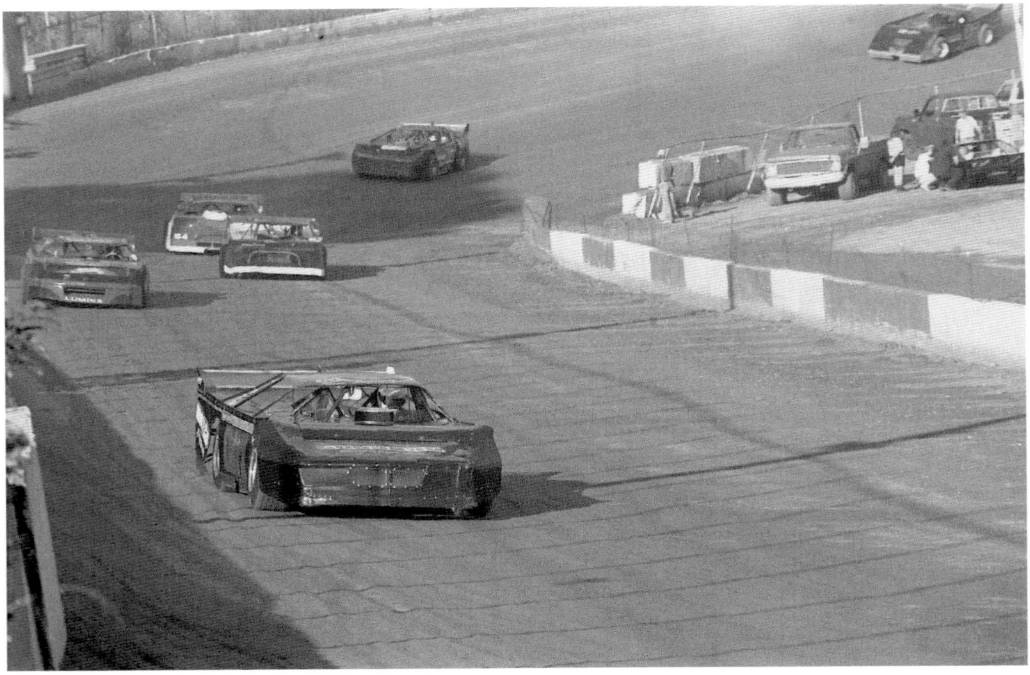

Roger Best (No. 007) leads a field of dirt Late Model stock cars down the front straightaway at Kingsport during the early 1990s. The Maryville, Tennessee, native earned track championships at Kingsport, Atomic, and Smoky Mountain speedways before becoming a regular in the Southern All-Stars series. (Photograph by the author.)

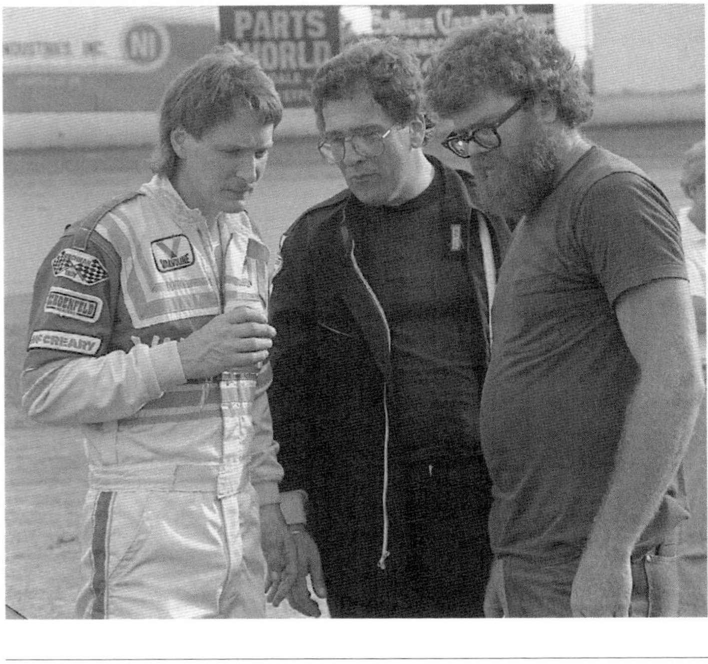

Roger Clendenin (left), Mike Memmer (center), and Lynn Shankle discuss the performance of their Late Model stock cars at Kingsport Speedway. All three were among the top contenders in dirt-racing action in the late 1980s. (Photograph by the author.)

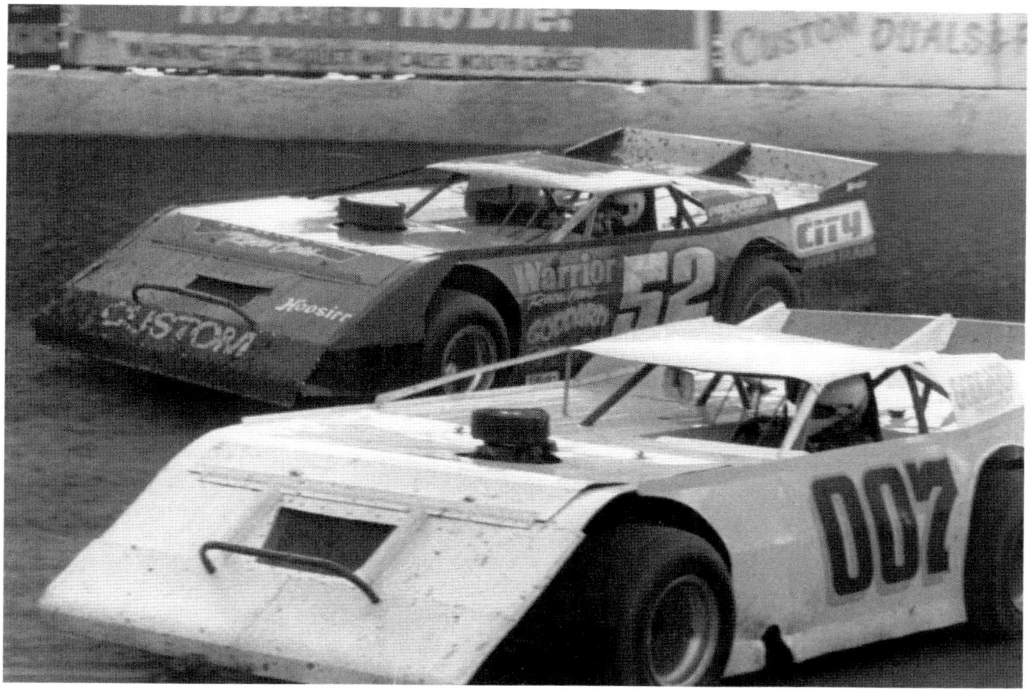

Scott Sexton (No. 52) tries the high lane around Roger Best (No. 007). Sexton, known as "Superman," won nearly 200 features in his distinguished career. Best was always a contender wherever he competed, winning many notable races and two Southern All-Stars series titles. (Photograph by the author.)

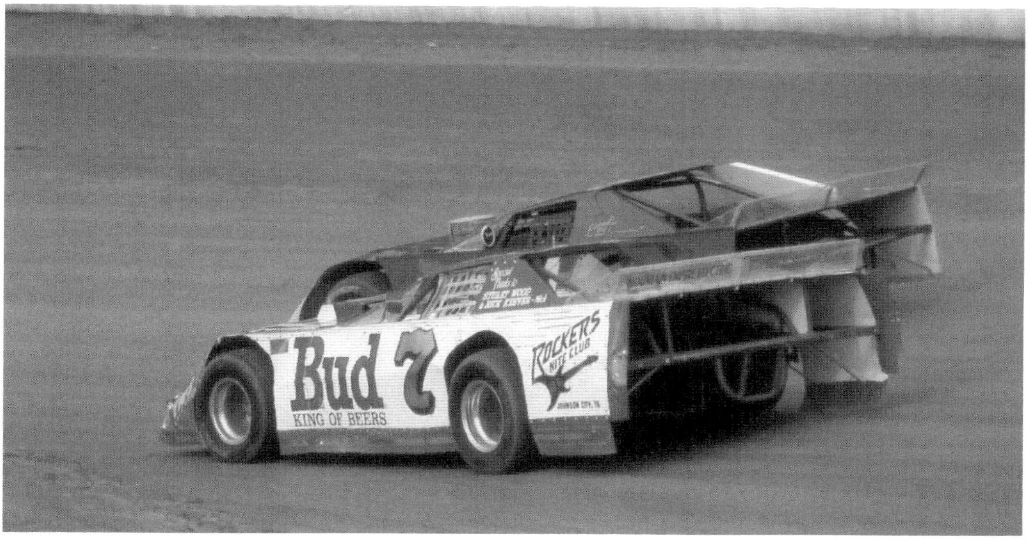

Dale Ball (No. 7) of Johnson City, Tennessee, drives on the inside of the machine of Danny Blevins (No. 4) as they race through turn four. Ball was the 1990 Kingsport Late Model season champion. His father, Walter Ball, was a dirt-racing standout who previously competed at Kingsport and other East Tennessee tracks. Blevins won multiple races and was always in contention. (Photograph by the author.)

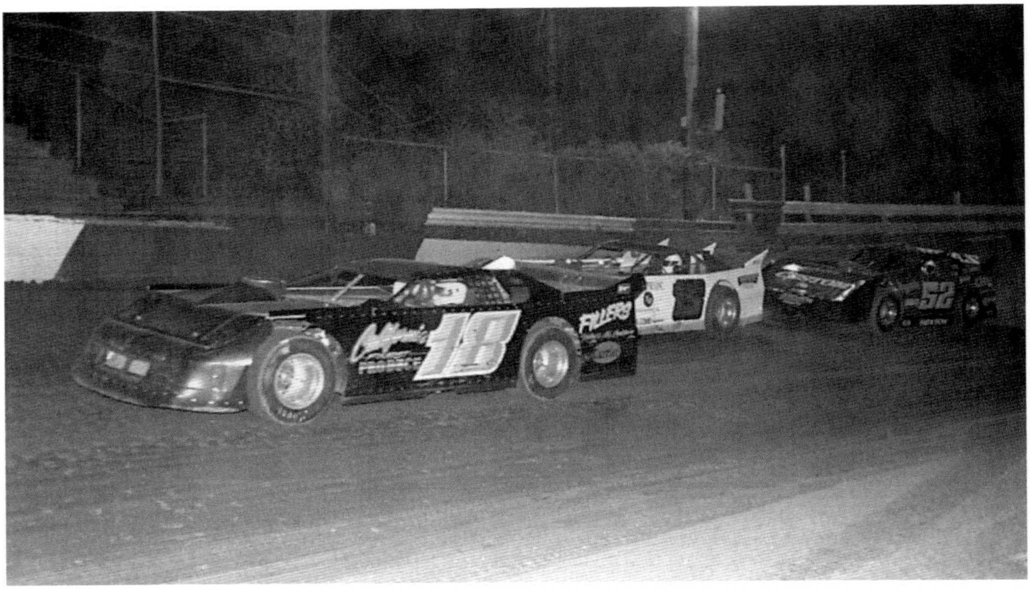

Dirt Late Models driven by Gary Myers (No. 18), Rick Norris (No. 15), and Scott Sexton (No. 52) roar off turn two and down the backstretch at Kingsport Speedway during action in the 1990s. Myers is a former track points champion, and all were regular threats to take the checkered flag. (Photograph by the author.)

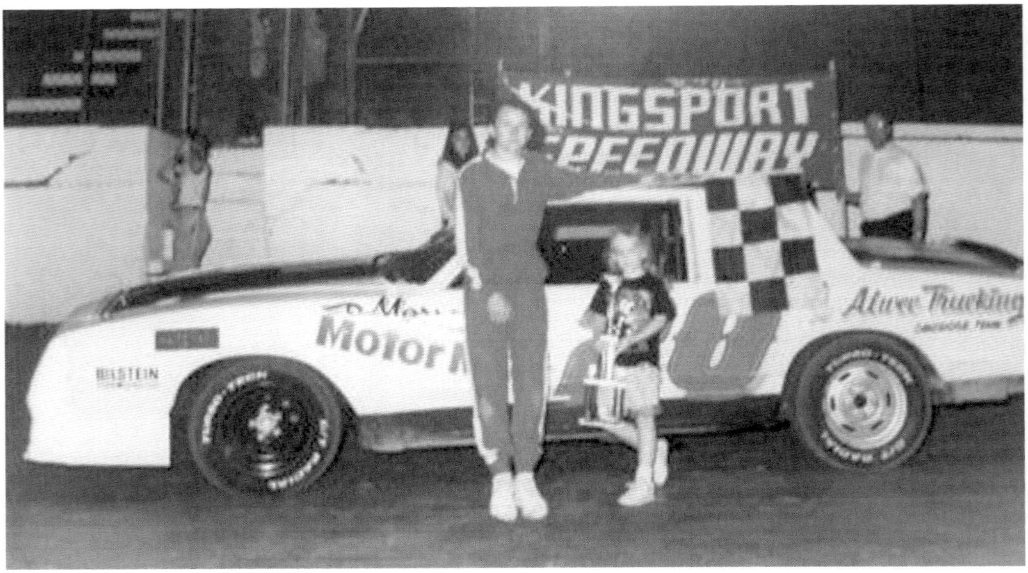

Current dirt Late Model star Jimmy Owens of Newport, Tennessee, won the first race he ever entered, a 1991 street stock contest at Kingsport Speedway. Owens, who is now known as the "Newport Nightmare," has more than 500 career victories, including many of the most prestigious races in Late Model racing. (Courtesy of Robert Walden.)

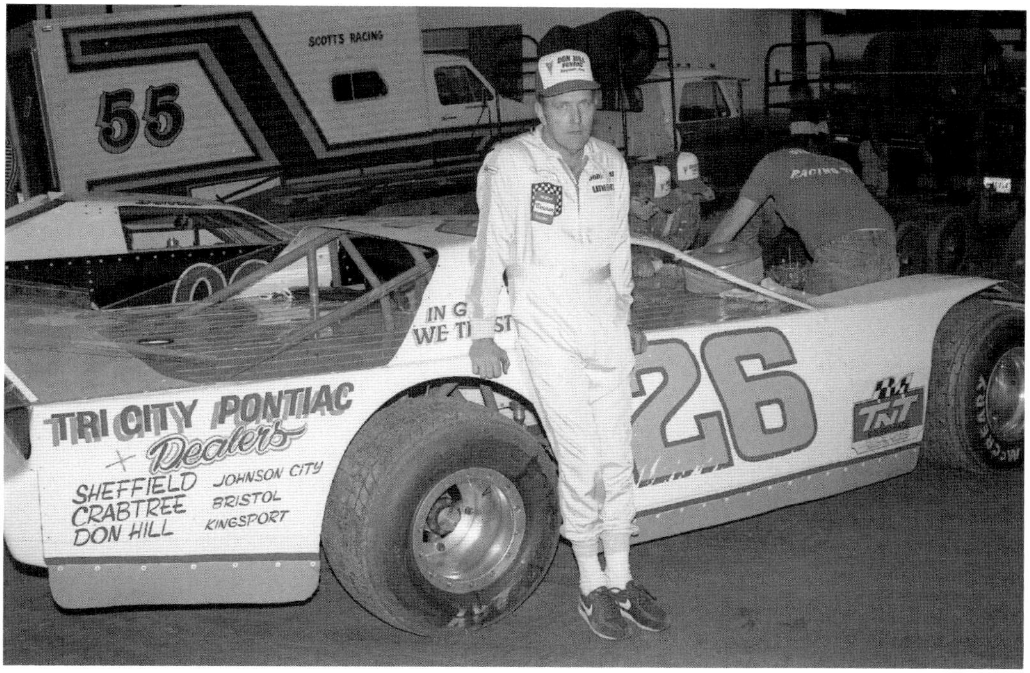

John A. Utsman of Bluff City, Tennessee, built much of his reputation driving Fords, but in 1988, he raced a Pontiac Trans Am powered by a Buick V-6 engine against the V-8 competition. The car was sponsored by local Pontiac dealers and won its share of races. (Photograph by Mike O'Dell.)

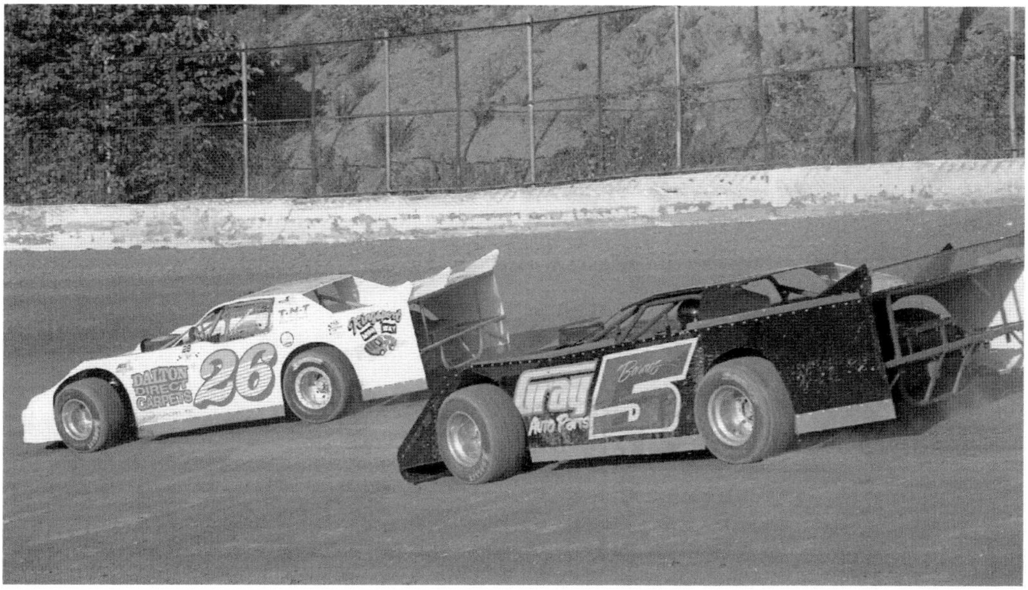

John A. Utsman (No. 26) leads Frankie Barnes (No. 5) in action at Kingsport. Utsman won 18 races in 28 starts at Kingsport and Volunteer speedways in 1993. After clinching both track championships, one of Utsman's cars was enshrined in the International Motorsports Hall of Fame in Talladega, Alabama, where it remains today. (Photograph by the author.)

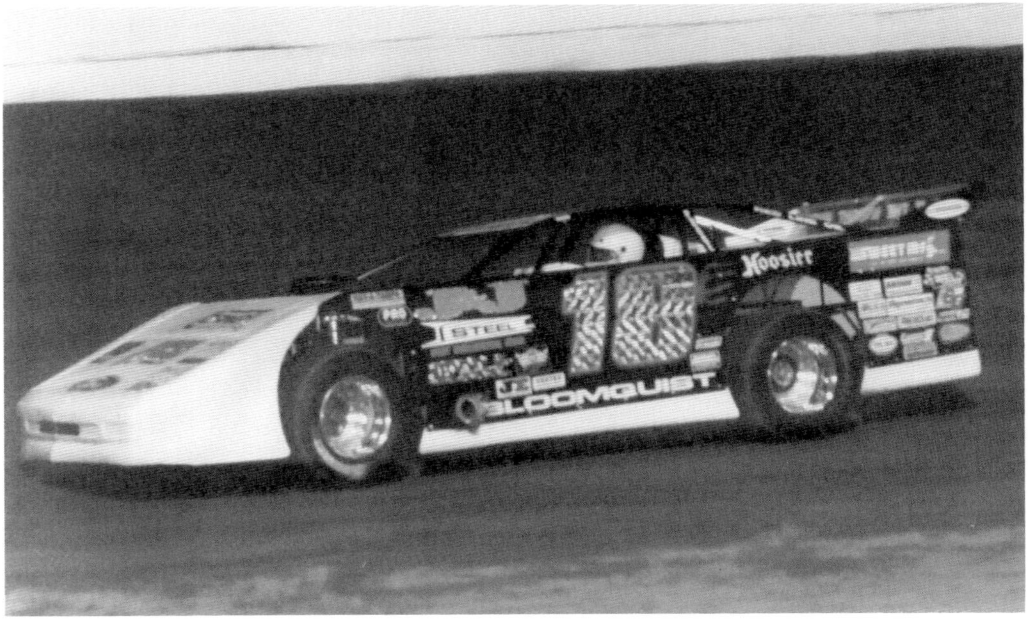

Years after Scott Bloomquist dominated the weekly action at Kingsport, the legendary dirt racer returned home to claim a Hav-A-Tampa touring series victory in August 1994. The hall-of-fame driver credits much of his success with lessons learned at Kingsport and other East Tennessee dirt ovals. (Photograph by Randall Perry.)

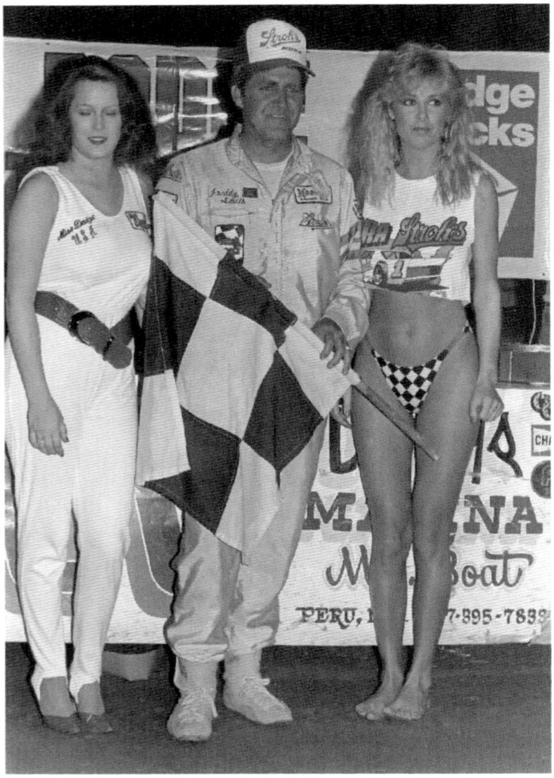

Freddy Smith was the big winner when the National Dirt Racing Association held its Ram Tough 100 at Kingsport Speedway in March 1985. Regarded as one of the greatest dirt racers of all time. Smith moved from North Carolina to East Tennessee and continued his winning ways. (Photograph by Mike O'Dell.)

5

Marquee Dirt Races

While Kingsport Speedway achieved its greatest acclaim during its NASCAR asphalt era, two events that generated some of its greatest exposure and largest-ever crowds happened in the 1980s dirt era.

In October 1985, the Kingsport-based National Dirt Racing Association staged its $250,000 Invitational race on its hometown track. An event packed with the promise of extensive advance promotion, the weight of national corporate sponsors, and network television coverage should have been the speedway's shining moment. However, fan attendance failed to live up to expectations, and—with so much money on the line—the event ultimately contributed to the sudden demise of the NDRA. A subsequent cover story in *Stock Car Racing* magazine describes how track conditions deteriorated, making passing nearly impossible. Buck Simmons ran away from an incredibly talented field of drivers.

Perhaps the ultimate irony was that NDRA founder Robert Smawley, a former motorcycle racer from Kingsport, previously promoted nearby rival Appalachian Speedway in its final years of operation. It seems the Kingsport track had the last laugh.

Just four years later, on July 6, 1989, Kingsport hosted one of its largest crowds, as thousands came to see NASCAR stars like Rusty Wallace, Dale Jarrett, and Michael Waltrip drive local dirt Late Model cars in an exhibition race.

Billed as the Race of Champions, the event was staged in cooperation with the Kingsport Chamber of Commerce, local auto-dealers, and the local newspaper. That event attracted even casual fans. A two-time Kingsport Grand National race winner, Richard Petty, also returned and served as the honorary starter, waving the green flag and signing a few thousand versions of his famous autograph.

The race was won by Rick Wilson, who, at that time, drove for Morgan-McClure Motorsports, the region's NASCAR team based in Abingdon, Virginia. Wilson outran future NASCAR hall of famers Wallace and Jarrett and former dirt standout Rodney Combs.

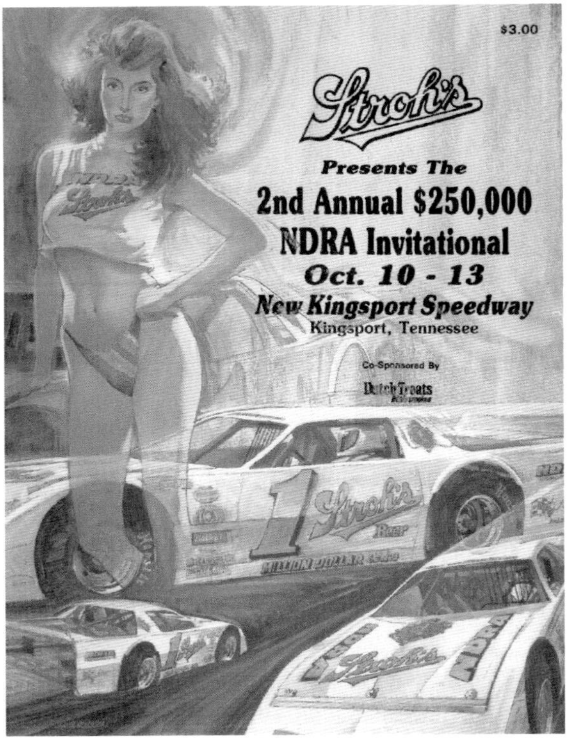

This is the cover of the souvenir program for the 1985 National Dirt Racing Association invitational race at Kingsport Speedway. The event and series featured significant corporate sponsorship and a payout of $250,000, the largest in dirt-racing history at that time. It received national television coverage from ESPN and WTBS and was broadcast live on the radio from Florida to Kentucky over a six-station network. (Author's collection.)

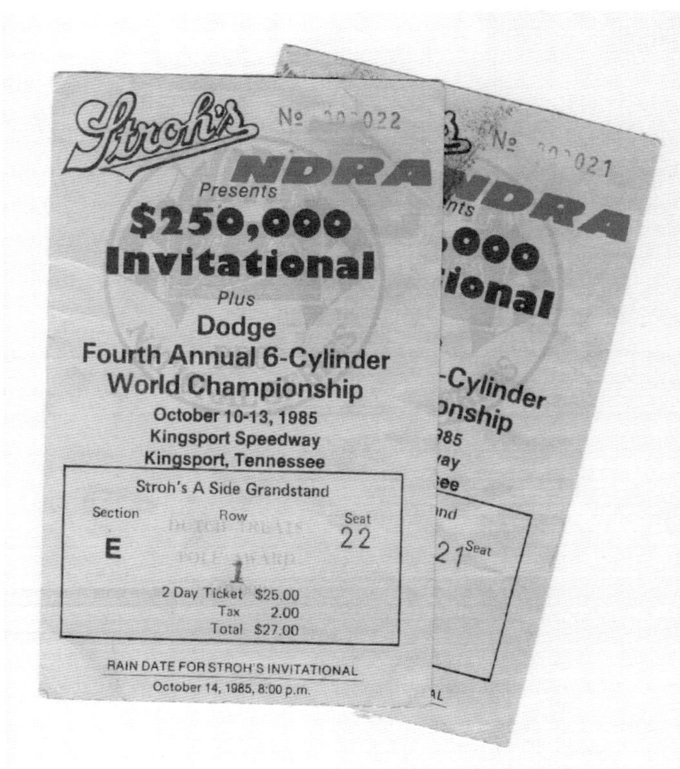

While the race was well attended and heavily promoted, promoter Robert Smawley did not sell enough of these tickets—at just $25 apiece—for the weekend to be profitable. The feature was run on a Sunday afternoon, rather than Saturday night, which is preferred by most promoters. (Author's collection.)

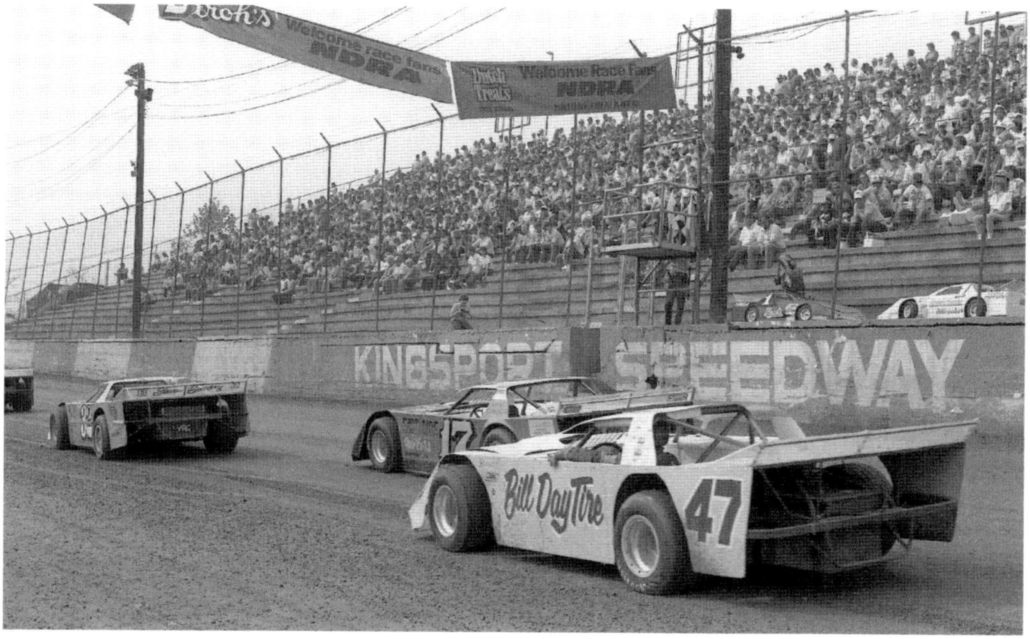

The four-day NDRA Invitational attracted 150 Late Model racers from all across the United States to Kingsport Speedway. Here, cars including Doug Ingalls (No. 47) and Glenn Gault (No. 32) make a pace lap before the front stretch grandstand. (Photograph by Mike O'Dell.)

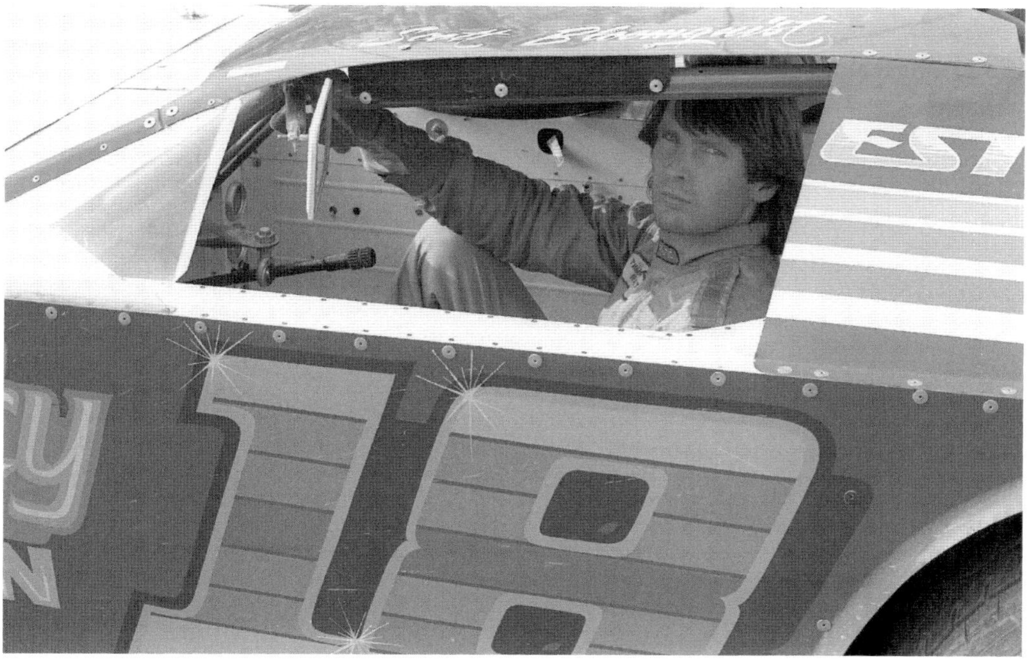

Scott Bloomquist was building a considerable reputation racing and winning on East Tennessee dirt tracks, but the NDRA race was one that got away. The Mooresburg, Tennessee, driver qualified 11th-fastest, but poor track conditions limited passing opportunities, and he finished fifth. (Photograph by Mike O'Dell.)

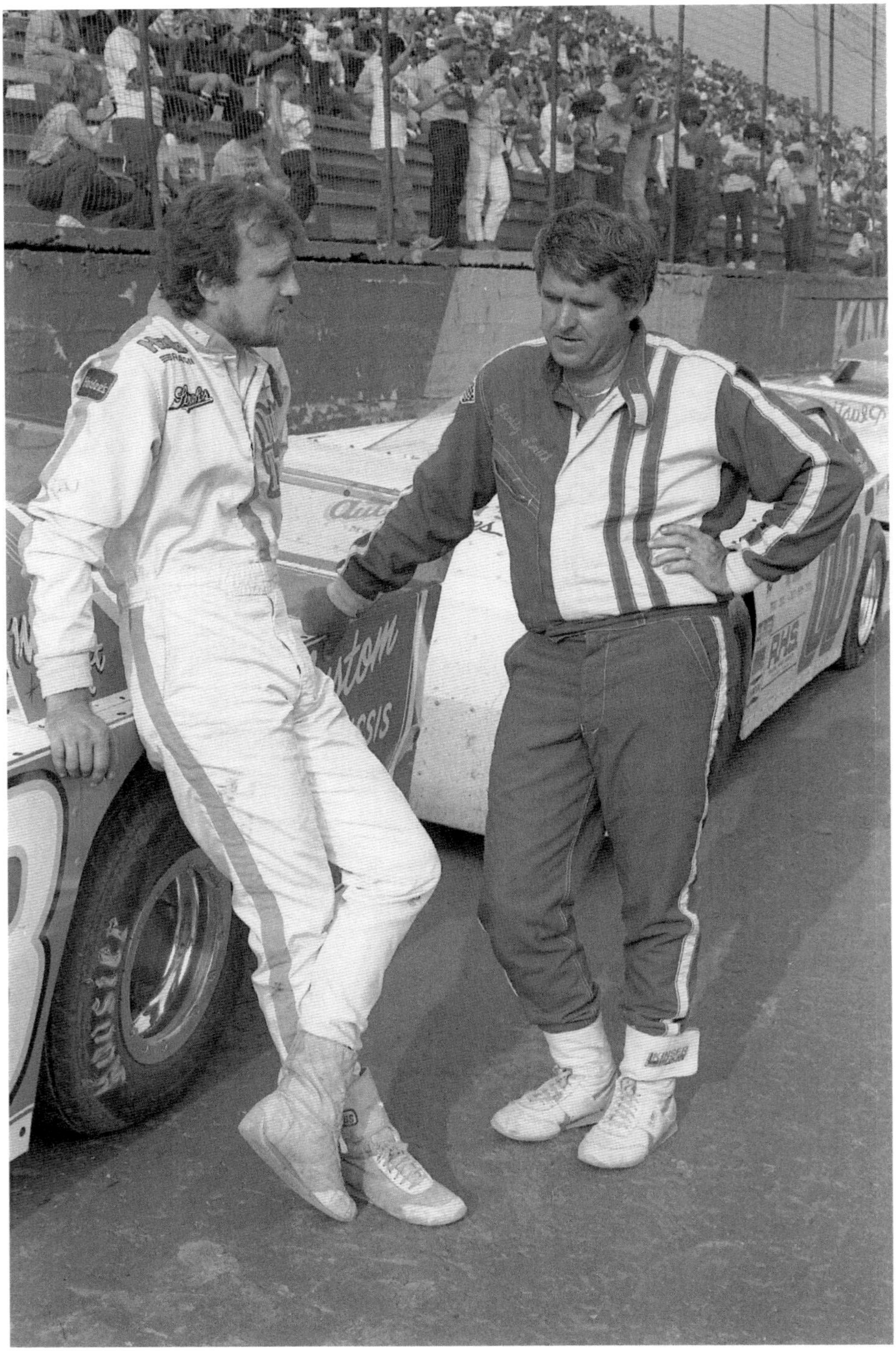

Drivers Willy Kraft (left) and Freddy Smith talk just prior to the green flag for the NDRA Invitational. Both drivers qualified well, but North Carolina native Smith finished fourth, while Minnesota native Kraft ran a disappointing 14th. Smith won Kingsport's previous 100-lap NDRA race in March 1985. (Photograph by Mike O'Dell.)

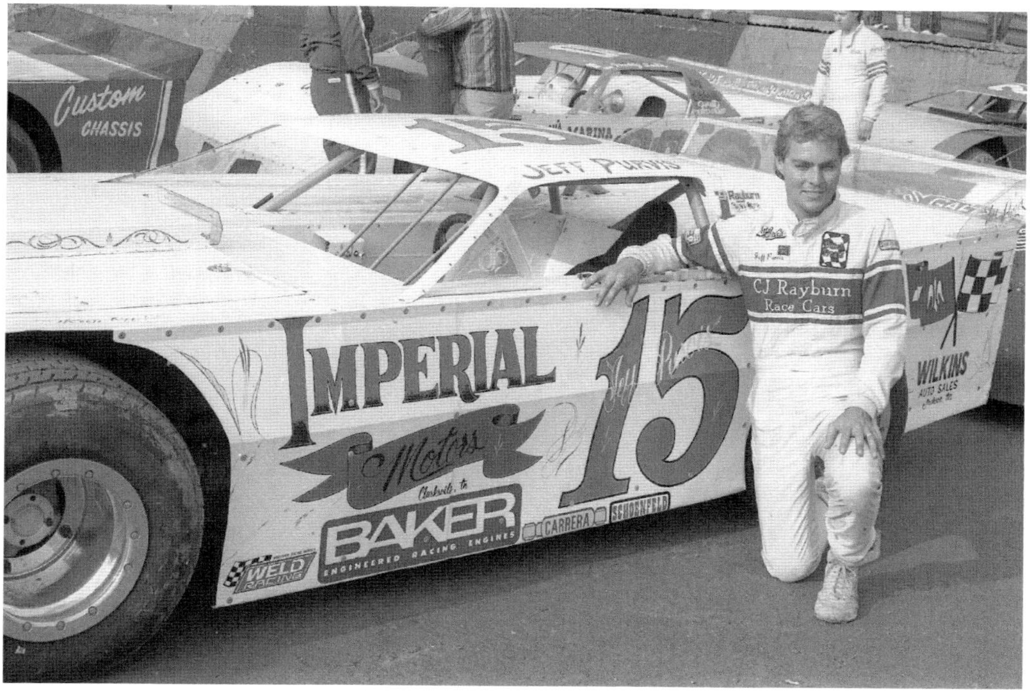

One of the prerace favorites was Jeff Purvis of Clarksville, Tennessee, the series points leader and defending national champion. After qualifying fifth, Purvis raced to a third-place finish. He also won the 1985 series title but never received the championship money, as NDRA experienced financial struggles. (Photograph by Mike O'Dell.)

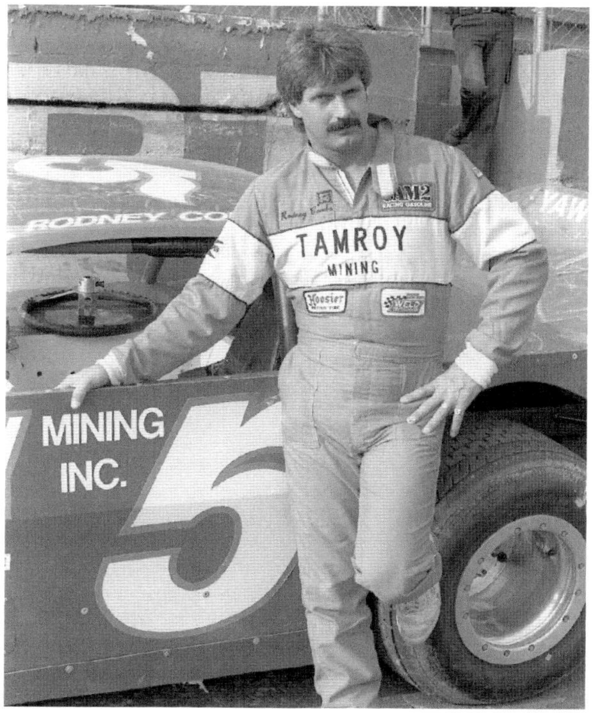

Former series champion Rodney Combs was also among the prerace favorites in the invitational. Combs started 16th in the 24-car field, but he brought out the race's first of five cautions when his brakes failed in turn four. (Photograph by Mike O'Dell.)

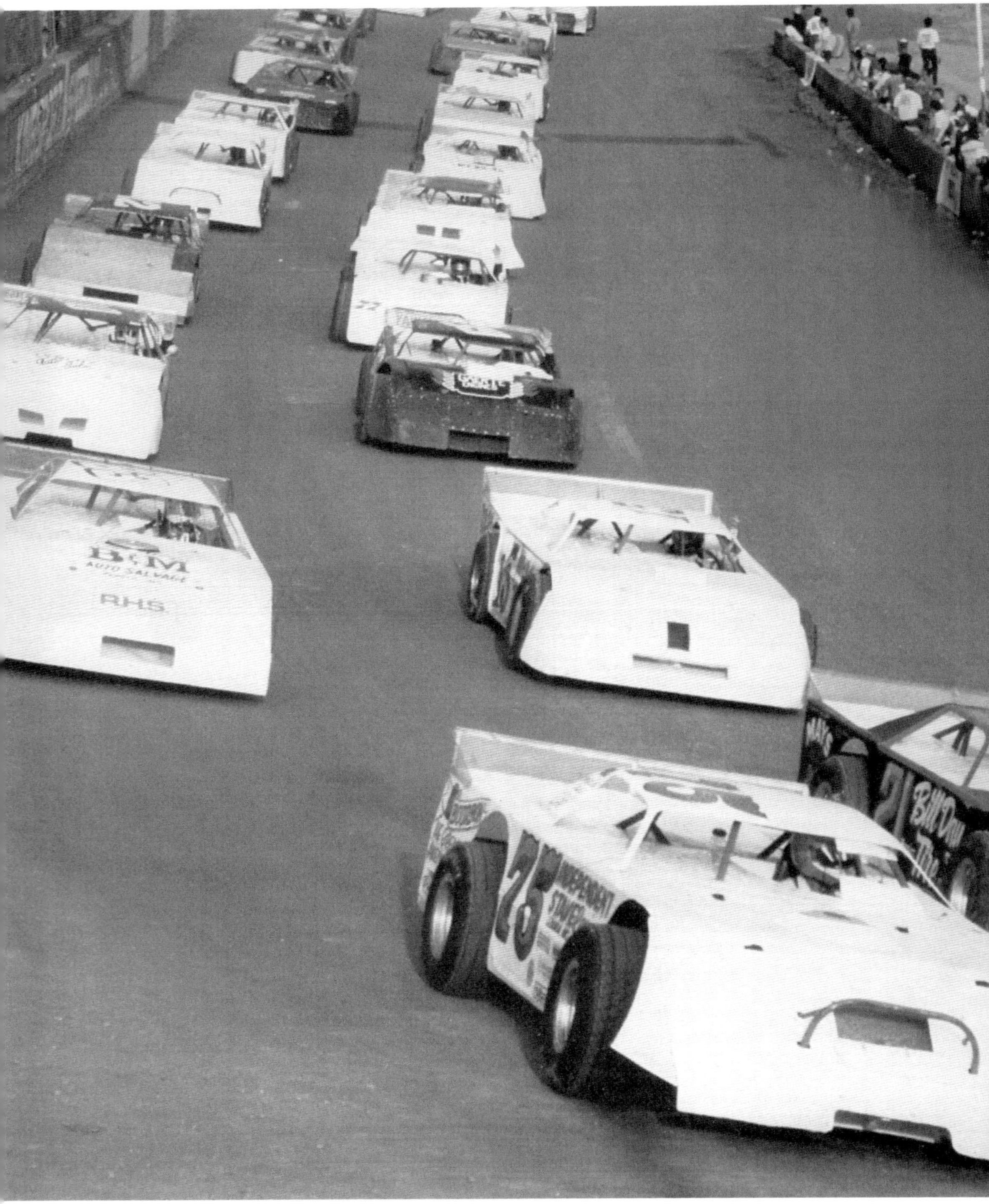

An all-star field of the nation's premier drivers circles Kingsport Speedway prior to the start of the $250,000 Invitational. Among those visible are Larry Phillips (No. 75), Billy Moyer (No. 21), Jeff Purvis (No. 15), and Willy Kraft (No. 83). (Author's collection.)

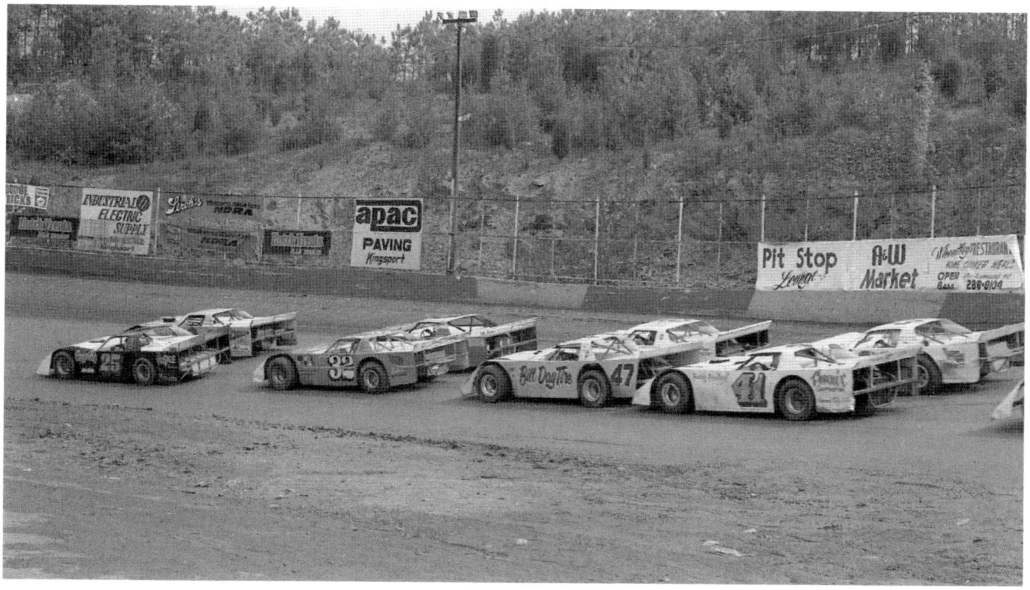

Another stellar group of drivers filled the consolation race, as Billy Clanton (No. 25) and Charles Powell III (No. 9) lead the field to the green flag. Also visible are Glenn Gault (No. 32), Doug Ingalls (No. 47), and Buddy Boutwell (No. 41), who ranked fourth in the national points entering the event but could not race his way into the feature. (Photograph by Mike O'Dell.)

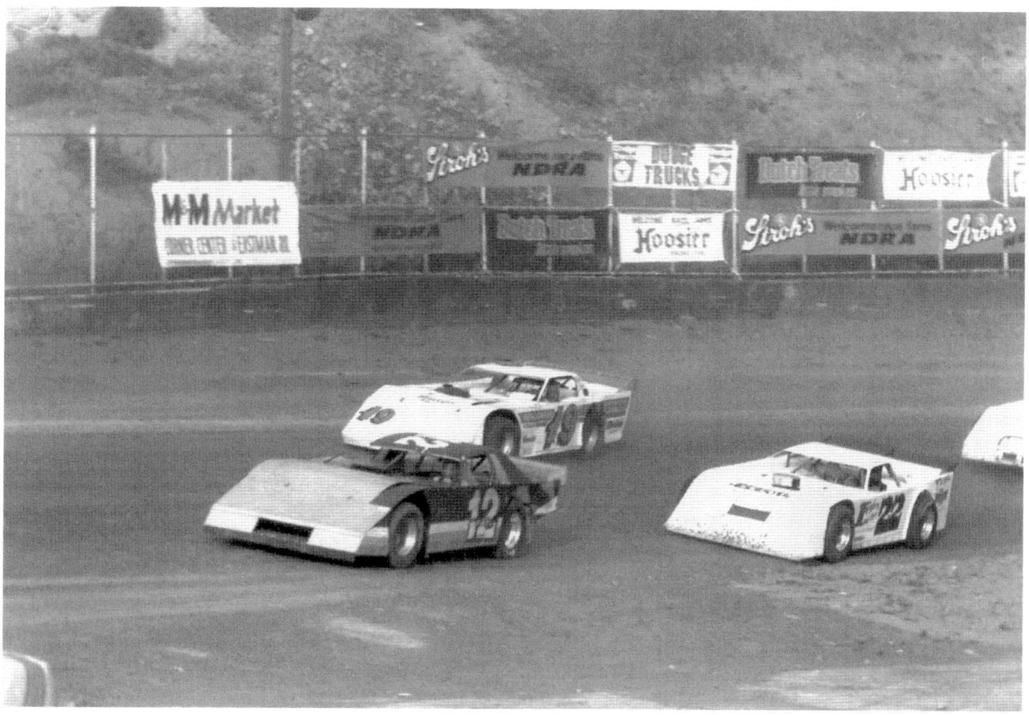

Rick Aukland (No. 12) leads Kenny Brightbill (No. 19), who takes his favored high line, and 1979 NDRA champion Leon Sells (No. 22) out of turn four during NDRA action at Kingsport. (Courtesy of Bradley Poulson and Michael Moats.)

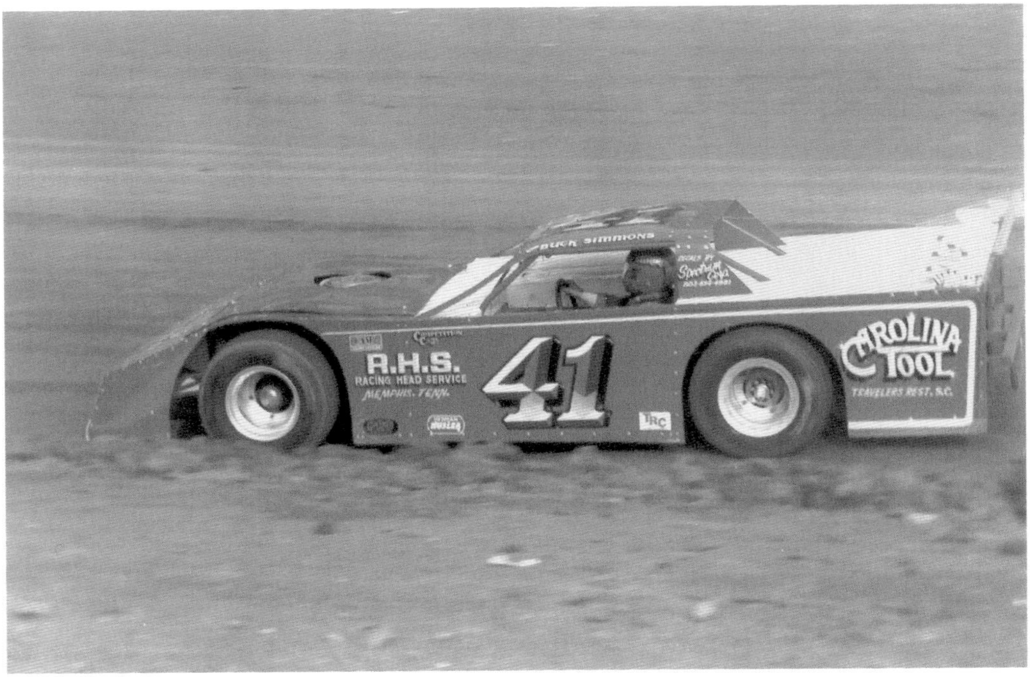

Buck Simmons (No. 41) enjoyed his richest payday in racing during the 1985 NDRA Invitational. Simmons received a $10,000 bonus for turning the fastest qualifying lap (16.080 seconds) on Friday, then collected the race's $20,000 top prize after leading all 100 laps on Sunday afternoon. Simmons (below) is all smiles celebrating with beauty queens representing the NDRA and series sponsors Dutch Treats and Stroh's beer. (Above, courtesy of Bradley Poulson and Michael Moats; below, photograph by Mike O'Dell.)

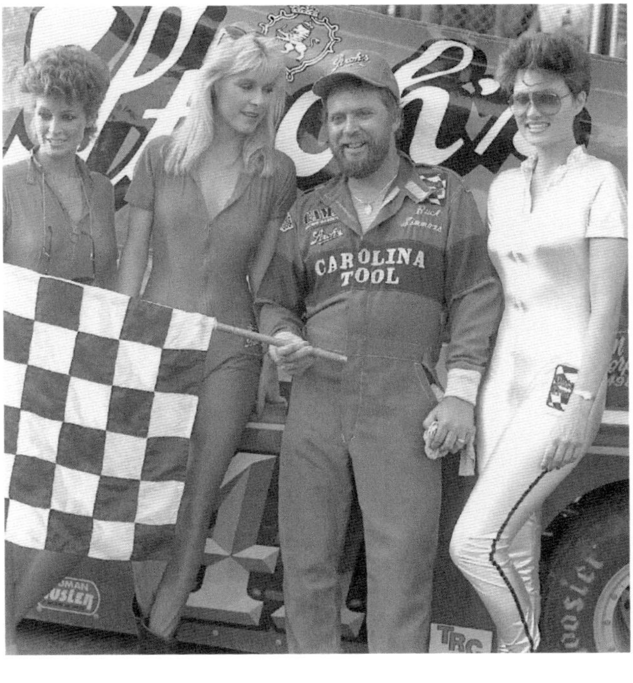

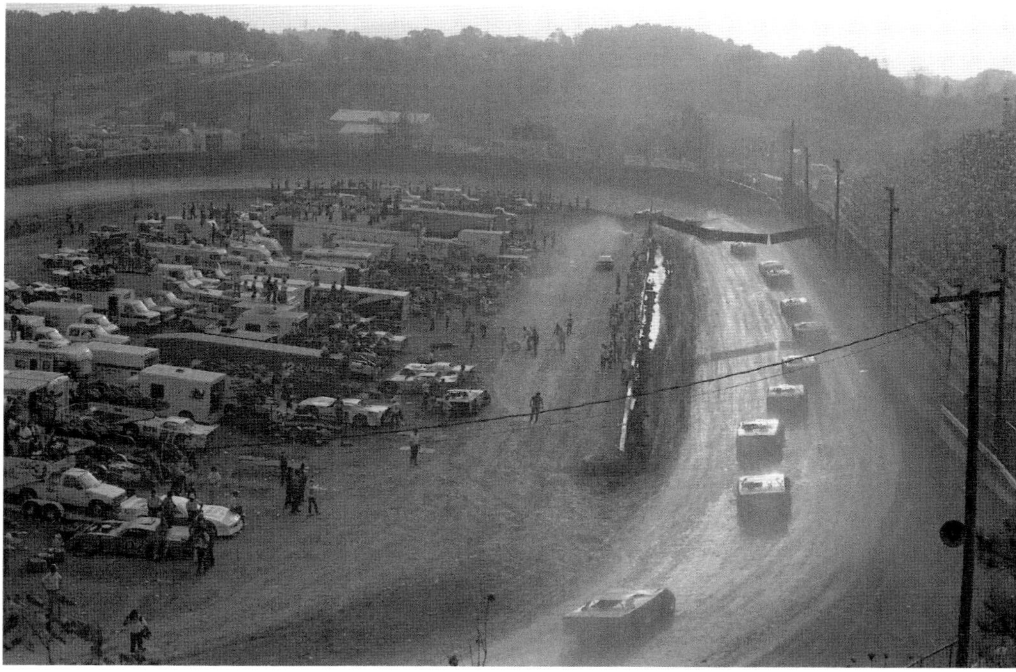

A dusty haze hangs over the Kingsport Speedway as drivers race during the NDRA Invitational weekend. The track became dry-slick, which hampered passing and forced most drivers to play follow-the-leader. (Photograph by Mike O'Dell.)

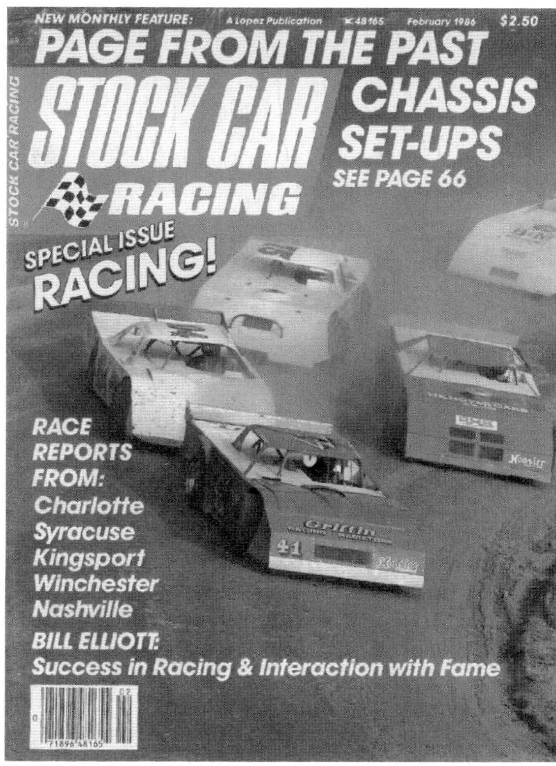

Results of the NDRA Invitational made the cover of the February 1986 issue of *Stock Car Racing* magazine, which includes extensive coverage inside. Note that the track name is listed on the cover—quite a feat for a weekly short track. Even today, that event remains among the largest in dirt-racing history. (Photograph by David Allio, courtesy of Drew Hierwarter's collection.)

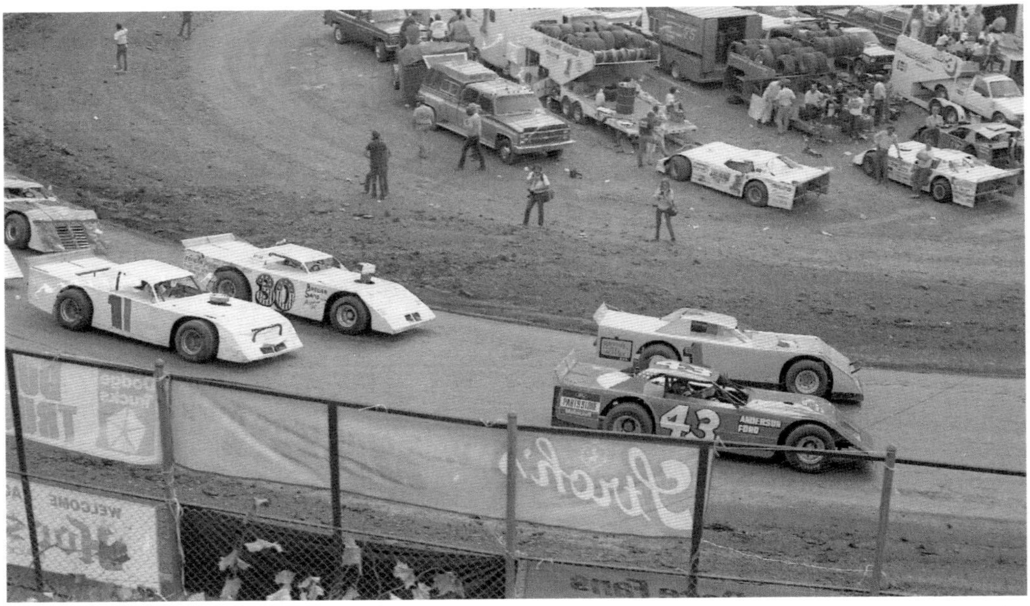

Fastest qualifier Ernie Irvan (No. 1) and Brogie Broyles (No. 43) lead the 20-car field for the $25,000 six-cylinder world championship race. Broyles led the first 41 laps before Irvan slipped by to claim the $5,000 first prize. Also pictured are the machines of Tommy Mungo (No. 30) and Laverne Jordan (No. 11). (Photograph by Mike O'Dell.)

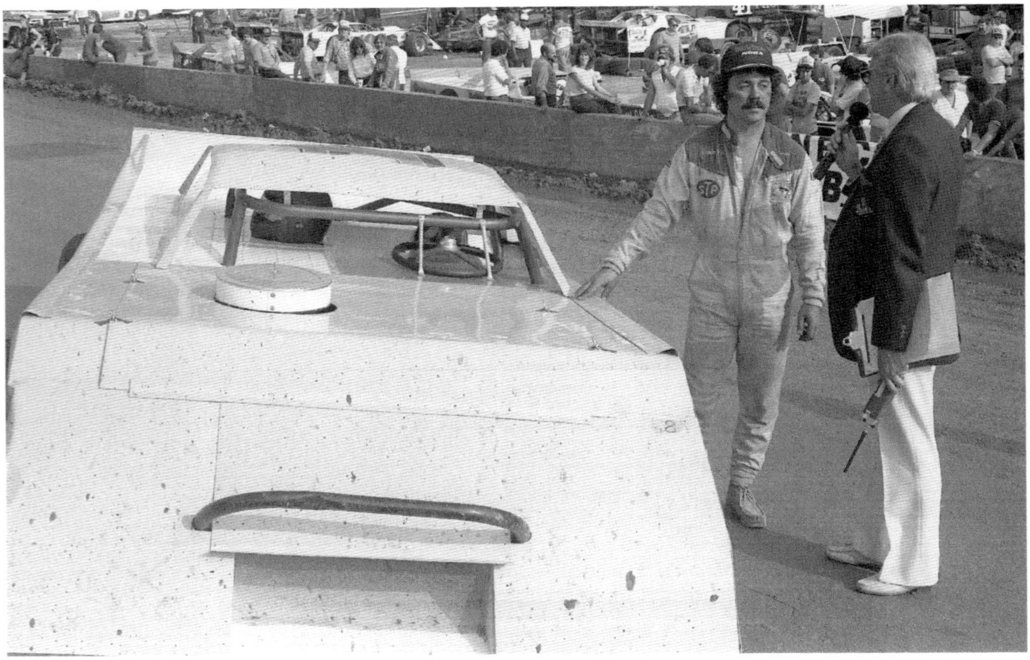

Ernie Irvan (left) speaks with announcer Skip Hough after winning the six-cylinder championship race. Irvan collected $5,000 for the win and $500 for being the fastest qualifier. A California native who relocated to North Carolina, Irvan went on to have a successful NASCAR career, including 15 premier series victories. (Photograph by Mike O'Dell.)

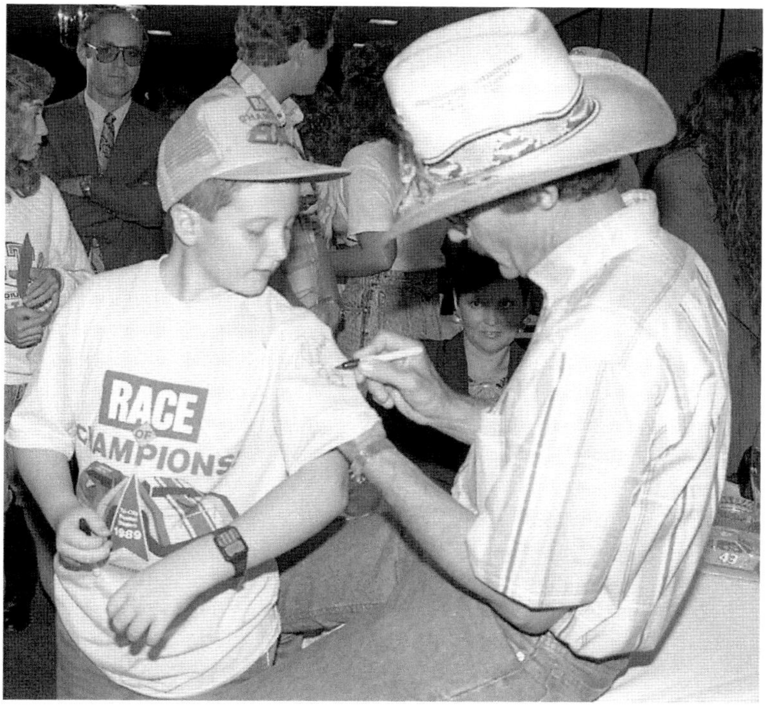

Stock car king Richard Petty signs autographs during an appearance at Kingsport Speedway's 1989 Race of Champions. Petty was the grand marshal for the event, which featured several NASCAR premier series drivers wheeling local Late Model stock cars. (Photograph by the author.)

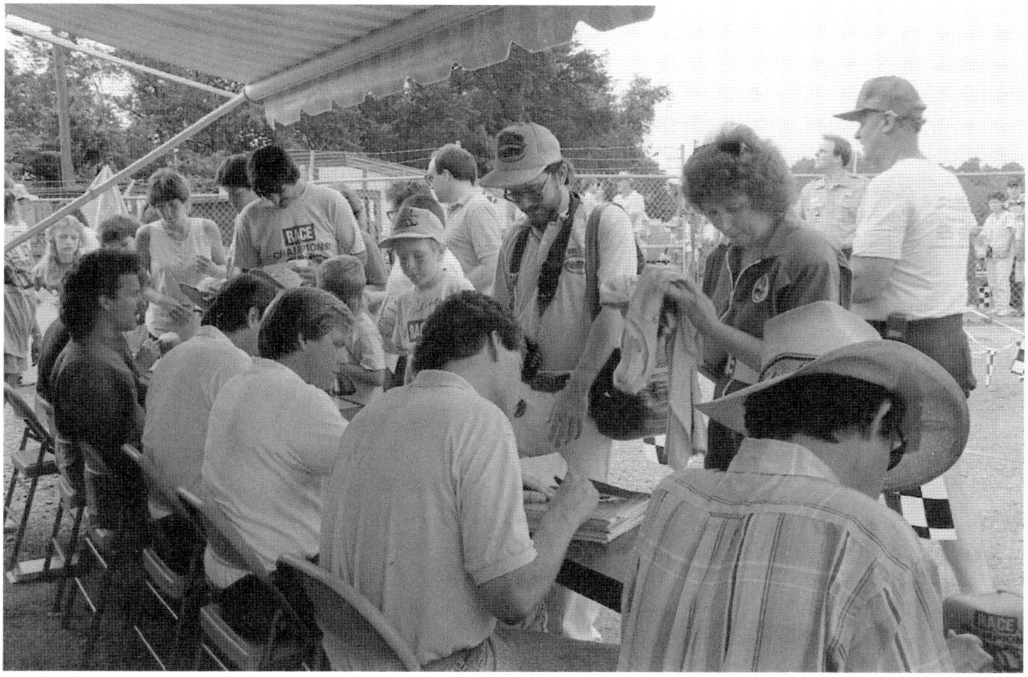

NASCAR drivers sign autographs for a long line of fans prior to the 1989 Race of Champions at Kingsport Speedway. Pictured, from left to right, are Kyle Petty, Dale Jarrett, Rick Wilson, Michael Waltrip, and Richard Petty. Not visible are Rusty Wallace and Rodney Combs. (Photograph by the author.)

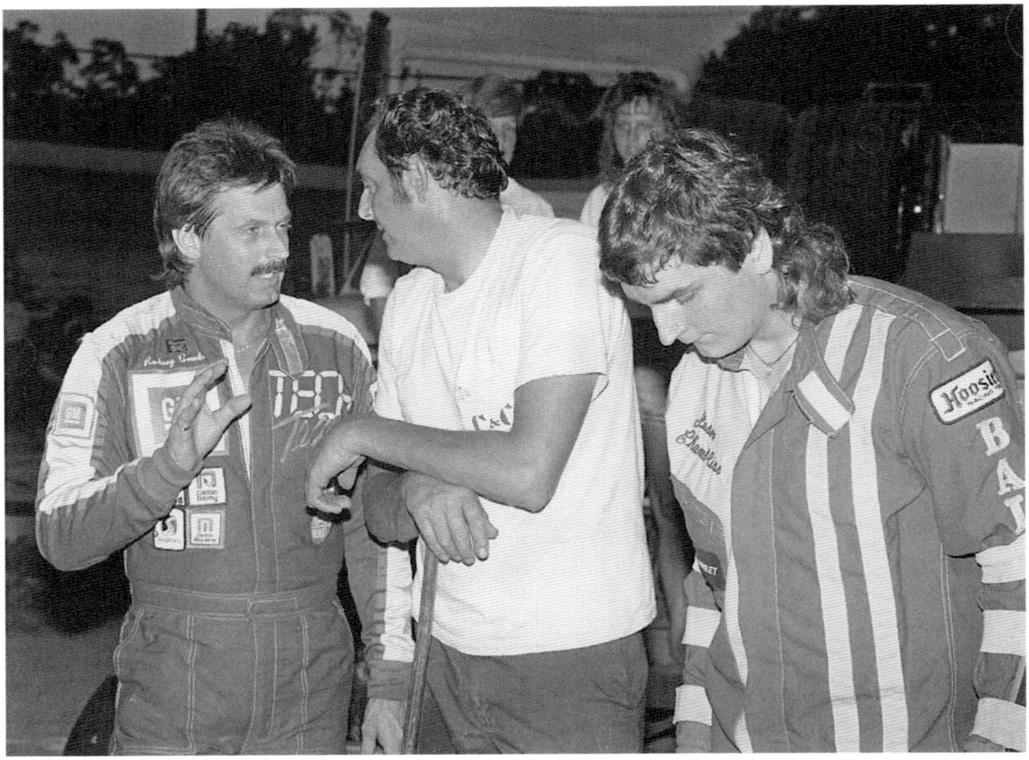

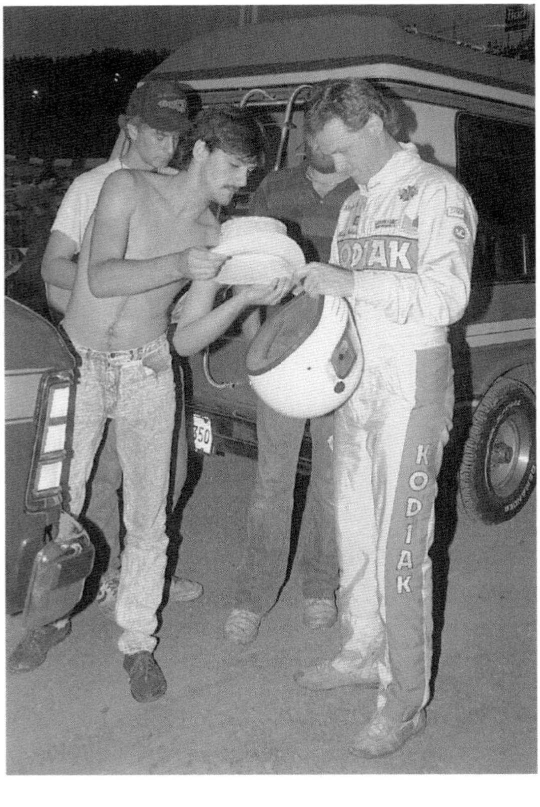

NASCAR driver Rodney Combs (left) talks with car owner Pete Chambliss (center) and driver Jason Chambliss. Combs, who was a dirt track standout before coming to NASCAR, drove their car in the Race of Champions and was the only participant with previous Kingsport experience. (Photograph by the author.)

Driver Rusty Wallace (right) signs autographs for fans in the pits at Kingsport Speedway's 1989 Race of Champions. Known as a short-track specialist, Wallace drove Roger Clendenin's car to a second-place finish. Wallace would capture his lone NASCAR premier series championship later that same season. (Photograph by the author.)

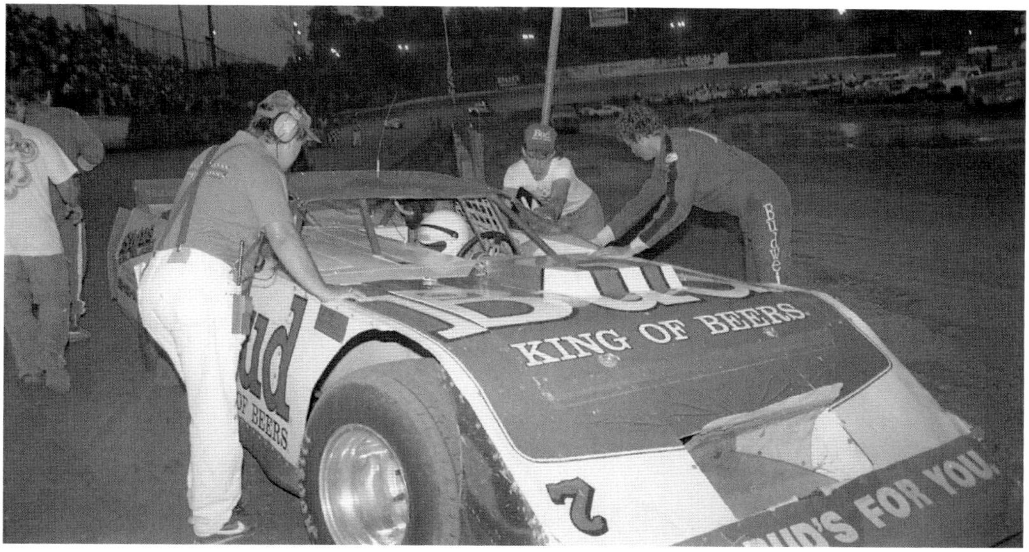

Dirt racer Dale Ball (right) helps push his car back for NASCAR driver Michael Waltrip to head onto the Kingsport Speedway track. Since both drivers are 6 feet 5 inches tall, Waltrip fit into the No. 7 machine. Waltrip would later win two Daytona 500s, become a team owner, television broadcaster, and the only Kingsport competitor to appear on television's *Dancing with the Stars*. (Photograph by the author.)

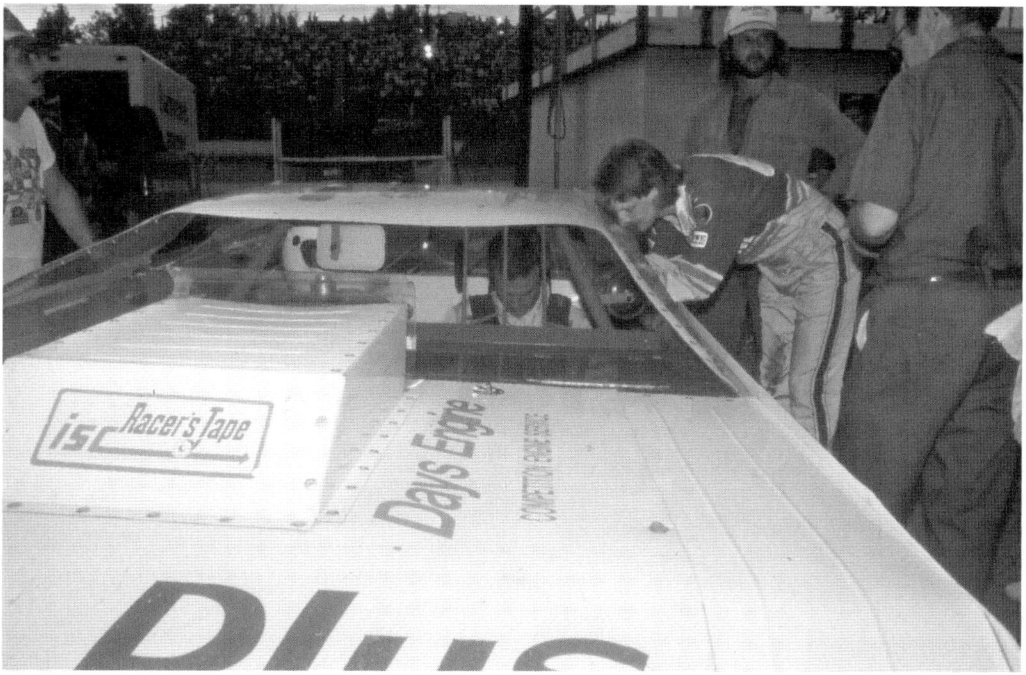

Roger Clendenin (right) leans in to speak with Rusty Wallace as Wallace gets strapped in to Clendenin's No. 27 machine for the Race of Champions. The event occurred just weeks after Wallace's infamous bump-and-run of Darrell Waltrip to win the Winston in Charlotte, North Carolina. (Photograph by the author.)

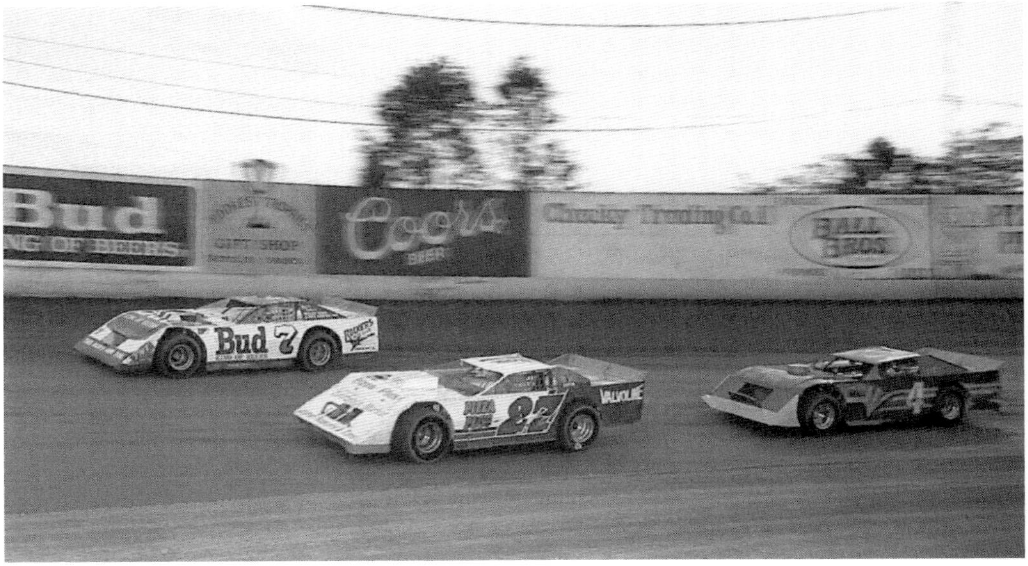

Rusty Wallace (No. 27) leads eventual Race of Champions winner Rick Wilson (No. 4) and Michael Waltrip (No. 7) through turns one and two. At that time, Wilson drove No. 4 in NASCAR's premier series, a machine fielded locally by Morgan-McClure Motorsports and prepared by crew chief Tony Glover of Kingsport. (Photograph by the author.)

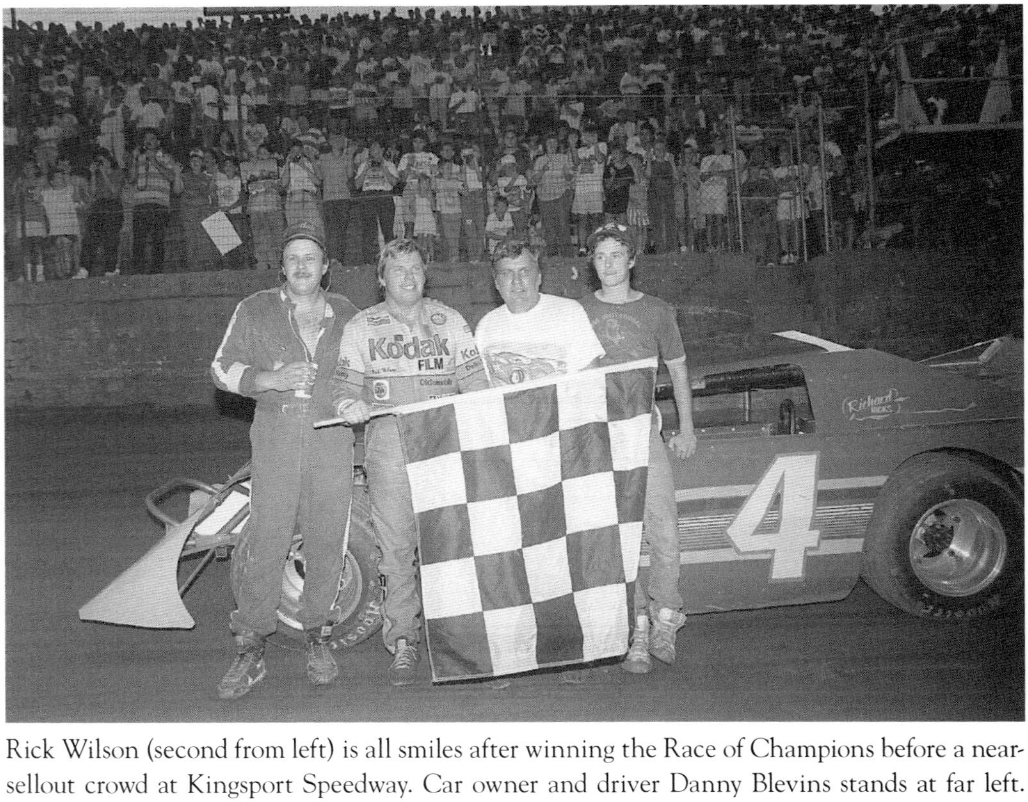

Rick Wilson (second from left) is all smiles after winning the Race of Champions before a near-sellout crowd at Kingsport Speedway. Car owner and driver Danny Blevins stands at far left. (Photograph by the author.)

6

Cementing a Future

Joe Loven was already searching for ways to rejuvenate the Kingsport Speedway even before acquiring the historic old track in 1994. Those plans included running only special events on the dirt oval, upgrading the facilities, promoting a more family-friendly atmosphere, and using a fifth-mile paved oval elsewhere on the property to showcase cars of Loven's Miniature Auto Race Car Association. This program, born in 1993, promoted competition among full-bodied go-karts that looked like miniature stock cars.

In August 1994, the track hosted what was then the premier touring dirt Late Model group, the Hav-A-Tampa Series, in conjunction with Bristol Motor Speedway's August race weekend. At that time, plans for 1995 called for additional races from that series, "World of Outlaws sprint cars and possibly the ARCA series on dirt," according to a public relations firm hired by Loven. Those plans never bore fruit, and the track held only a couple of races in 1995.

The dirt-track atmosphere had apparently worn out its welcome, so Loven weighed options. For the second time in Kingsport history, the answer was found at nearby Bristol Motor Speedway. It was Loven's concrete firm that solved a serious dilemma for then Bristol owner Larry Carrier. That track's asphalt surface kept breaking apart, and winners like Alan Kulwicki would complain about the track while accepting Carrier's money. So, Carrier hired Loven in 1992 to replace Bristol's asphalt with concrete. After some early objections, this surface cemented Bristol's future. Loven now believed that the same approach could save Kingsport, so his crews began preparing the surface and carefully pouring sections of a new racetrack.

Weather delayed its opening by a couple of weeks, but Kingsport sprang back to life in late April 1996 with a renewed NASCAR sanction and financial support from R.J. Reynolds and its Winston brand, the same company that instigated pulling NASCAR premier series races from Kingsport and other smaller venues in the early 1970s.

For the next seven seasons, Kingsport was alive with the roar of engines and the cheers of the crowd.

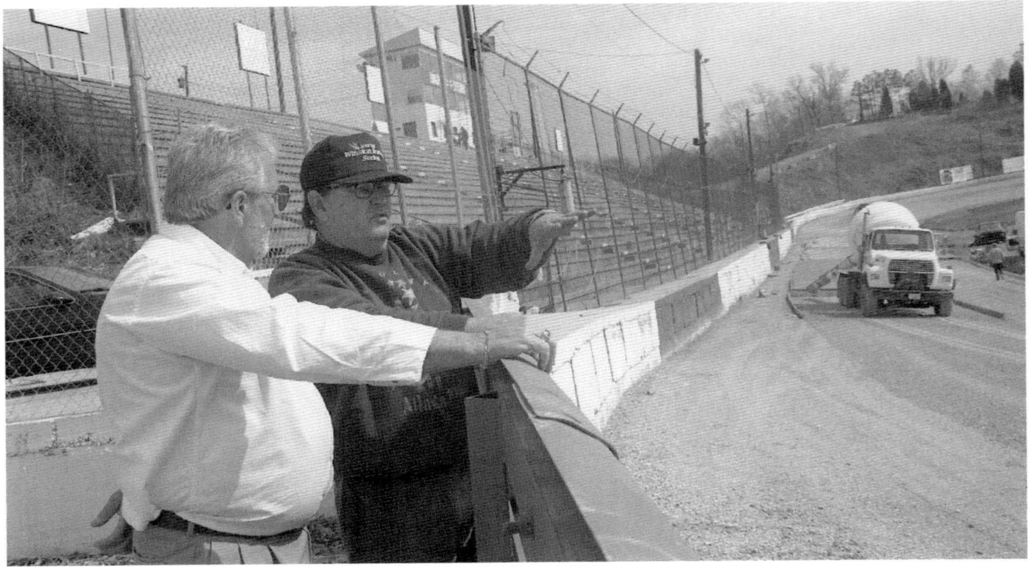

Joe Loven (right) gestures as he explains his plans for revitalizing Kingsport Speedway to promoter Harold Crook. Loven owns a concrete business, so he decided to cover the former dirt surface with that product and return to the NASCAR weekly racing fold for the 1996 season. (Photograph by the author.)

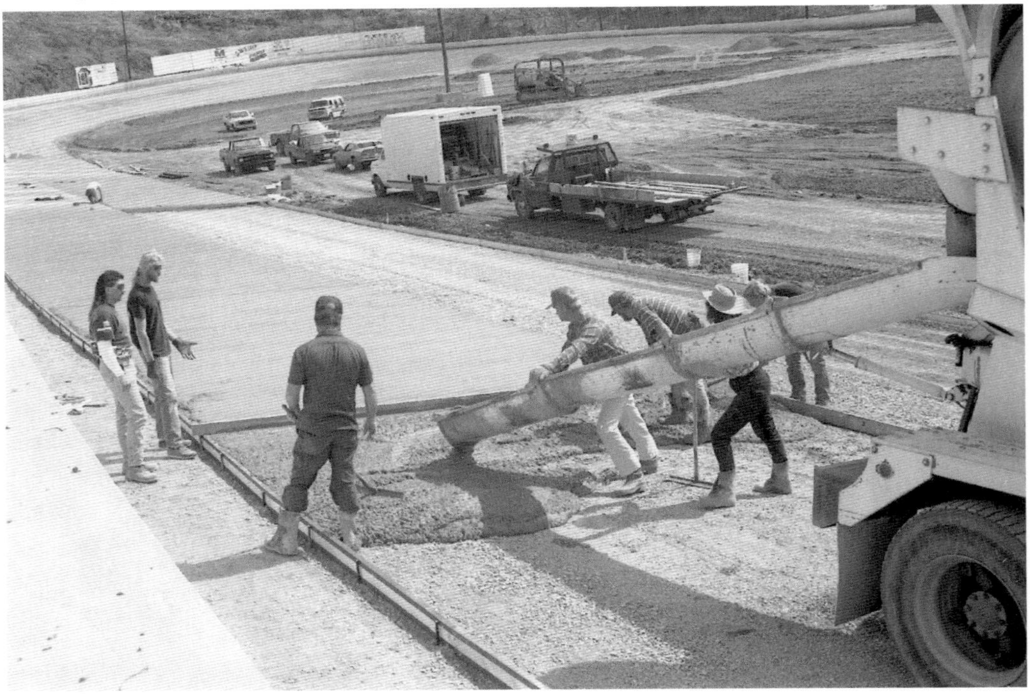

Workers carefully pour sections of concrete on the front straightaway at Kingsport Speedway in 1996, much like they did in 1992, when Joe Loven's crew redid the surface at Bristol Motor Speedway. The success of the Bristol surface provided impetus for Loven to make a similar change at his track. (Photograph by the author.)

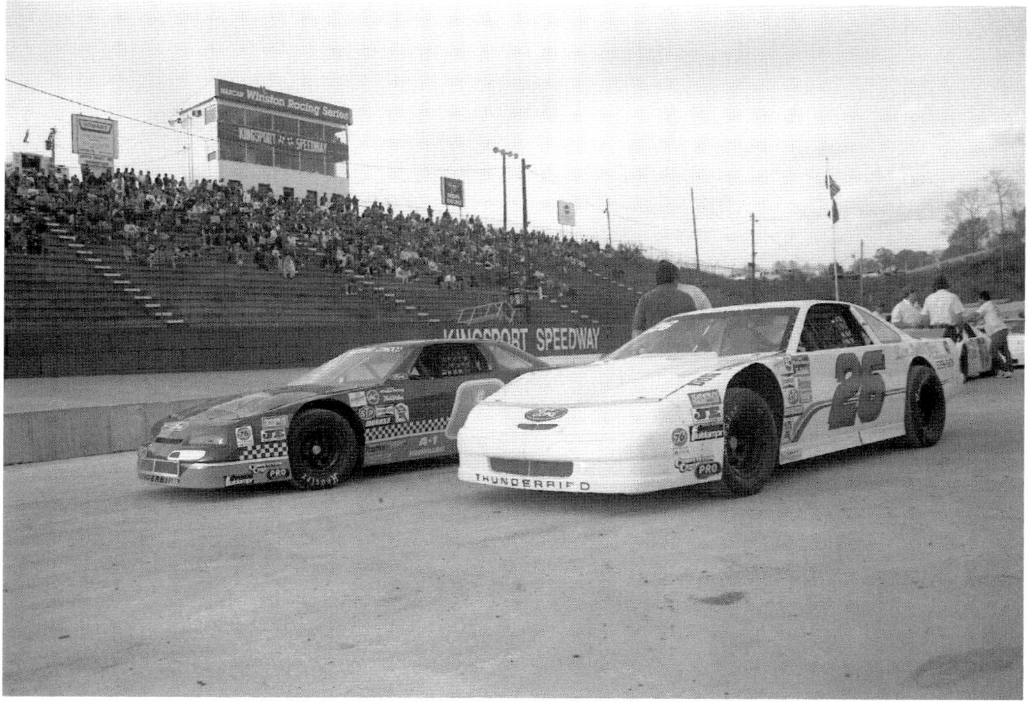

The machines of Mark Ketron (No. 26) and Wayne Hale (No. 6) line up on pit road during reopening night on April 26, 1996. A good crowd turned out to watch competitive racing action in the track's first NASCAR-sanctioned race in more than a decade. (Photograph by the author.)

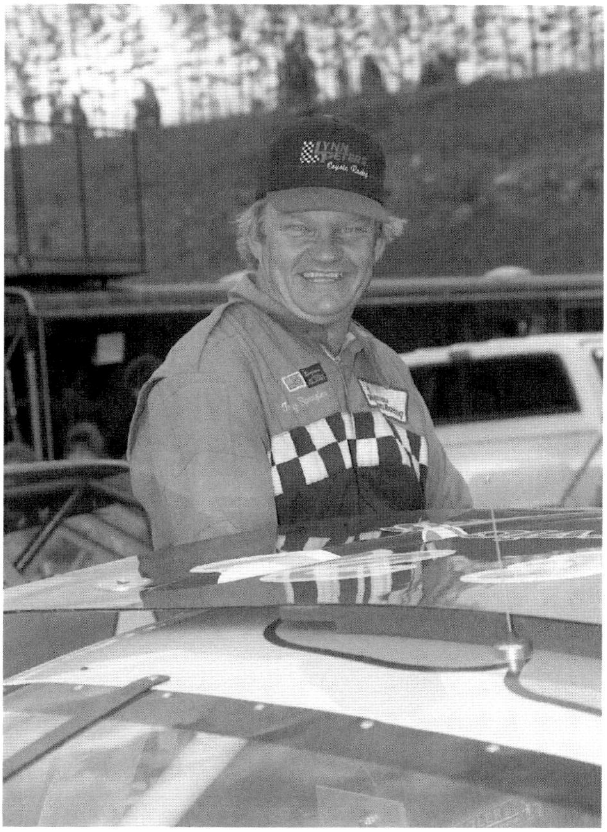

Tommy Spangler of Bristol, Virginia, is all smiles as he climbs into his racer for Kingsport's reopening race in April 1996. Spangler won the championship at nearby Lonesome Pine Raceway the previous year and was always a contender at Kingsport. (Photograph by the author.)

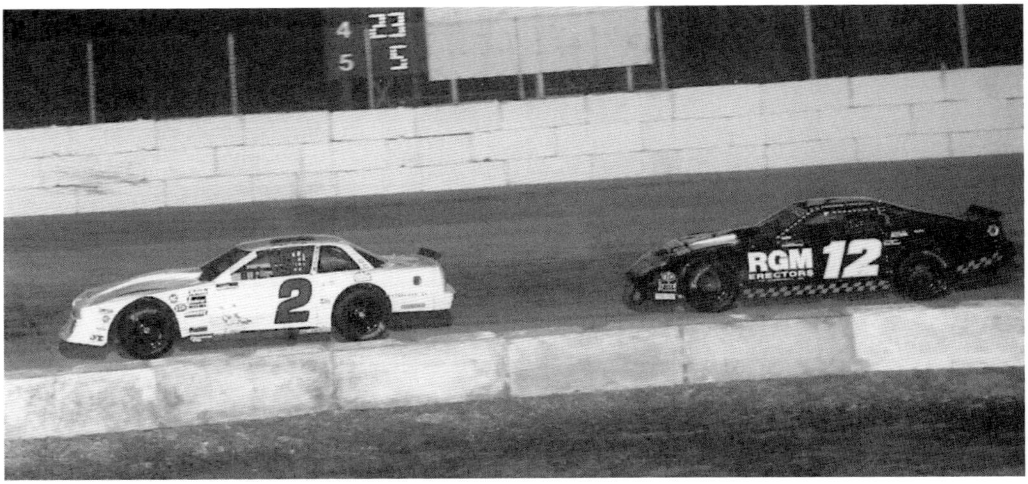

Boyd Sult (No. 2) spent more than half of that first race reeling in fast qualifier Ronnie Thomas (No. 12). After passing Thomas, Sult went on to win the 100-lap Late Model feature. Sult said he only decided to travel to Kingsport earlier that day, after he and his crew completed work on the race car. (Photograph by the author.)

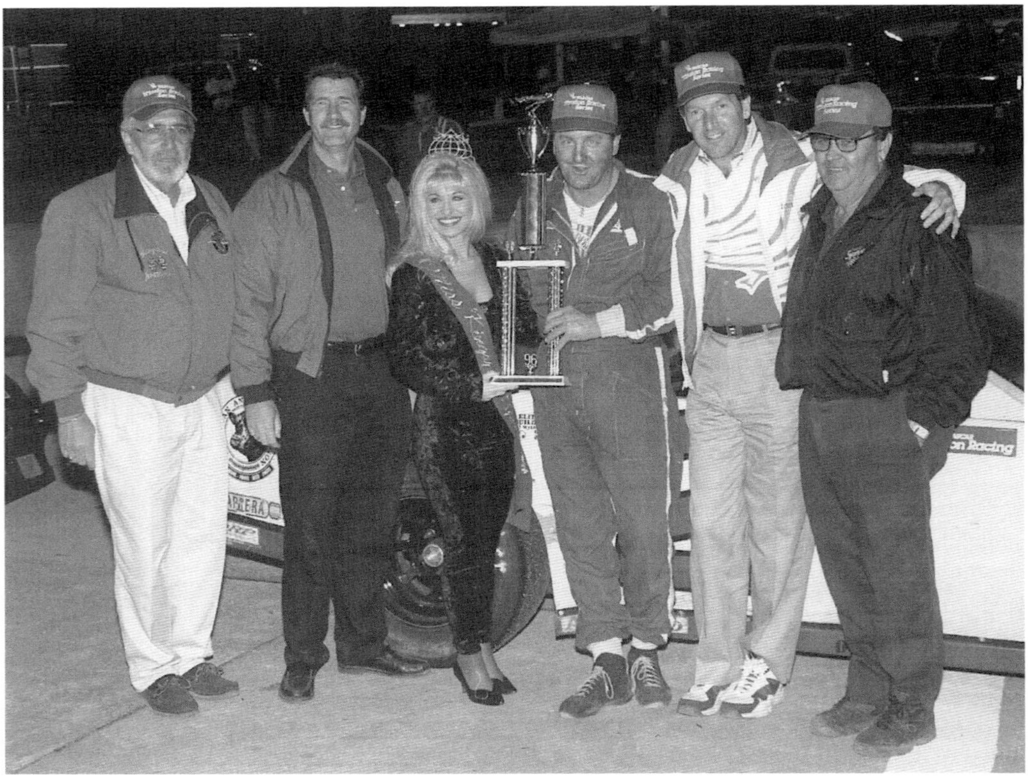

Winner Boyd Sult accepts the trophy from Miss Kingsport Speedway, Raulette Fuller, after winning the 100-lap feature. Shown here are, from left to right, promoter Harold Crook, NASCAR vice president Dennis Huth, Fuller, Sult, Winston's Dan Henley, and speedway owner Joe Loven. (Photograph by the author.)

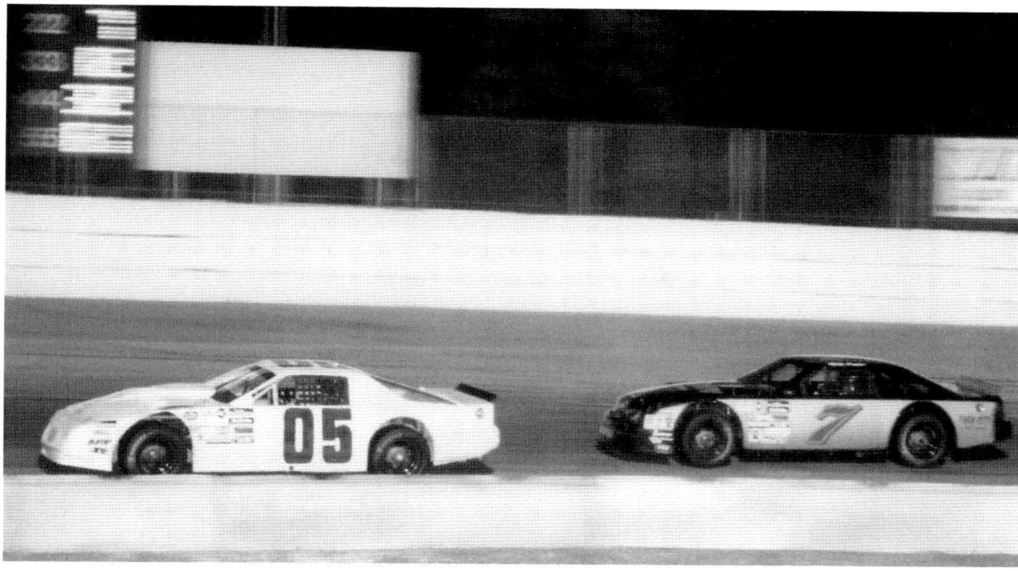

Veteran racers Jeff Agnew (No. 05) of Floyd, Virginia, and Mike Porter (No. 7) of Princeton, West Virginia, regularly battled on the Kingsport concrete in the late 1990s. Porter previously raced in the NASCAR Busch Series, where he won the pole for its very first race at Daytona in 1982. (Photograph by the author.)

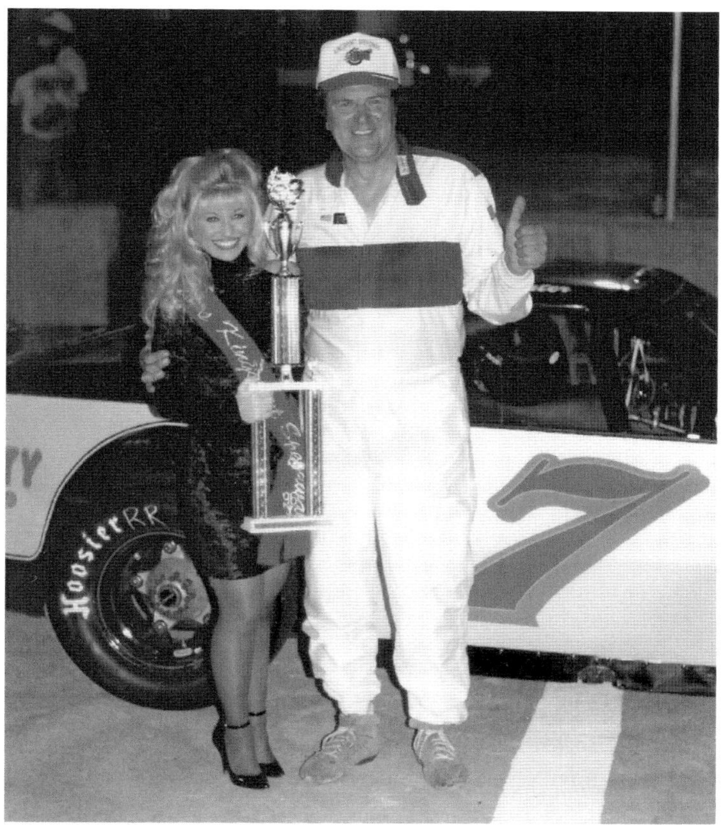

Mike Porter is all smiles after collecting the trophy for a 1996 Kingsport Speedway NASCAR Late Model win from Miss Kingsport Speedway, Raulette Fuller. Porter posted 19 wins during a remarkable 1996 season at Kingsport and Lonesome Pine speedways, the most of any Winston Racing Series driver in the nation. (Photograph by the author.)

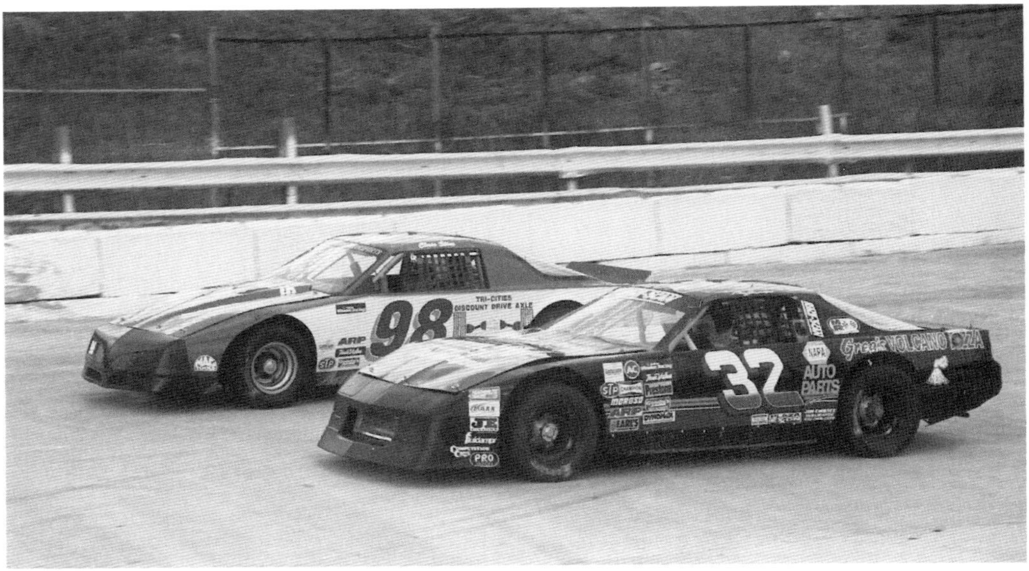

Robbie Ferguson (No. 32) races his Chevrolet against the Pontiac of Chris Stine (No. 98) through the corners at Kingsport Speedway. Ferguson finished a close second to Jeff Agnew in the 1996 track title race, falling just 30 points short. Ferguson posted 31 top-five finishes in 36 races. (Photograph by the author.)

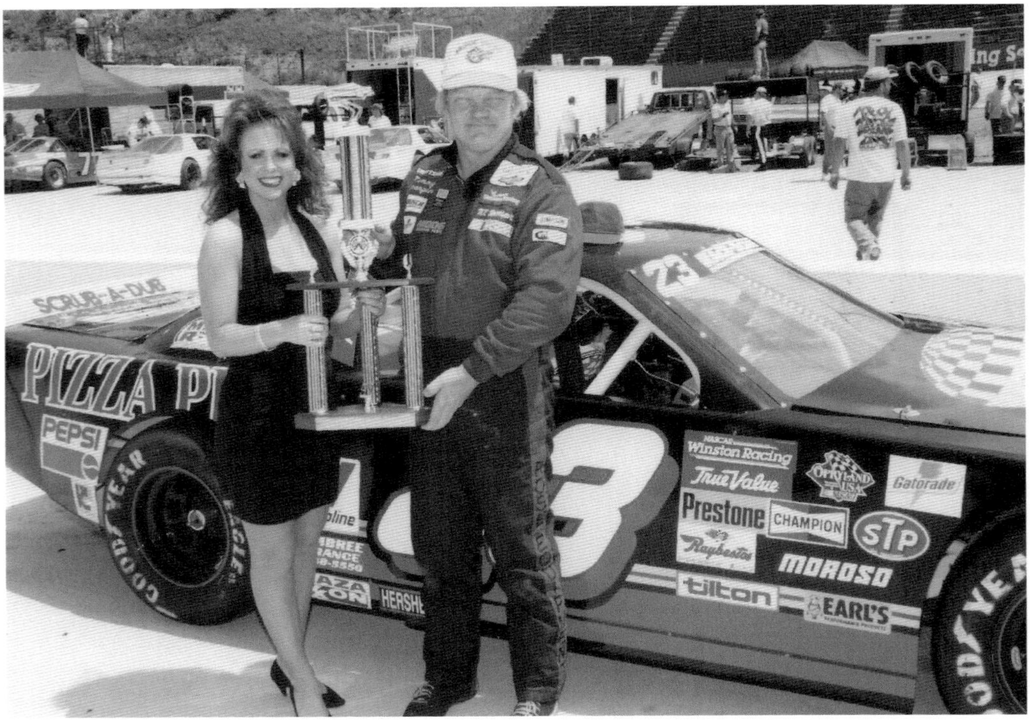

Tommy Spangler accepts a trophy following a feature race win during the 1997 season at Kingsport Speedway. Spangler finished in the top 20 in points in Kingsport's 1996 and 1997 seasons. (Photograph by Randall Perry.)

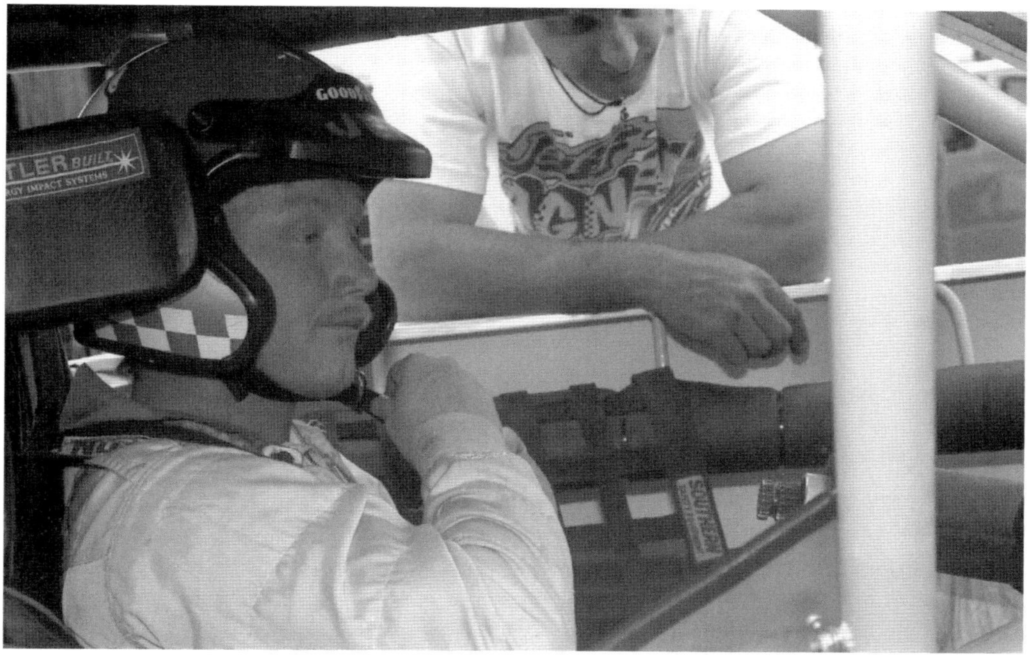

Above, Jeff Agnew buckles the chinstrap of his helmet before rolling onto the track at Kingsport Speedway in 1996. He won that season's track Late Model championship and finished sixth in the NASCAR Blue Ridge region with nine victories in 22 races. Agnew is seen below in 1997, when he forged 20 wins in 38 starts to win another Kingsport title over Robbie Ferguson and finish just behind national champion Dexter Canipe in the Blue Ridge region. (Above, photograph by the author; below, photograph by Randall Perry.)

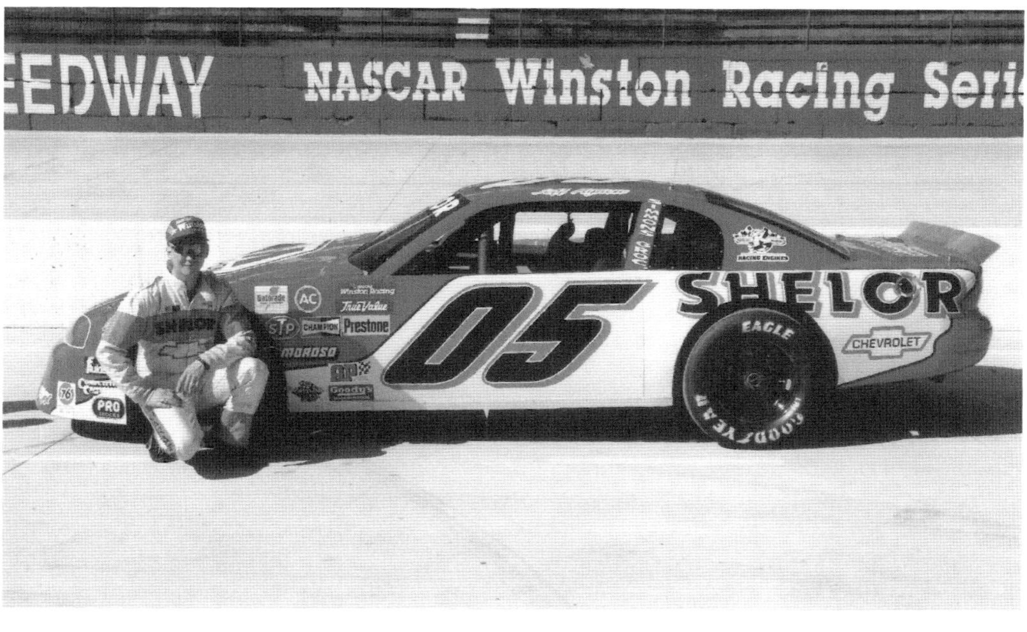

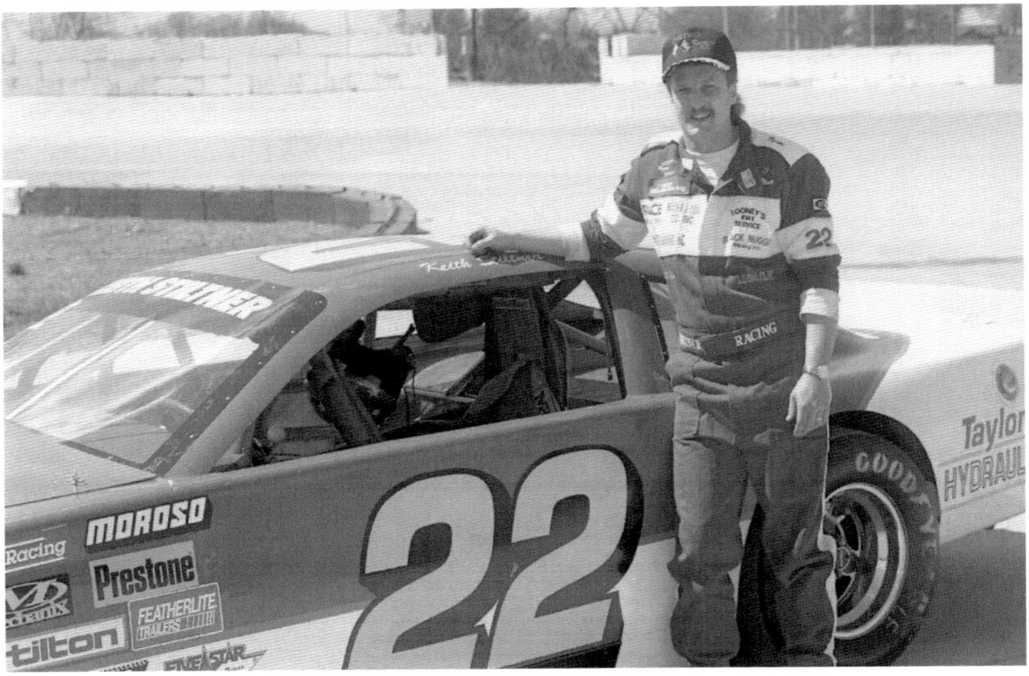

Keith Stiltner of Grundy, Virginia, succeeded Jeff Agnew as a two-time Kingsport track champion. In 1998, he posted two wins and had 23 top-five finishes for the title and a 10th-place regional finish. In 1999, Stiltner amassed nine wins in 19 starts and finished second in the Blue Ridge region behind champion Shane Huffman. (Photograph by the author.)

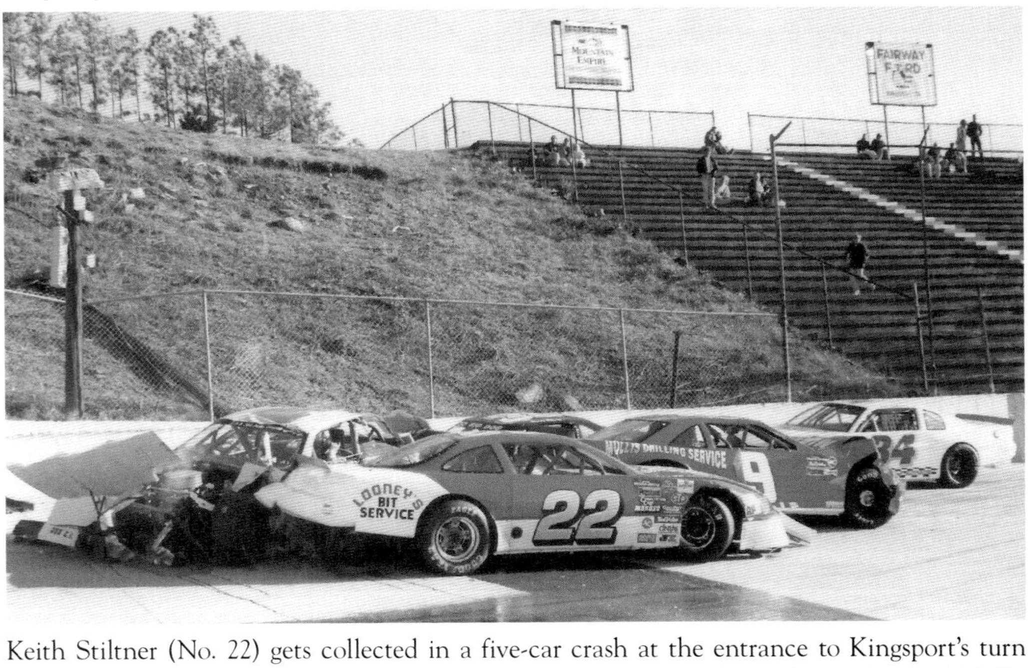

Keith Stiltner (No. 22) gets collected in a five-car crash at the entrance to Kingsport's turn three. Among those involved are Tim Nichols (No. 04), Danny Blevins (No. 38), Chad Mullis (No. 9), and Terry Stone (No. 34). (Photograph by Randall Perry.)

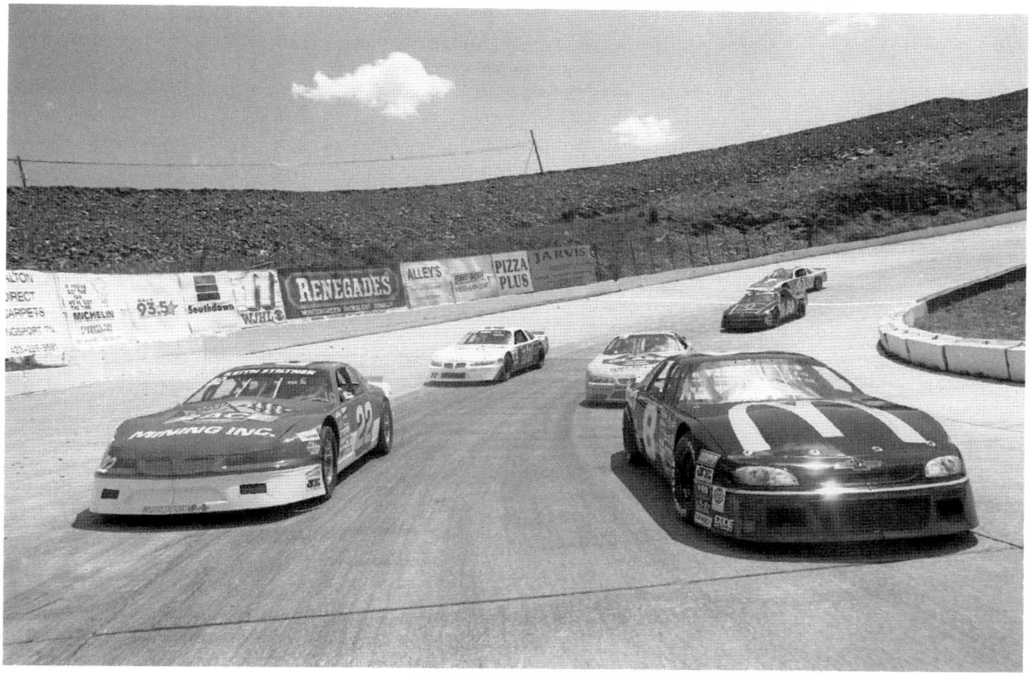

The machines of Keith Stiltner (No. 22) and Scott Ferrell (No. 8) lead a pack of Late Model stock cars through turns three and four for the 1998 season. The photograph was taken for a special racing supplement in the *Sullivan County News* as Kingsport Speedway celebrated its 34th season during NASCAR's 50th-anniversary season. (Photograph by the author.)

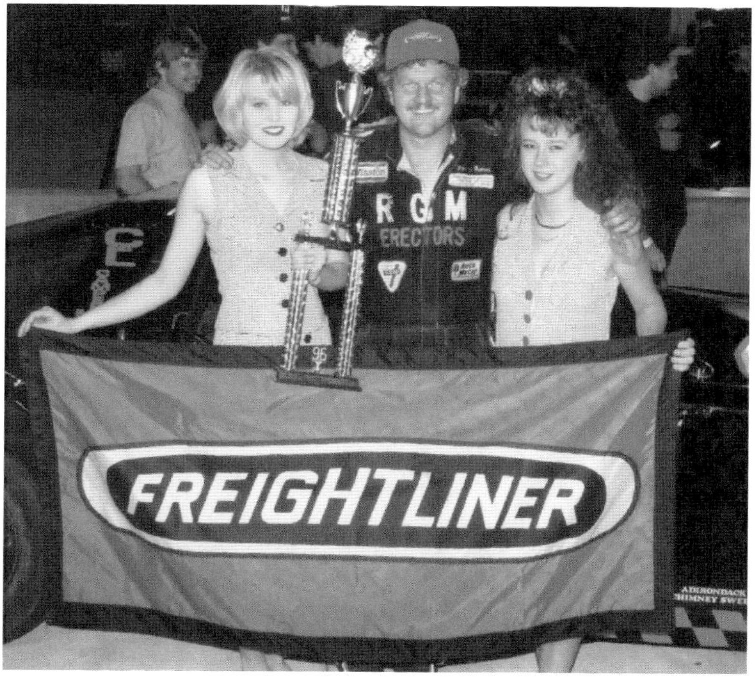

Ronnie Thomas of Christiansburg, Virginia, celebrates a 1996 NASCAR victory at Kingsport. Thomas was the 1978 NASCAR premier series rookie of the year and competed at that level for nearly a decade. He later scored more than 100 wins in NASCAR weekly series action and made regular visits to Kingsport. (Photograph by Randall Perry.)

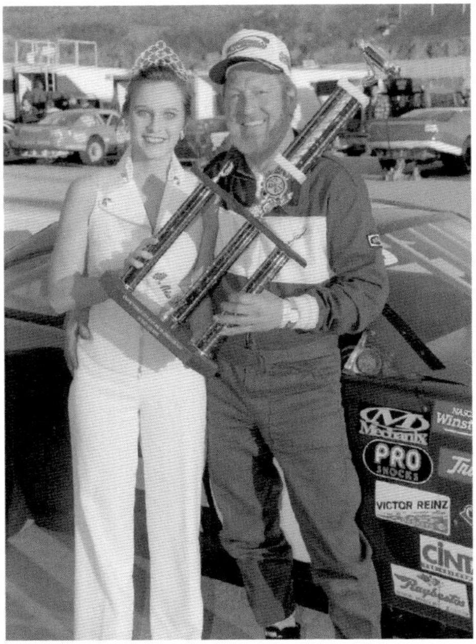

Veteran racer Paul Shull, a North Carolina native who moved to Virginia, has been winning at Kingsport Speedway since the 1970s. He is a two-time track champion in the Limited Sportsman class in 1997–1998, formerly raced Late Models, and once finished ahead of Dale Earnhardt, Geoff Bodine, and Dale Jarrett in a race at Bristol. (Photograph by Randall Perry.)

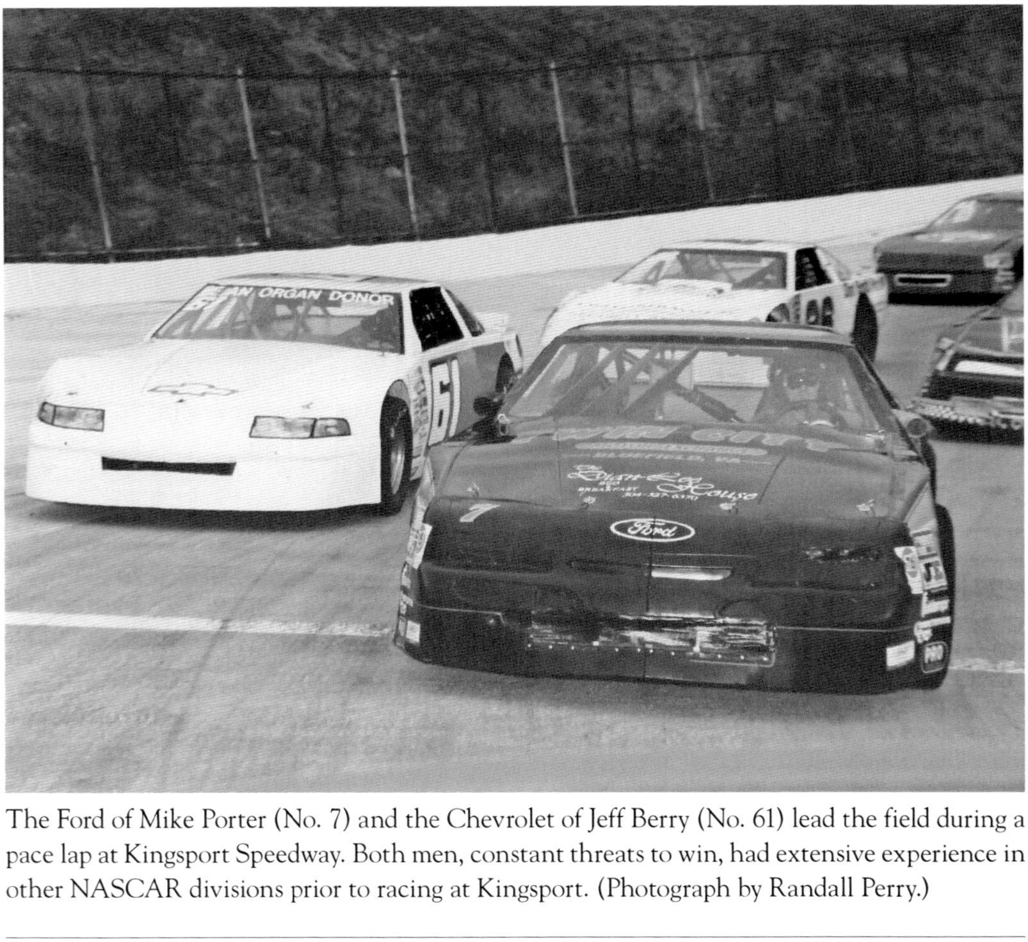

The Ford of Mike Porter (No. 7) and the Chevrolet of Jeff Berry (No. 61) lead the field during a pace lap at Kingsport Speedway. Both men, constant threats to win, had extensive experience in other NASCAR divisions prior to racing at Kingsport. (Photograph by Randall Perry.)

Wade Day, seen here with his wife, Jessica, swept both the Kingsport Speedway and Blue Ridge region NASCAR championships in 2000. Day, age 23, of Blountville, Tennessee, wheeled a car owned by Gloria and Matt Wolfe to 14 victories in 20 starts, in only his second season of racing Late Models. (Photograph by Randall Perry.)

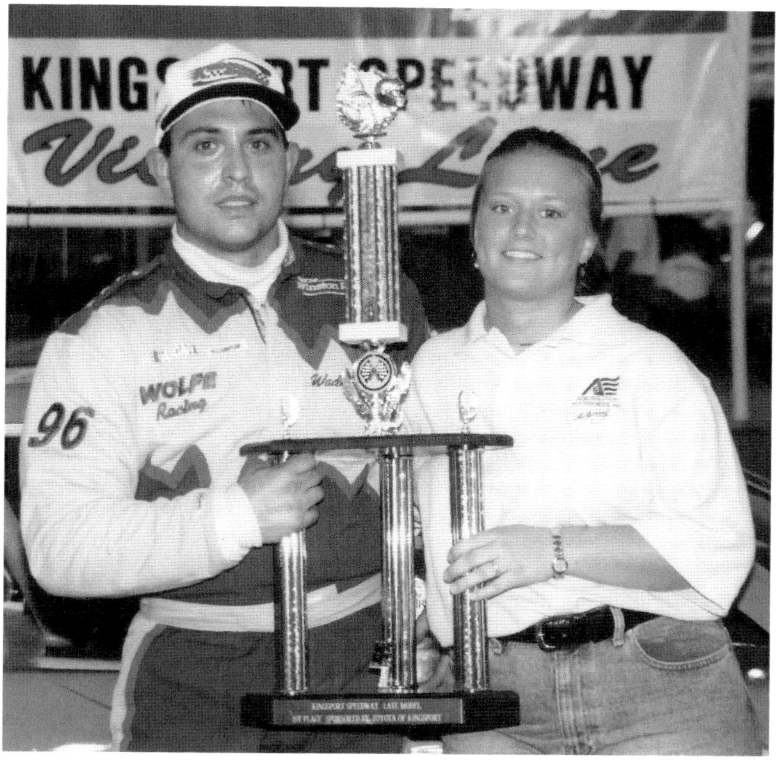

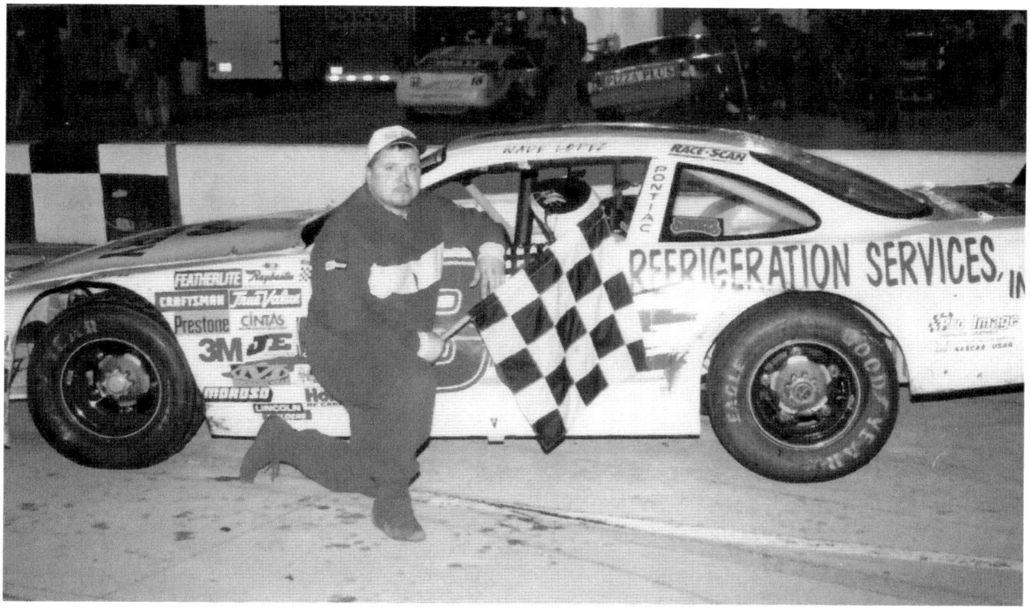

Wade Lopez of Abingdon, Virginia, won a hard-fought battle to wrestle the 2001 Kingsport Late Model championship from Jeff Berry. Lopez finished two spots ahead of Berry in the season finale Top Dawg 150 race to claim the title by nine points. Lopez had one victory and 16 top-five finishes. (Photograph by Randall Perry.)

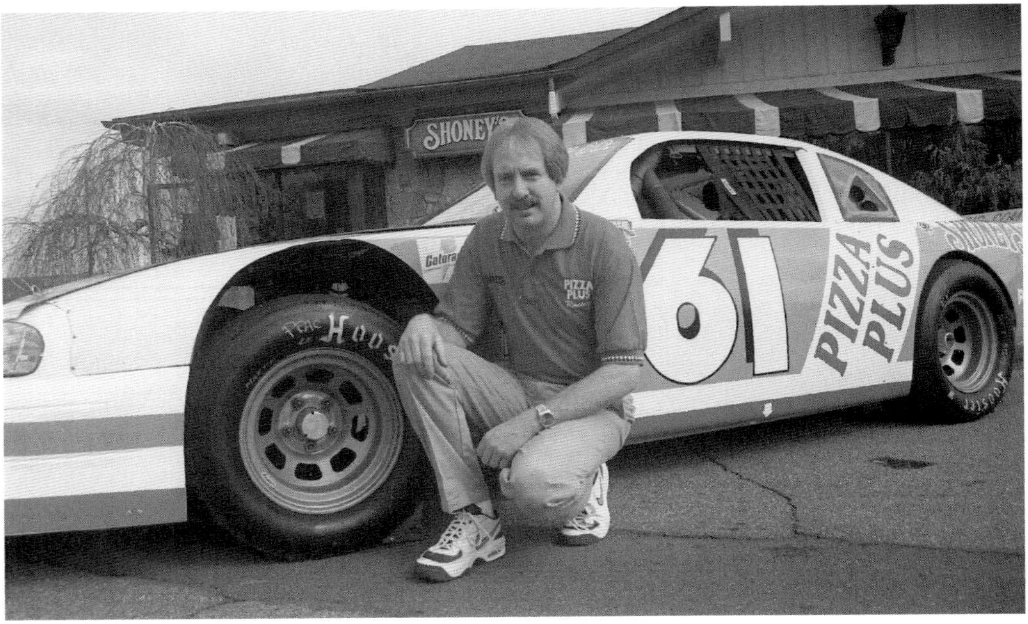

Jeff Berry began competing at Kingsport Speedway in the 1970s in the Hobby class before advancing to the Late Model division and nearly winning the 2001 track championship. It was truly a home-track advantage for the hometown driver, whose race shop was across the street from the track. (Photograph by the author.)

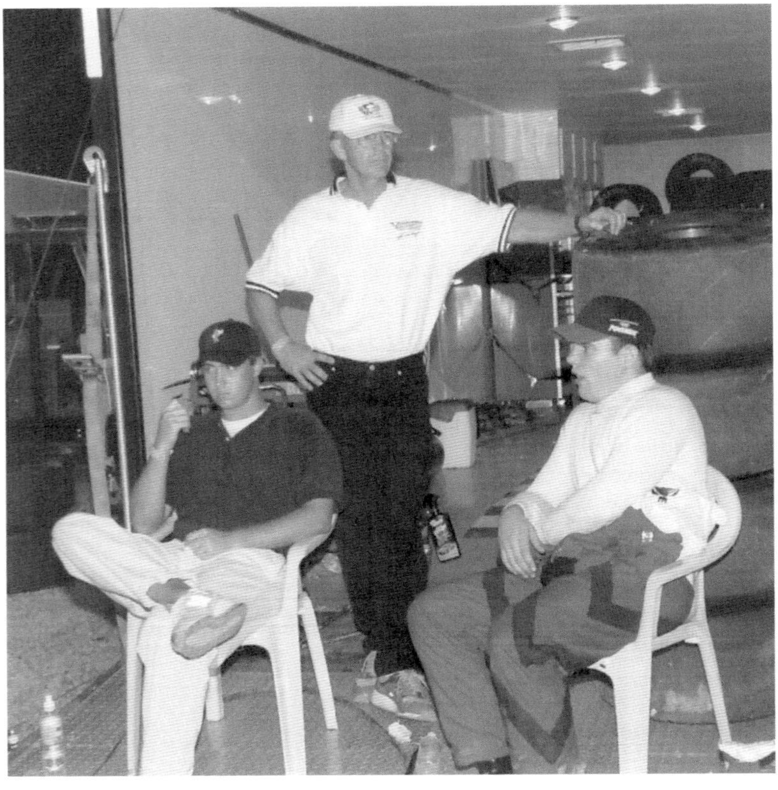

Joe Gibbs (standing), a NASCAR premier series team owner and NFL championship–winning coach, made multiple visits to Kingsport in the 1990s with his sons J.D. (left) and Coy, who was competing in Late Model stock cars. (Photograph by Randall Perry.)

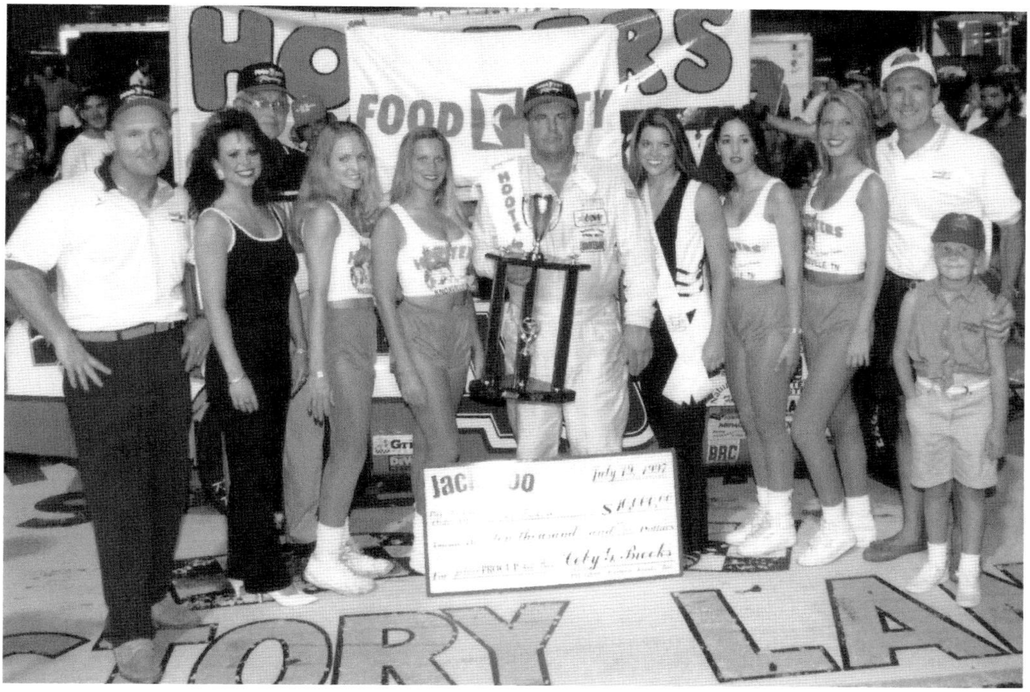

Gene Morgan enjoyed the winner's circle celebration at the Food City 250 for the Hooter's Pro Cup Series in July 1997, but officials later took the victory and gave it to Chad Chaffin after an infraction was discovered. It was the sixth race in the first official year of that series and its only Kingsport appearance. (Photograph by Randall Perry.)

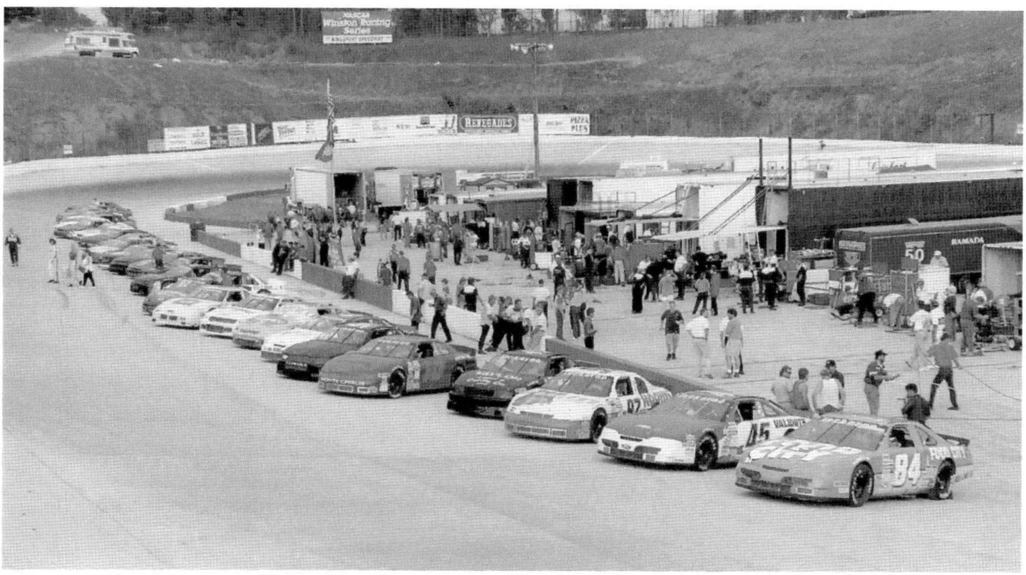

The 30-car field is lined up for the 1997 Food City 250 Hooter's Pro Cup series race at Kingsport. Eventual winner Chad Chaffin (No. 84) was also the fastest qualifier at 78.151 miles per hour in his Food City–sponsored Ford. He collected $10,000 of the race's $50,000 payout. (Photograph by Randall Perry.)

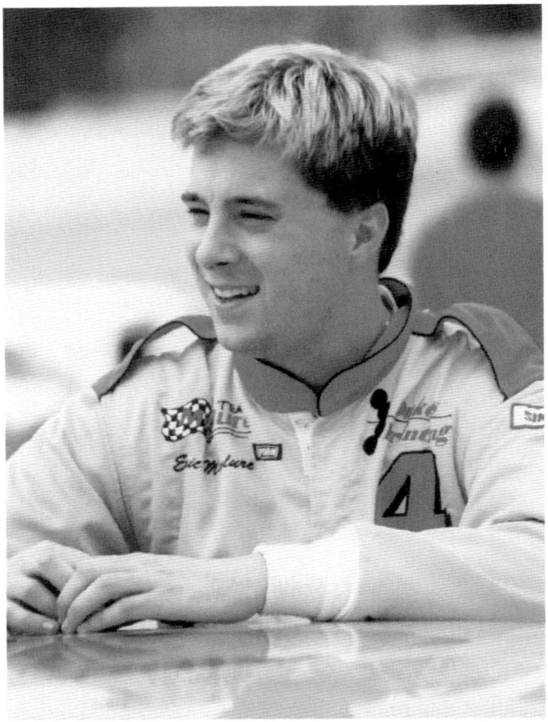

Before racing in the NASCAR Xfinity and Nationwide series, Eric McClure of Chilhowie, Virginia, competed at Kingsport and Lonesome Pine speedways. At the local tracks, McClure campaigned a No. 4 Chevrolet painted like the premier series entries fielded by his family's Morgan-McClure Motorsports. (Photograph by Randall Perry.)

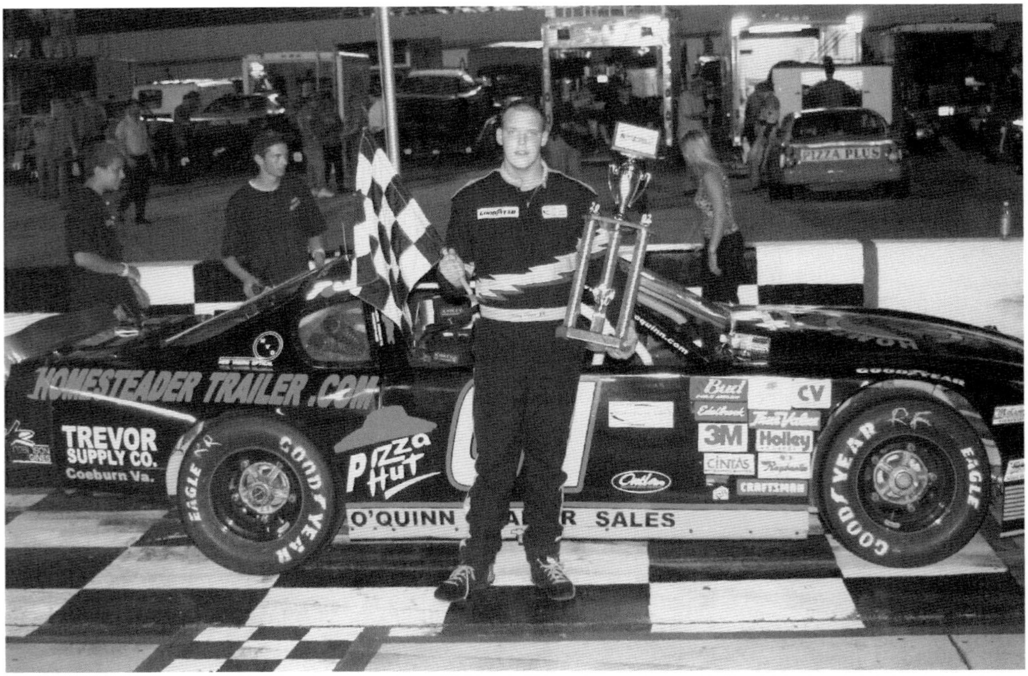

Danny O'Quinn of Coeburn, Virginia, became a regular winner at the Kingsport and Lonesome Pine tracks in 2000 and 2001. He went on to become the 2002 UARA national champion and eventually began driving in the former NASCAR Busch Series for car owner Jack Roush. O'Quinn captured the 2006 rookie of the year award. (Photograph by Randall Perry.)

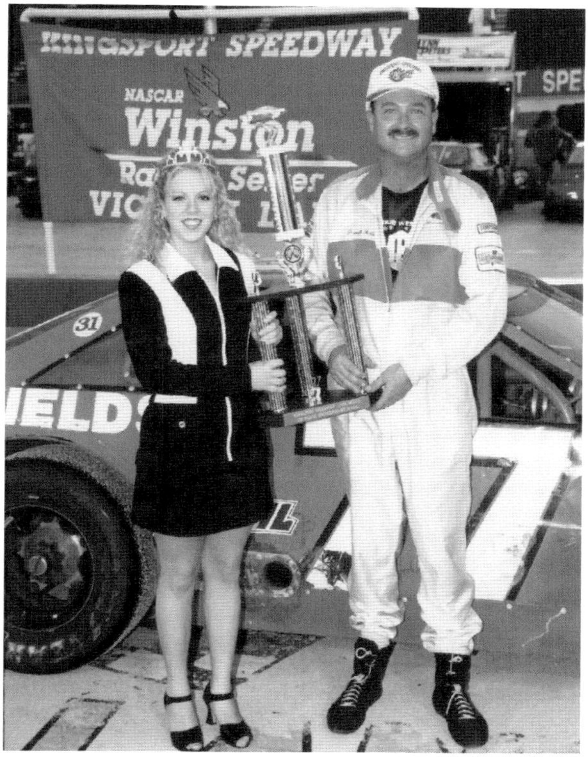

Darrell Holman of Abingdon, Virginia, won races at Kingsport Speedway in the 1990s, following a successful career in the NASCAR Dash series. More recently, Holman has worked with his son Caleb in a variety of racing series. (Photograph by Randall Perry.)

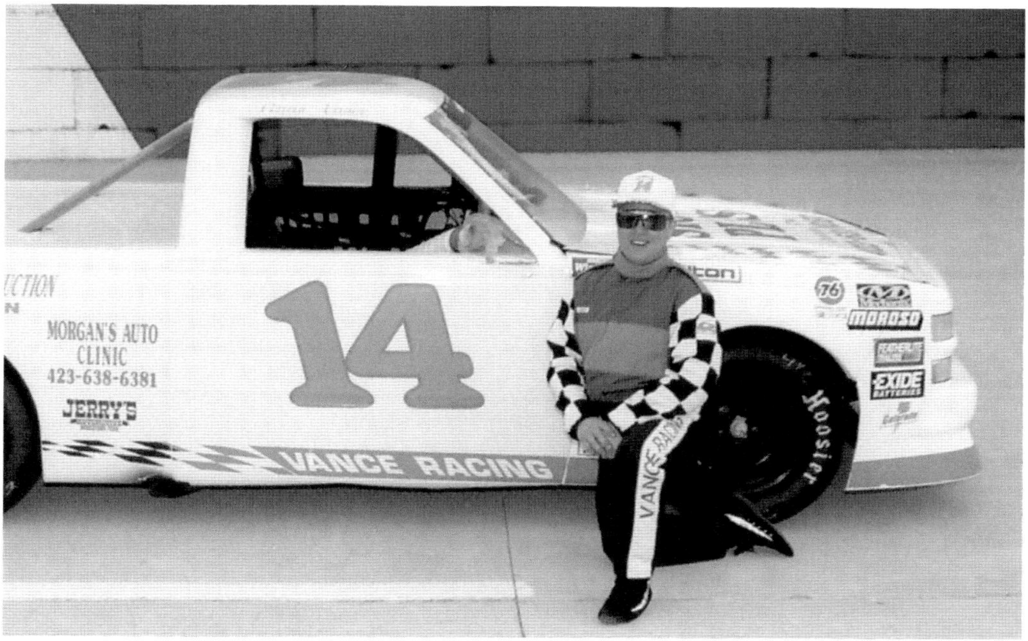

Brian Vance followed his father's tire tracks to become a successful short-track competitor. He was Kingsport's 1999 street stock champion and later managed the racetrack for Galaxy Motorsports. In 2008, he was named race director for the NASCAR Whelen Modified series. (Photograph by Randall Perry.)

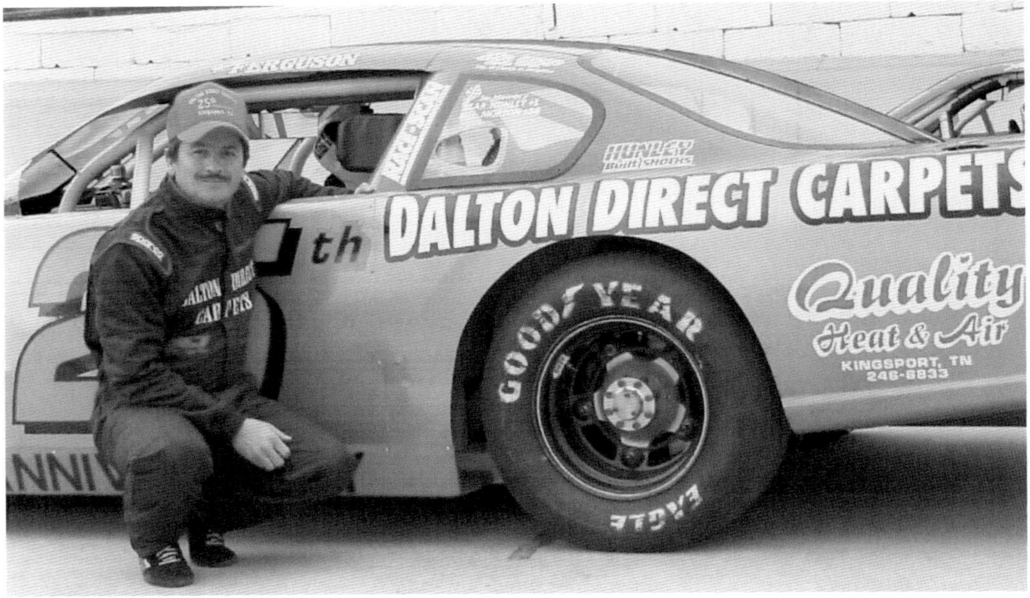

Robbie Ferguson has enjoyed a remarkable short-track racing career, including his 2002 Kingsport Speedway track championship. Ferguson has raced at Kingsport for decades, whether the surface was dirt, asphalt, or concrete. (Photograph by Randall Perry.)

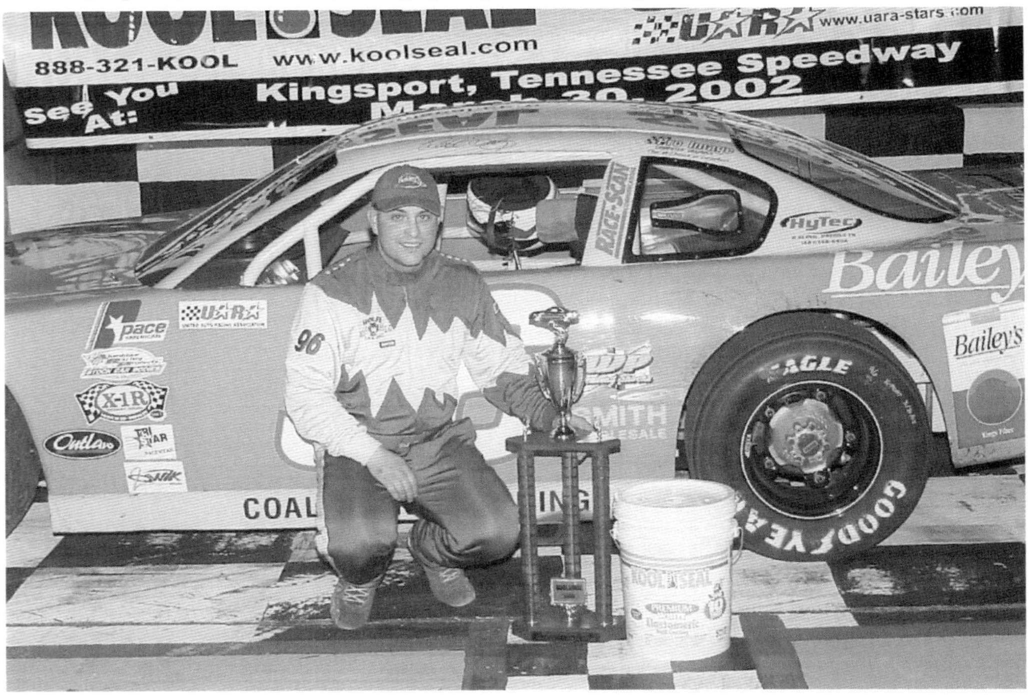

Former track champion Wade Day prevailed at the Kool Seal 150 in April 2002. The race, which was rained out on its original date, was the first Kingsport appearance for the new United Auto Racing Association (UARA). Keith Stiltner and Danny O'Quinn won Kingsport's other UARA races that season. (Photograph by Randall Perry.)

7

Return of the Roar

For all of the buzz surrounding Kingsport's mid-1990s revival, the air quickly escaped that balloon when promoters of Galaxy Motorsports withdrew after the 2002 season. Track owner Joe Loven was then focused on promoting his Volunteer Speedway dirt oval and did not have any prospects to take over operating Kingsport. The track sat lifeless for seven years. During the summer of 2009, its demise appeared more imminent than ever.

Longtime fans and racers mourned the lengthy silence and speculated about a dim future. Perhaps, they fretted, the property would wind up as nondescript apartments, condominiums, or, heaven forbid, another convenience store or storage warehouse. An industrial park replaced nearby Appalachian Speedway. Perhaps a similar fate awaited Kingsport.

Mourners would drive out Morelock Street, wind their way past the backstretch grandstand entrance and around the sharp curve, and pull off the street atop the hill overlooking the track. Shutting off their engines, they would step out and stare, their mind's eyes filling with legends racing fender to fender—Richard Petty or Jack Ingram on the asphalt; Buck Simmons or Scott Bloomquist carving up the dirt.

Then, one blustery November afternoon, something marvelous, something seemingly unimaginable shattered the midweek silence. It was a race car; no, two cars. Unmuffled engines fired up and rolled out to circle the concrete.

Miraculously, Kingsport Speedway awakened from its slumber. United Auto Racing Association president Kerry Bodenhamer needed a place to stage his season finale. After conversations with friend and track owner Joe Loven, a deal was reached.

Race day dawned clear and sunny, and a sizable, enthusiastic crowd turned out. That race led to two more the following year and sparked renewed interest. Former NASCAR driver Robert Pressley, who served as crew chief for his son Coleman at that time, recalled the roar from attending Kingsport races with his father, Bob, in the 1970s. There were big crowds and big-time drivers.

Did the old track really still have some life? Would it be worth investing time and money to find out? The rebirth that followed would not have happened without those early UARA races.

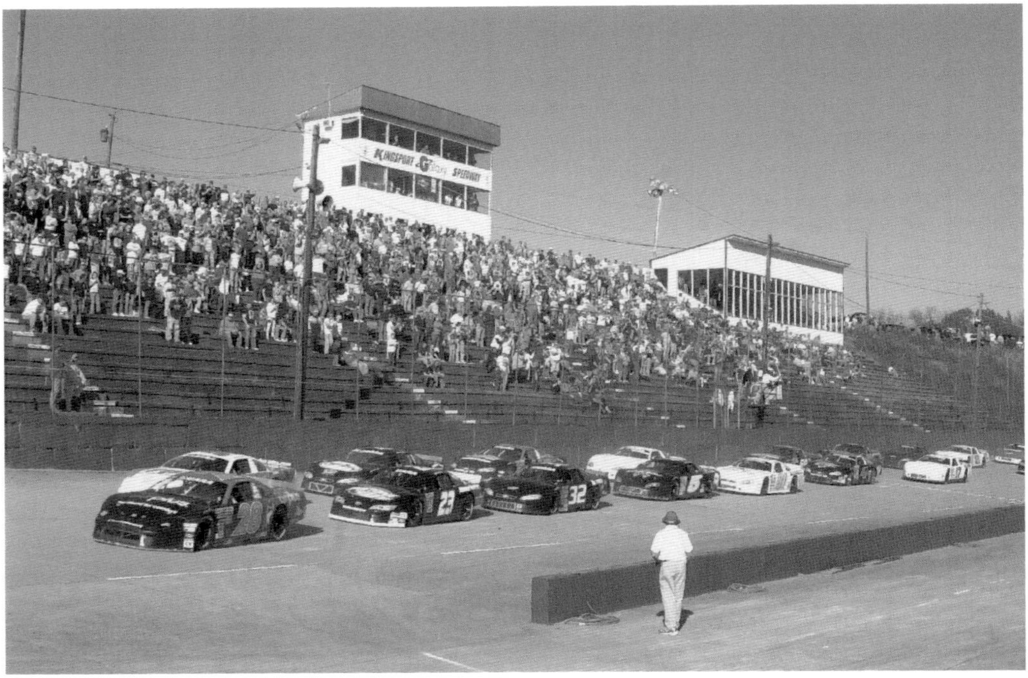

Fastest qualifier Brandon McReynolds (No. 28) leads the field into the first turn during the first lap of the UARA 150 at Kingsport Speedway in November 2009. The race was the season finale for the United Auto Racing Association's Stars series and marked the first competition at the track since 2002. (Photograph by Drew Hierwarter.)

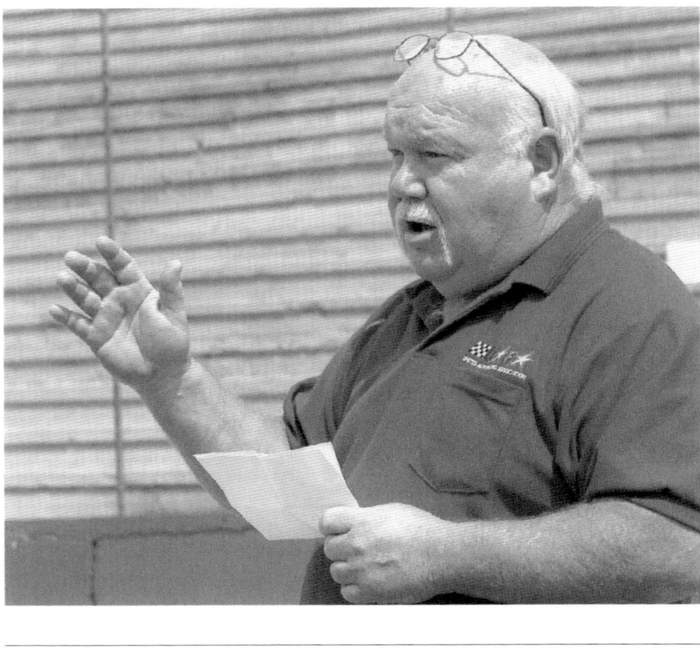

Kerry Bodenhamer speaks to drivers running in his United Auto Racing Association Late Model series. Bodenhamer and track owner Joe Loven worked together to bring racing back to Kingsport in 2009, eventually sparking a return to regular competition. (Photograph by Drew Hierwarter.)

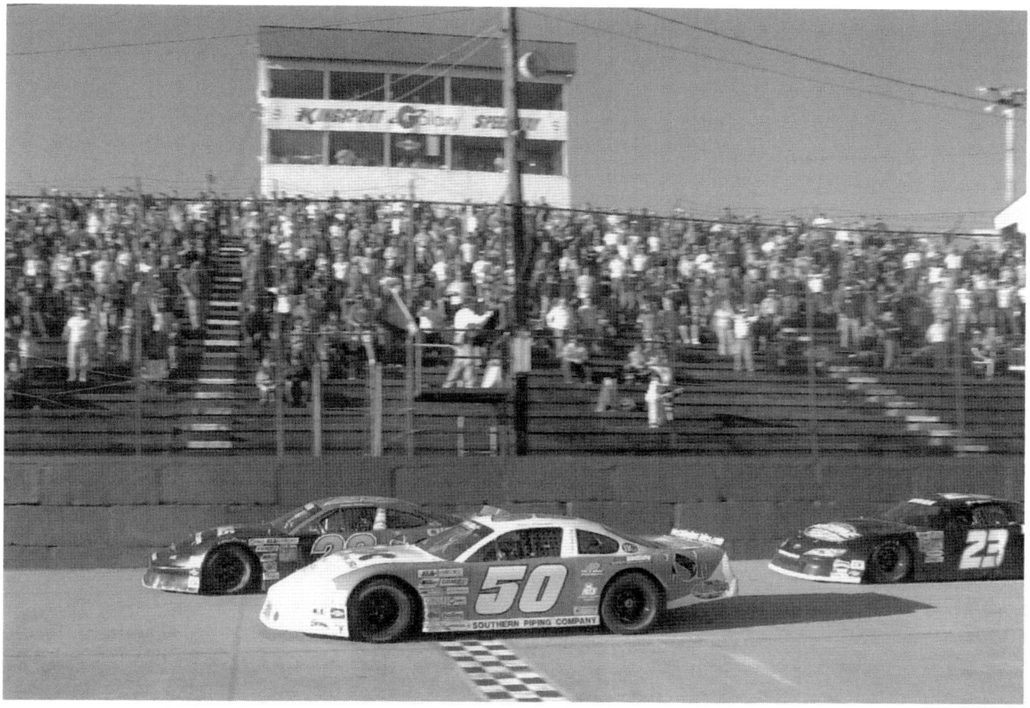

Fans were on their feet as Brandon McReynolds (No. 28) edged Jamey Caudill (No. 50) by a fender to win the inaugural UARA 150 at Kingsport Speedway in November 2009. Matt McCall (No. 23) finished third in the 26-car field and claimed the 2009 UARA series points championship over Caudill. (Photograph by Drew Hierwarter.)

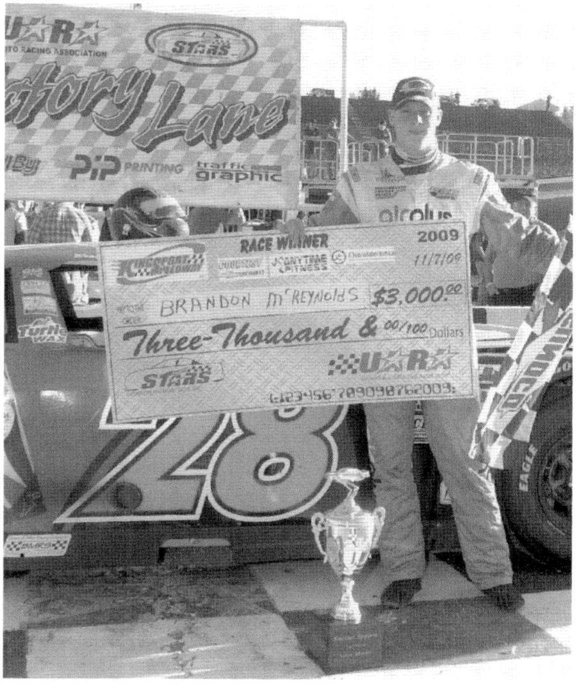

UARA 150 winner Brandon McReynolds celebrates in Kingsport Speedway's victory lane after claiming the $3,000 top prize. McReynolds, the son of former NASCAR premier series crew chief and television analyst Larry McReynolds, has gone on to race in other NASCAR series. (Photograph by Drew Hierwarter.)

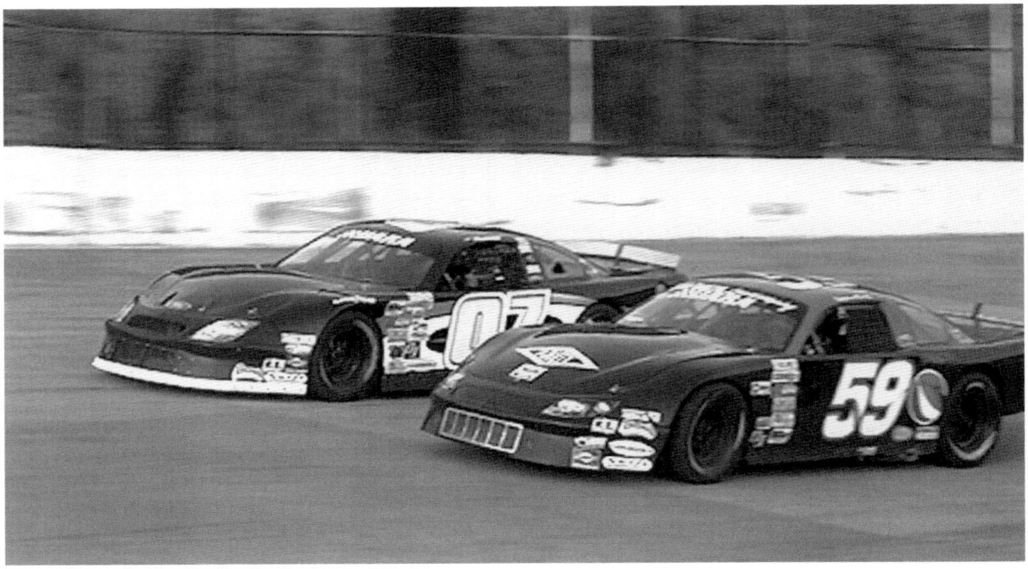

Coleman Pressley (No. 59) and Clint King (No. 07) race for the lead during the UARA 150 at Kingsport in March 2010. King won, and Pressley finished sixth, after setting the fastest time during qualifying. Pressley's grandfather Bob was a standout racer who won a number of races at Kingsport, and his father, Robert, competed in all of NASCAR's top series. (Photograph by Drew Hierwarter.)

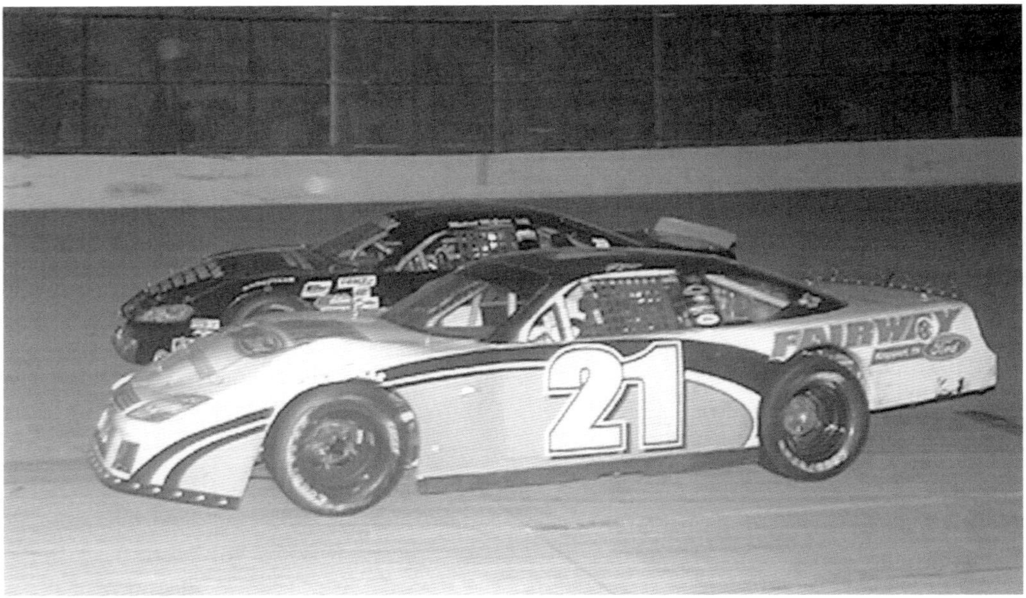

Hometown racer John King (No. 21) overcame a poor qualifying effort to post a strong fifth-place finish in the UARA 150 at Kingsport Speedway in March 2010. King's machine was sponsored by Fairway Ford of Kingsport. (Photograph by Drew Hierwarter.)

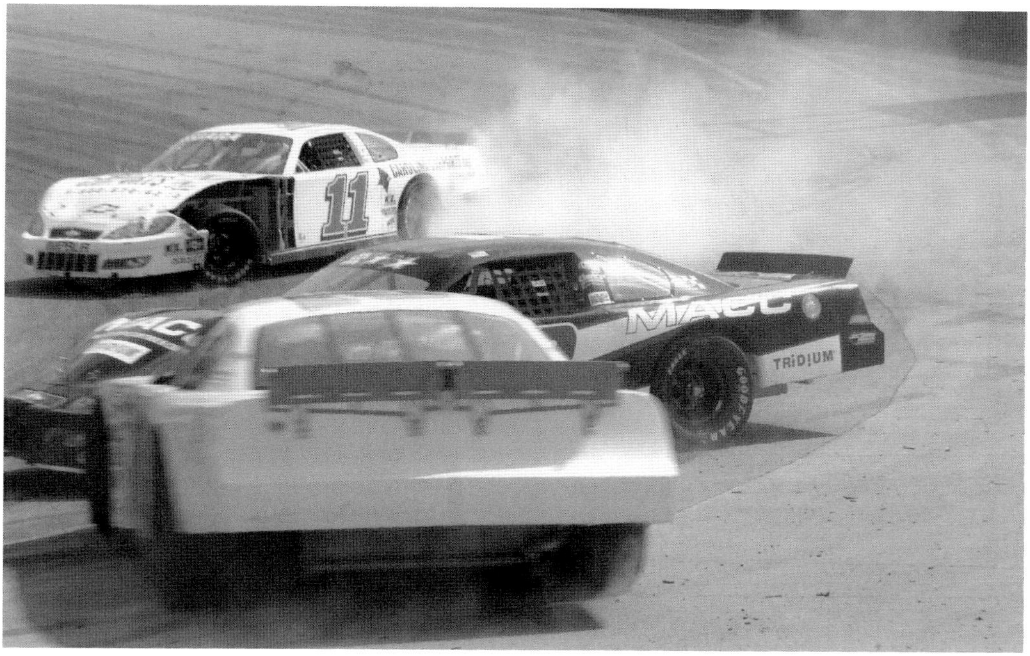

The Chevrolet of Robert Johnson (No. 11) displays typical short-track crash damage following a first-turn incident during Kingsport's Courtesy Chevrolet 150 in August 2010. Johnson is the son of NASCAR legend Junior Johnson. Scott Turlington (No. 48) and Garrett Campbell (No. 12) were also involved. Both Turlington and Johnson bounced back to post top-10 finishes. (Photograph by Drew Hierwarter.)

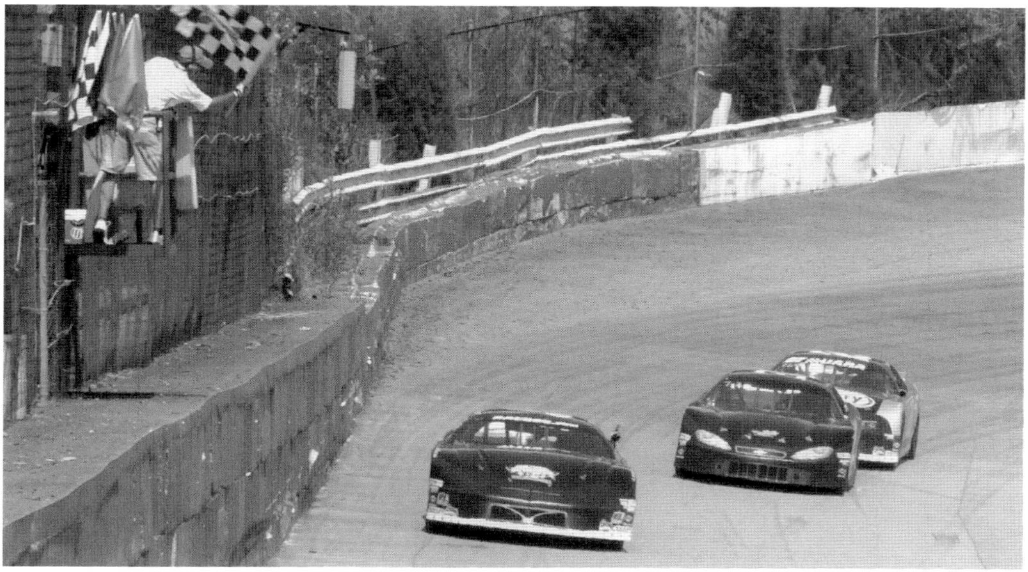

Brennan Poole waves to the fans while streaking beneath UARA flagman Danny Willard's checkered flag to win the Courtesy Chevrolet 150 in August 2010. Poole, a Texas native who starred in the Automobile Racing Club of America and advanced into NASCAR, was closely followed by Kyle Grissom and Lee Tissot. (Photograph by Drew Hierwarter.)

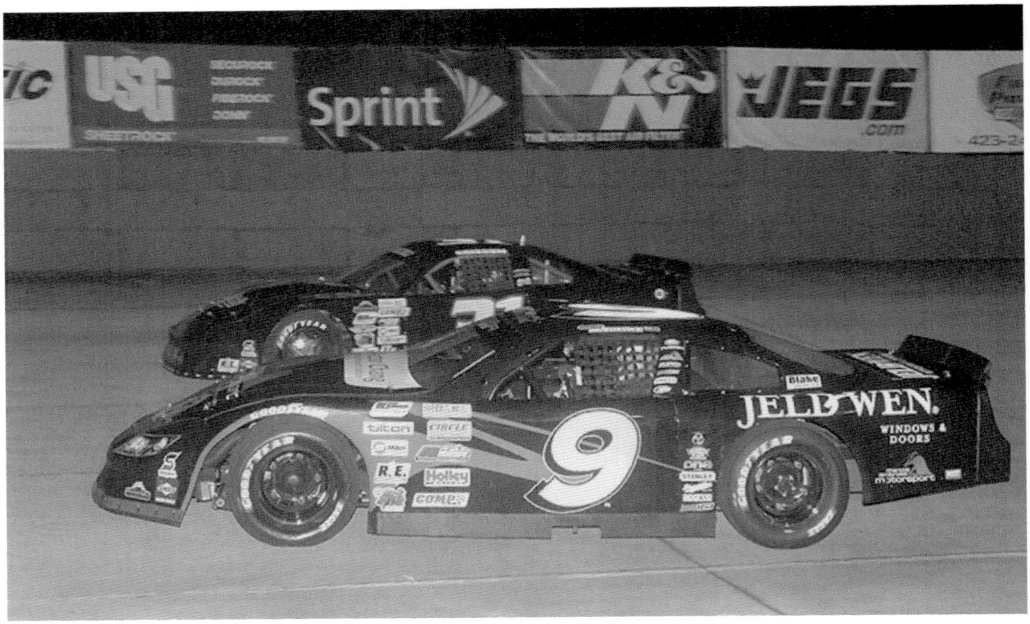

Australian racer George Miedecke (No. 9), driving a Ford owned by former NASCAR star Marcos Ambrose, had a spirited battle with Kyle Grissom (No. 31) during the UARA Courtesy Chevrolet 150 in April 2011. Miedecke spun Grissom on the final lap and took the checkers, but he was disqualified for rough driving. He went on to become that season's rookie of the year. (Photograph by Drew Hierwarter.)

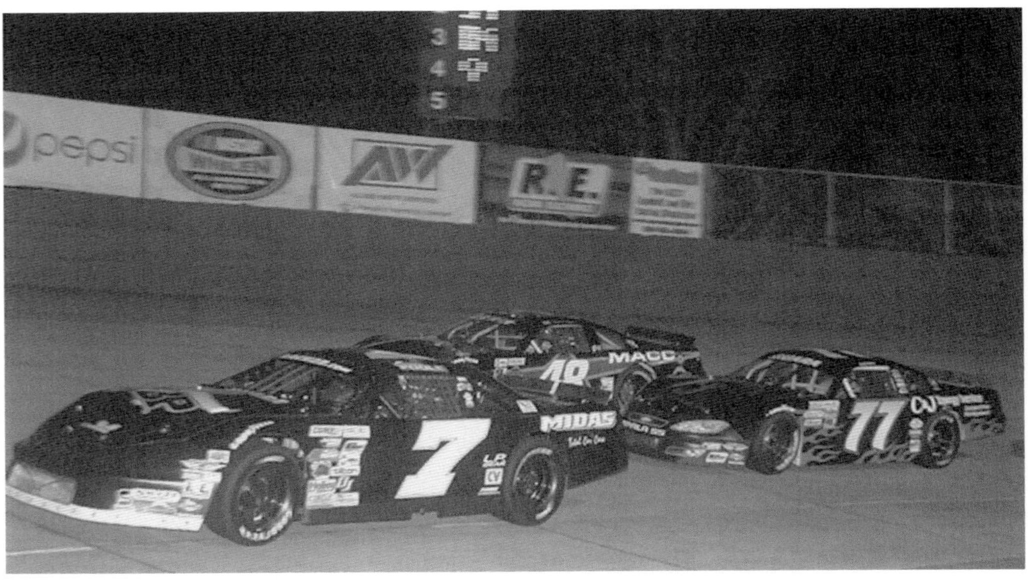

Brennan Poole (No. 7) leads Alex Yontz (No. 77) and Scott Turlington (No. 48) on his way to winning the UARA Courtesy Chevrolet 150 at Kingsport Speedway in April 2011. It was Poole's second straight victory at Kingsport. (Photograph by Drew Hierwarter.)

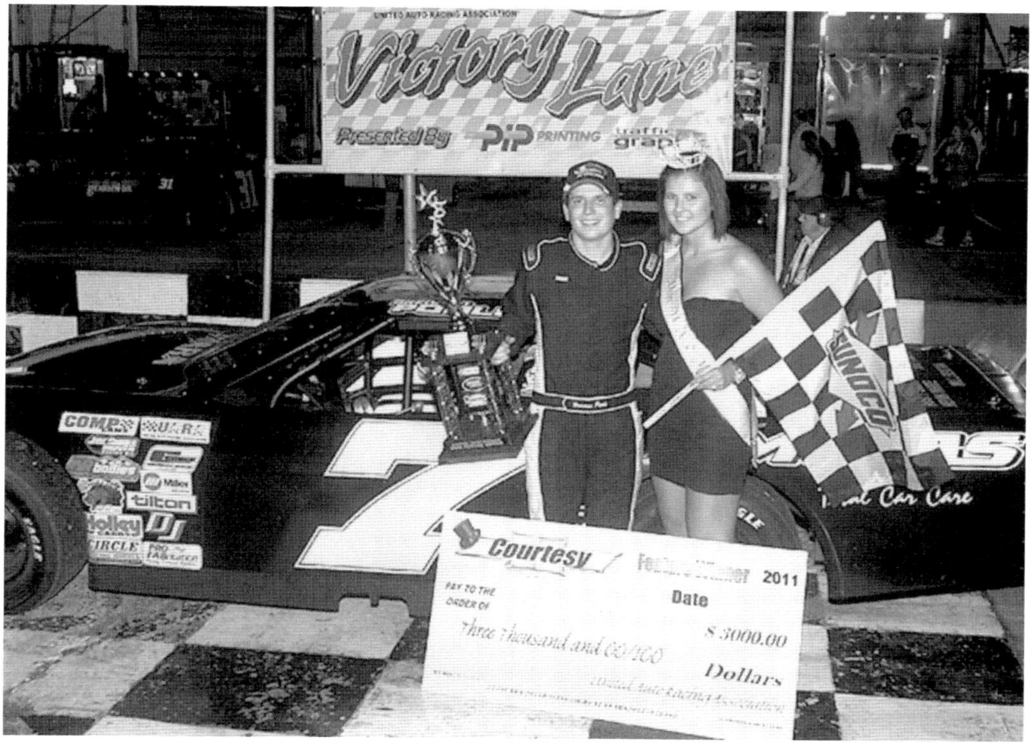

Brennan Poole shares Kingsport Speedway's victory lane with Miss UARA, Brittany Poe, after winning the UARA Courtesy Chevrolet 150 in April 2011. He finished second on the track, but was awarded the win after the leader was disqualified. Poole went on to claim that year's UARA Stars season championship. (Photograph by Drew Hierwarter.)

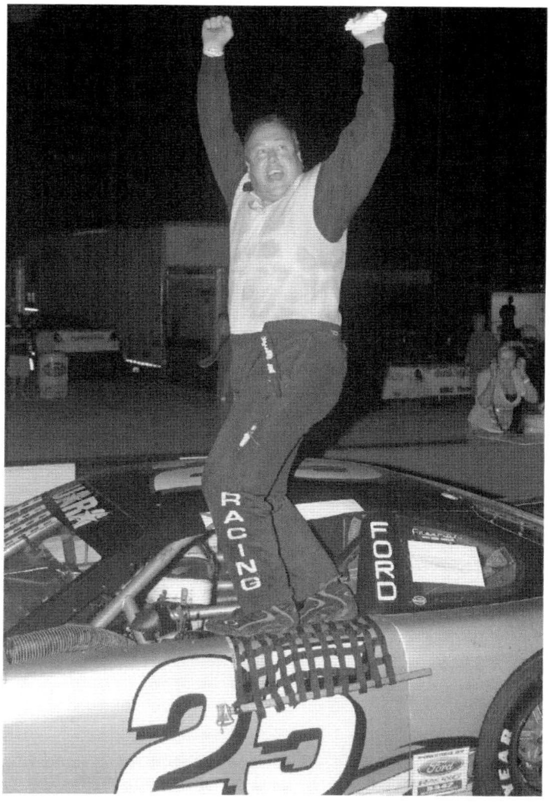

An ecstatic Lee Tissot jumps on his car and celebrates winning the Courtesy Chevrolet 150 UARA series feature in August 2011. Tissot, who competed regularly at Kingsport Speedway that year, led every lap in his Ford. The former series champion held off Kyle Grissom for the victory. (Photograph by Randall Perry.)

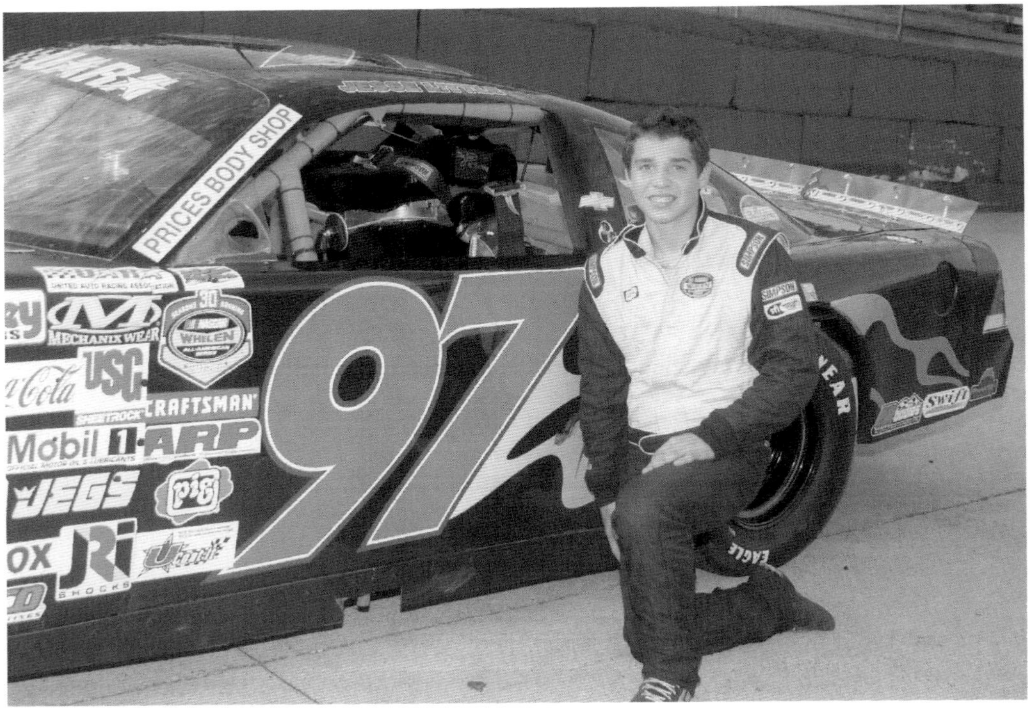

Rising NASCAR driver Jesse Little made his Kingsport Speedway debut in 2011 at age 14, competing in the Courtesy Chevrolet 150 UARA race. He is the son of former NASCAR driver and current NASCAR executive Chad Little. His mother, Donna, grew up in East Tennessee. (Photograph by Randall Perry.)

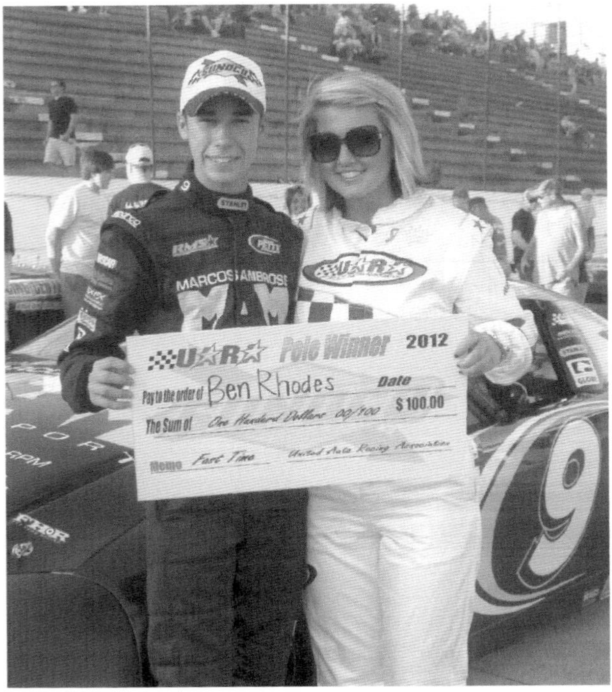

Current NASCAR driver Ben Rhodes of Louisville, Kentucky, accepts the Sunoco Pole Award from Miss UARA, Brittany Poe, prior to the UARA 150 at Kingsport Speedway in May 2012. Rhodes wheeled the No. 9 Ford owned by Marcos Ambrose to the fastest qualifying lap, but finished a disappointing 15th. (Photograph by Drew Hierwarter.)

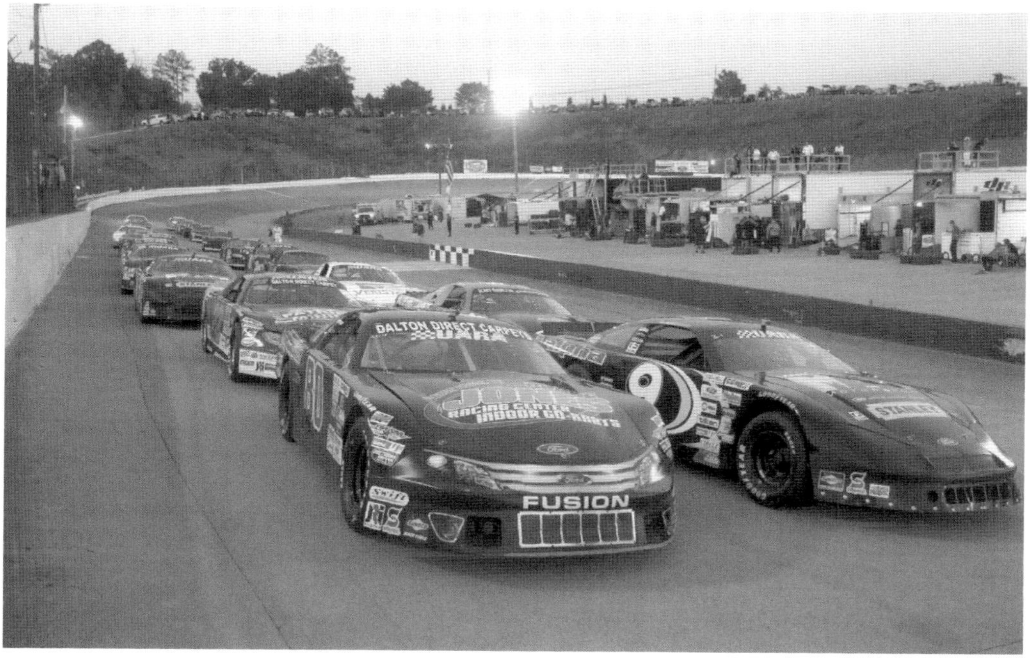

An all-Ford front row of Ben Rhodes (No. 9) and Blake Jones (No. 80) leads a 22-car field to the green flag during the UARA 150 at Kingsport Speedway in May 2012. Neither young driver figured in the outcome, as Coleman Pressley edged out Sammy Jasper and Coleman's cousin Kaleb Pressley. (Photograph by Drew Hierwarter.)

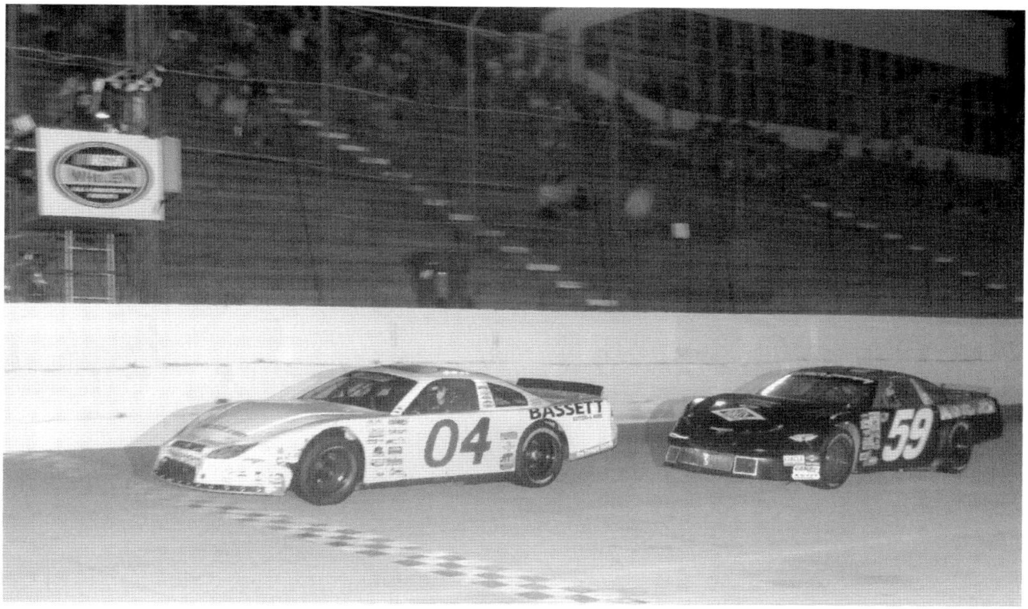

Ronnie Bassett Jr. (No. 04) was disqualified and stripped of an apparent victory by race officials following the completion of the UARA Stars 150 race at Kingsport Speedway in May 2012. Coleman Pressley (No. 59), the 2010 series champion, was elevated from runner-up to race winner. (Photograph by Drew Hierwarter.)

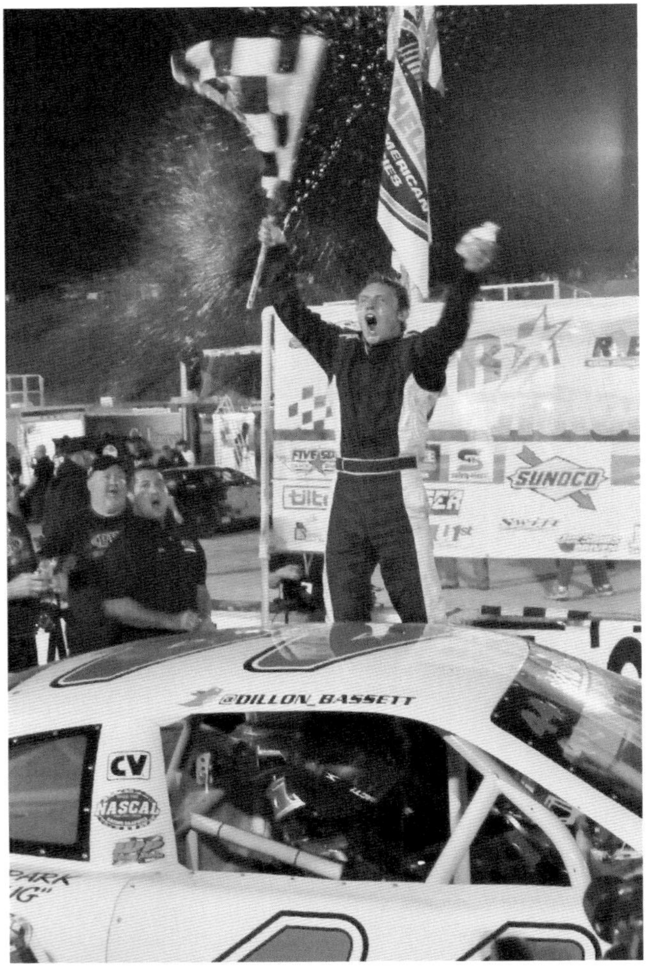

An exuberant Dillon Bassett celebrates winning the UARA 150 at Kingsport Speedway in September 2012. His win, combined with a ninth-place finish by points leader Travis Swaim, allowed Bassett to close the gap in their battle for the UARA season championship. (Photograph by Randall Perry.)

Dillon Bassett (No. 44) passes Daniel Pope (No. 16) during the UARA 150 at Kingsport Speedway in September 2013. Bassett started ninth, but worked his way through the field to score his second consecutive win at the "Concrete Jungle." (Photograph by Drew Hierwarter.)

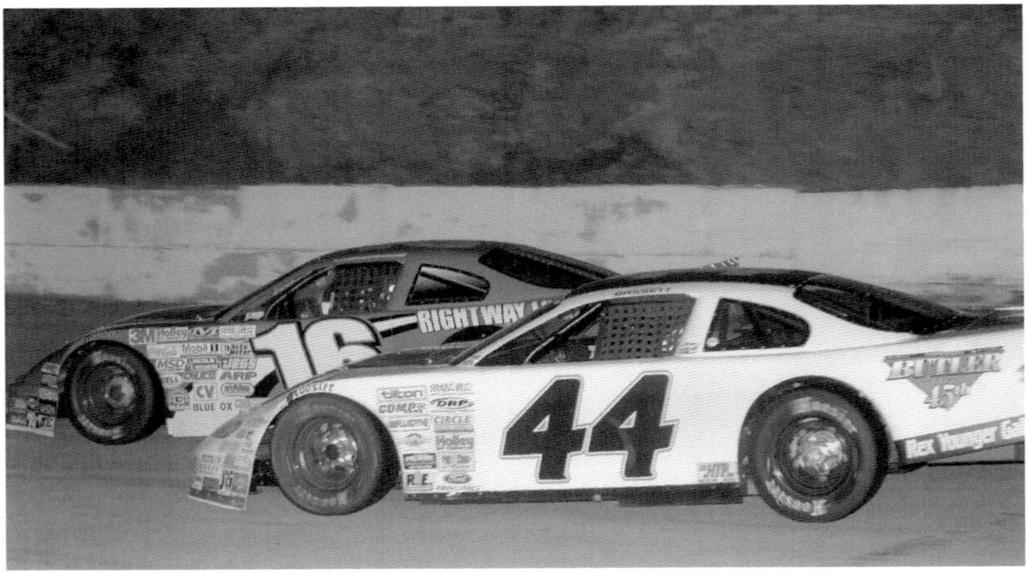

8

THE CONCRETE JUNGLE

Karen Tunnell was one of those diehard race fanatics who sometimes drove out Morelock Street, made the sharp left turn, and pulled into a well-worn spot at the top of the hill overlooking Kingsport Speedway, wishing somehow the rumble of engines would again shatter the venerable old track's silence.

Racing returned to Kingsport with regularity in 2011, as Robert Pressley, whose father, Bob, raced and won many times during Kingsport's golden era, accepted the challenge of rejuvenating the track. Pressley regained the NASCAR sanction and assembled a full season schedule. When Tunnell learned of Pressley's plans, she was among the first to call and offer to work there.

Pressley oversaw the program for three seasons, rebuilding the featured Late Model class, support divisions, sponsors, and relationships. But Pressley did not renew the lease after the 2013 season, choosing instead to pursue other opportunities.

Track owner Joe Loven then reached out to longtime friends Ervin and Keith Stiltner, who were already leasing Virginia's Lonesome Pine Raceway at the time. "We talked with Joe about it and we talked with Robert about it," Ervin Stiltner said. "We've been around racing forever. You can't make any money at it, but it's a lot of fun and the people are really good."

They agreed to terms. This time, it was Tunnell's phone that rang. Much more than a fan, Tunnell has spent many years working as a race official at Kingsport and many other area tracks, and her husband has competed. "It's a dream really. It's a challenge running both tracks but I'm really blessed and the response at Kingsport has been great," she said. Tunnell learned much from working for Pressley and met the challenge with seemingly boundless energy.

Kingsport Speedway celebrated its 50th-anniversary season in 2015. Fans could congregate on the concrete grandstands, just as so many have done since Ken Murray first installed them in 1968. Or they could relax on the hillside overlooking the third and fourth turns as racers by the dozen swapped paint and wrinkled sheet metal in search of another checkered flag.

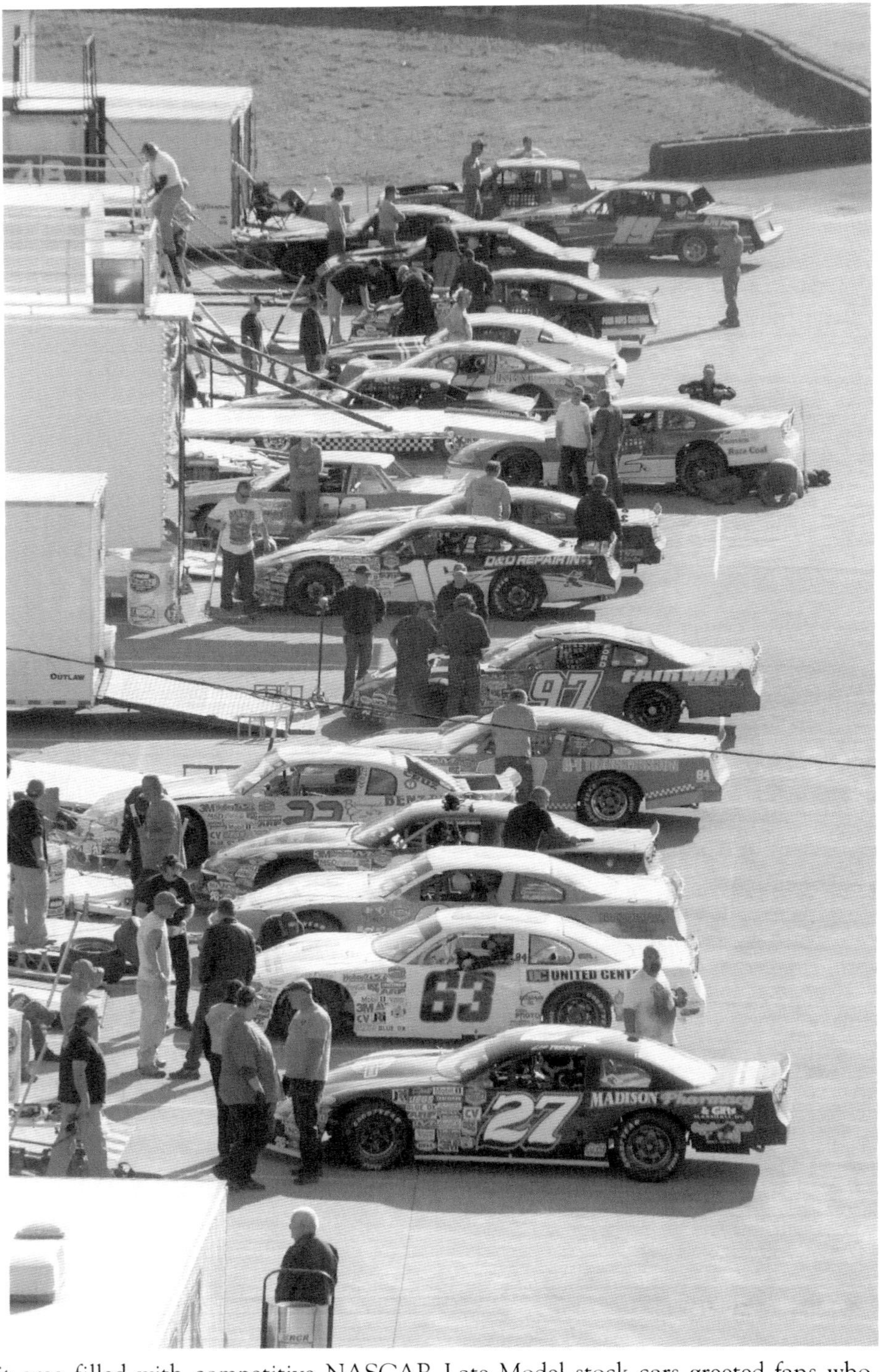

A pit area filled with competitive NASCAR Late Model stock cars greeted fans who came out to Kingsport Speedway in 2011. Drivers from the Tri-Cities, East Tennessee, Southwest Virginia, North Carolina, and other areas converged on Friday nights and Sunday afternoons. (Photograph by Randall Perry.)

Robert Pressley enjoyed a notable career driving in NASCAR's top three divisions between 1989 and 2005, including 12 combined victories. He took on the challenge of promoting the Kingsport track starting in 2011, returning it to NASCAR sanction and operating it for three successful seasons. (Photograph by Randall Perry.)

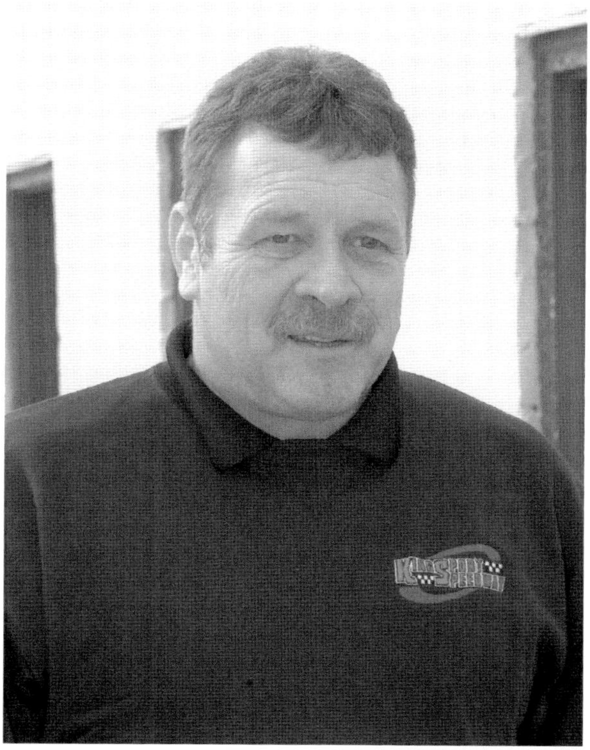

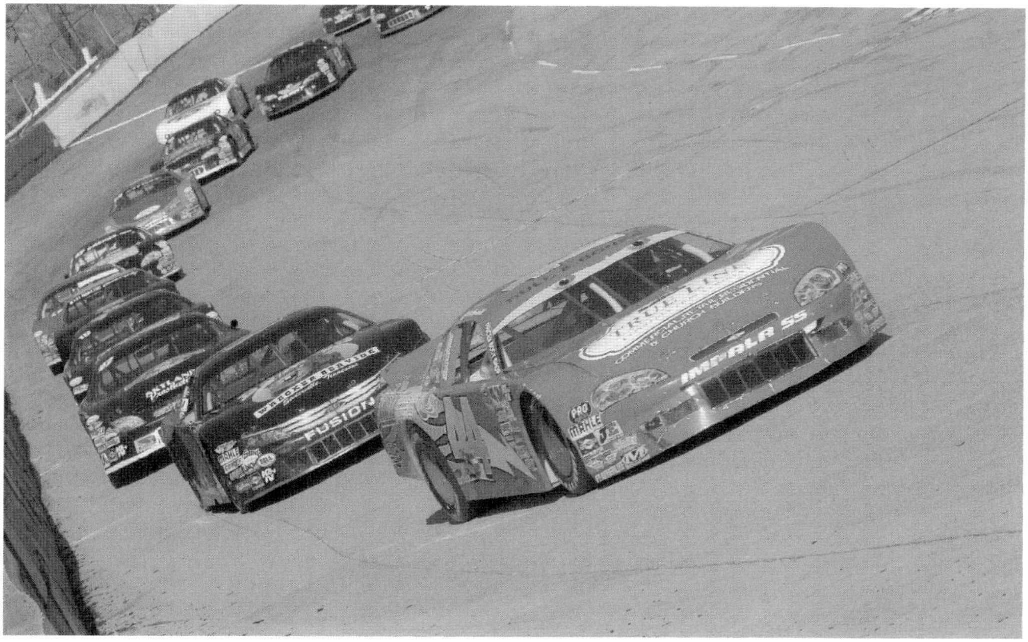

Nate Monteith (No. 44) leads the pack into turn one at Kingsport Speedway during the 2011 season. Monteith dominated that year, scoring 10 victories and 21 top-five finishes in 21 starts to win the track and Tennessee NASCAR All-American series championships. He finished 10th in the United States. (Photograph by Randall Perry.)

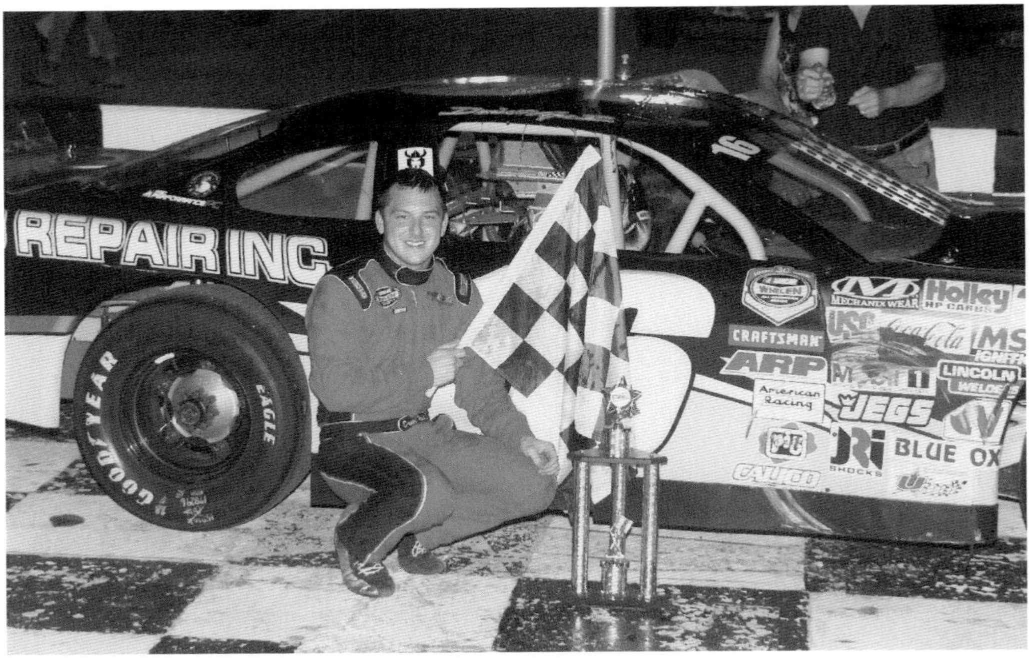

Daniel Pope made the 10-hour round trip each week from his Smyrna, Tennessee, home to compete at Kingsport during the 2011 season. Those road miles paid off, as Pope garnered three Late Model victories and posted a third-place finish in the Kingsport standings. (Photograph by Randall Perry.)

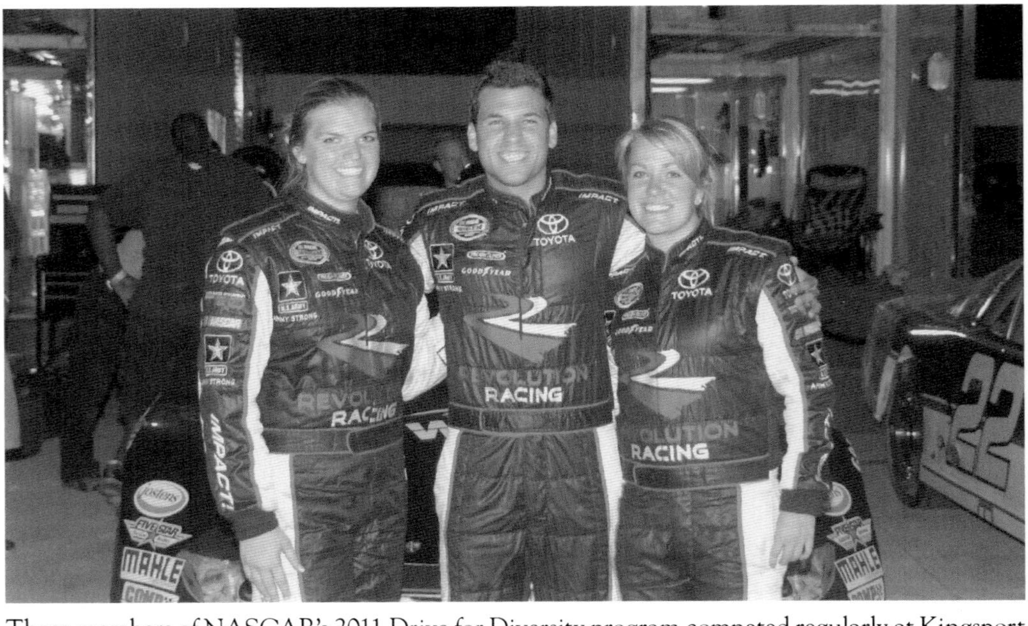

These members of NASCAR's 2011 Drive for Diversity program competed regularly at Kingsport in 2011. Shown are, from left to right, Tayla Orleans of North Carolina, Bryan Ortiz of Puerto Rico, and Mackena Bell of Nevada. Ortiz scored a best of fourth, and Orleans had five top-10 finishes in six Kingsport starts. (Photograph by Randall Perry.)

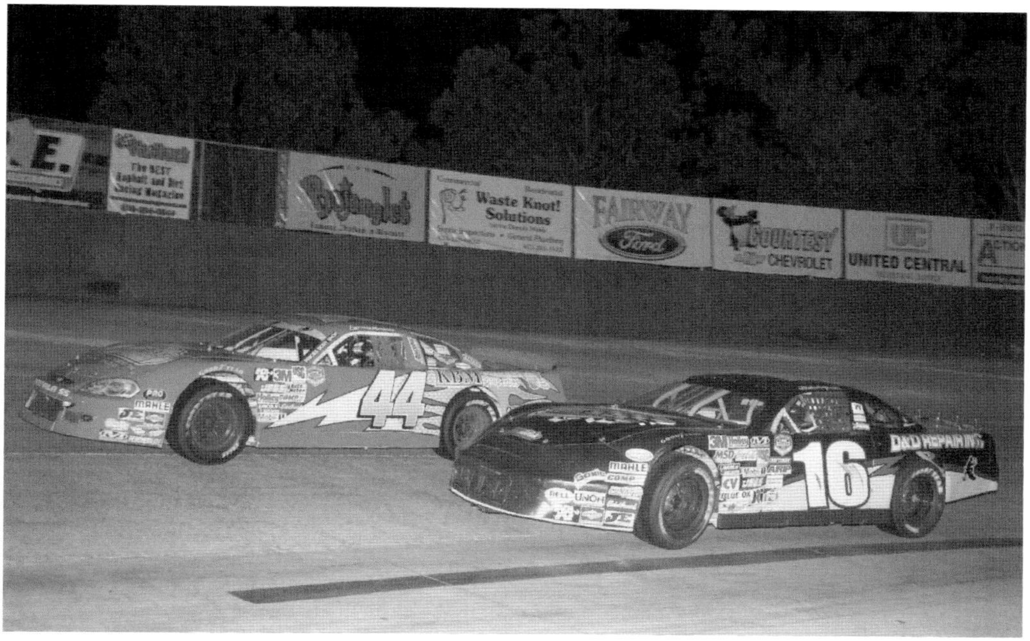

Nate Monteith (No. 44) and Daniel Pope (No. 16) battle for the lead during a 2011 Late Model race at Kingsport. Monteith wound up the season with 10 victories, and Pope won three times. (Photograph by Randall Perry.)

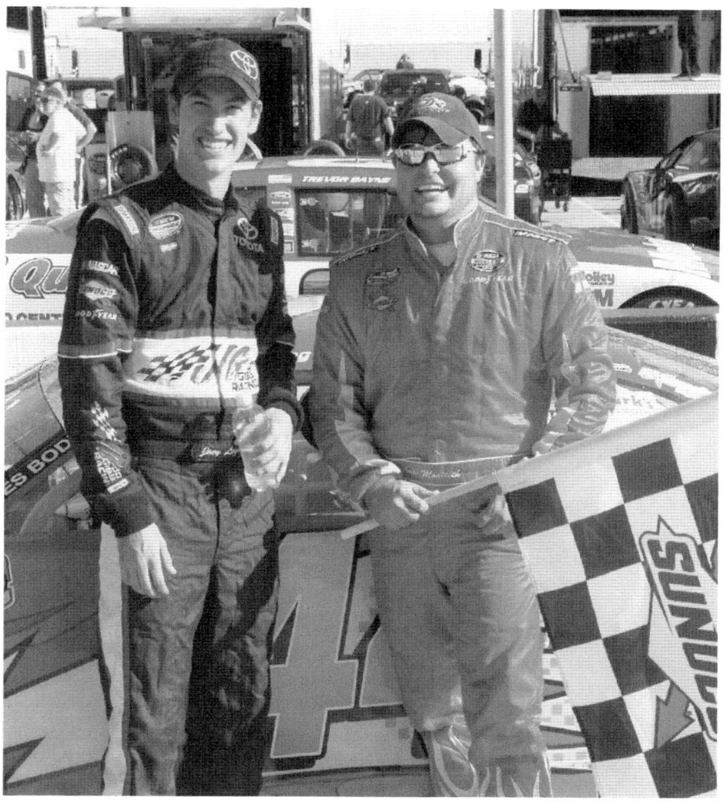

NASCAR premier series driver and Daytona 500 champion Joey Logano (left) congratulates Nate Monteith following the latter's victory in the 2011 Tennessee Championship 125 Late Model race. Logano finished a solid second, driving a car prepared by Robert and Coleman Pressley. (Photograph by Randall Perry.)

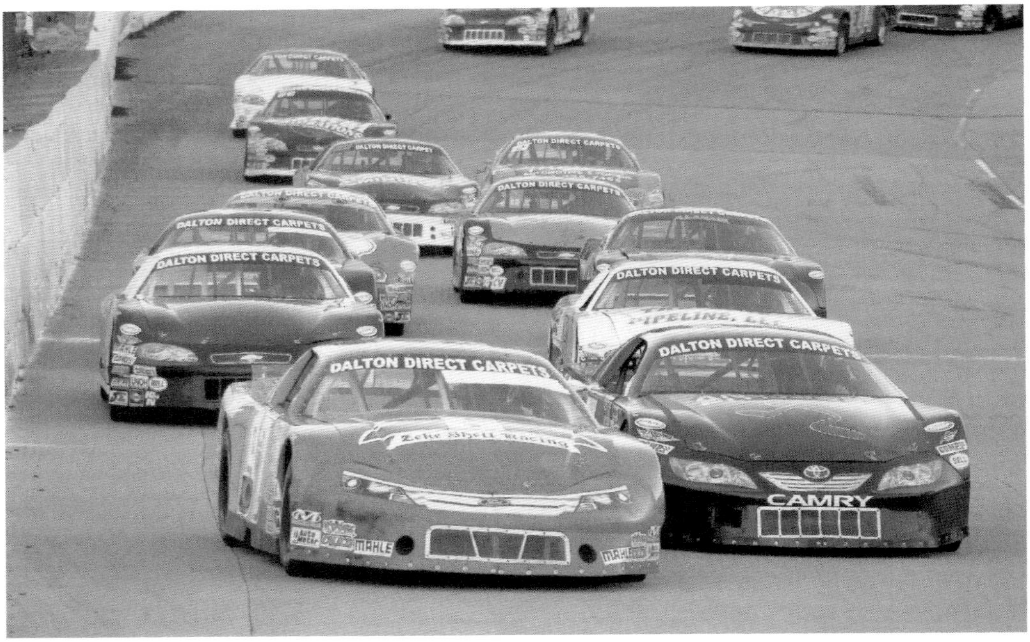

Zeke Shell (No. 97) leads the pack down the front straightaway during Late Model action in 2012. That was a breakout season for Shell, who scored two victories and finished second in the track's NASCAR points standings. (Photograph by Randall Perry.)

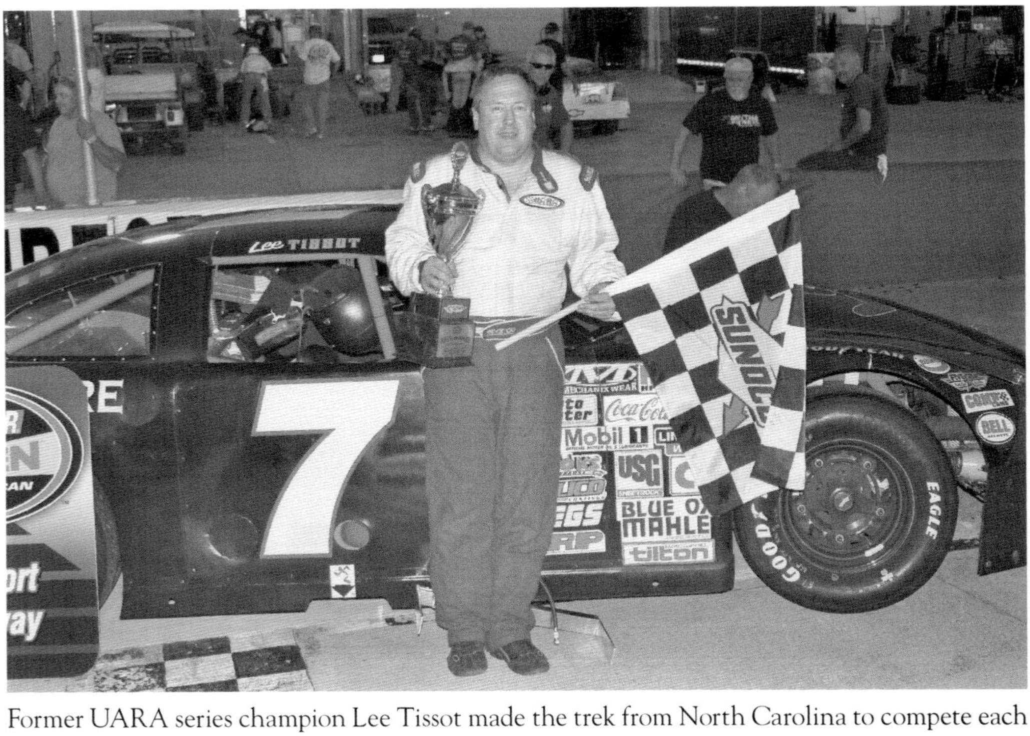

Former UARA series champion Lee Tissot made the trek from North Carolina to compete each week at Kingsport Speedway in 2012. He scored this one victory and finished in the top five in the final season standings. (Photograph by Randall Perry.)

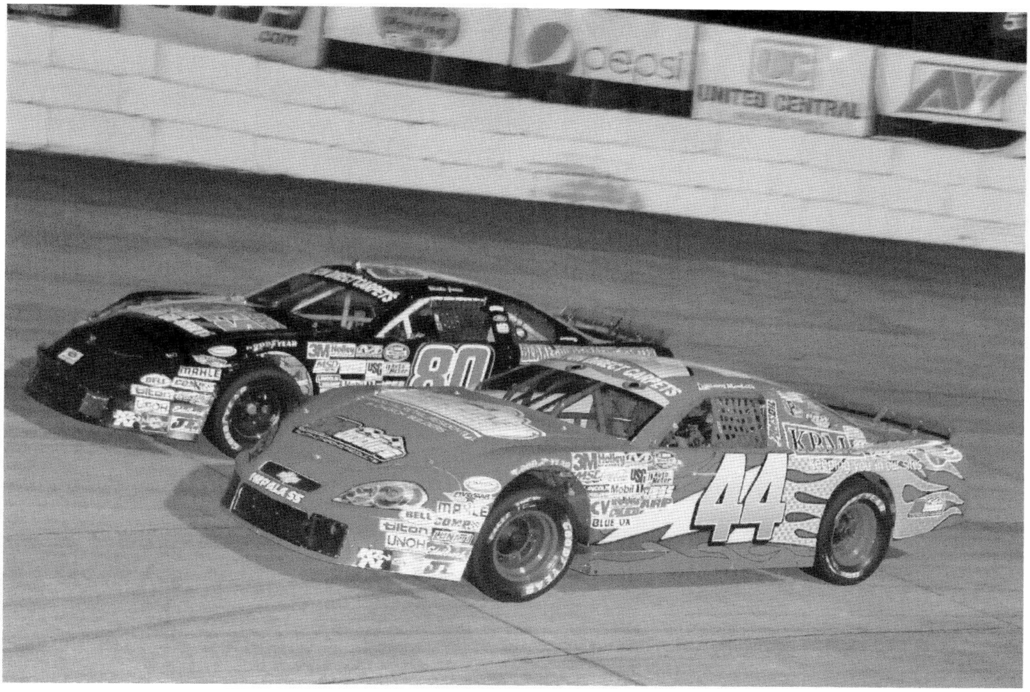

Above, Nate "Lightning" Monteith (No. 44) runs the inside line with his Chevrolet against Blake Jones (No. 80). Monteith replicated his 2011 performance by scoring 10 victories and claiming the Kingsport and Tennessee state NASCAR championships. Monteith (right) had reason to smile, collecting 10 additional Kingsport trophies and finishing fourth in the national NASCAR All-American standings. (Both, photograph by Randall Perry.)

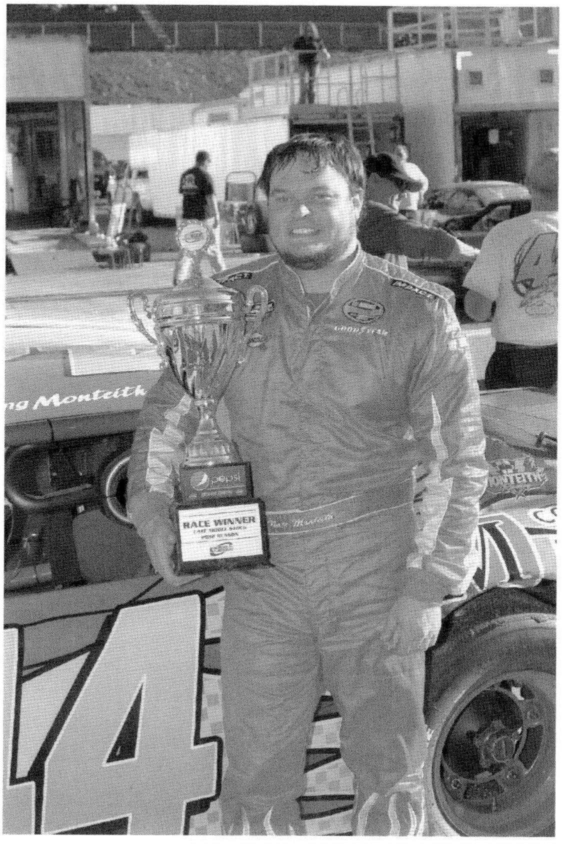

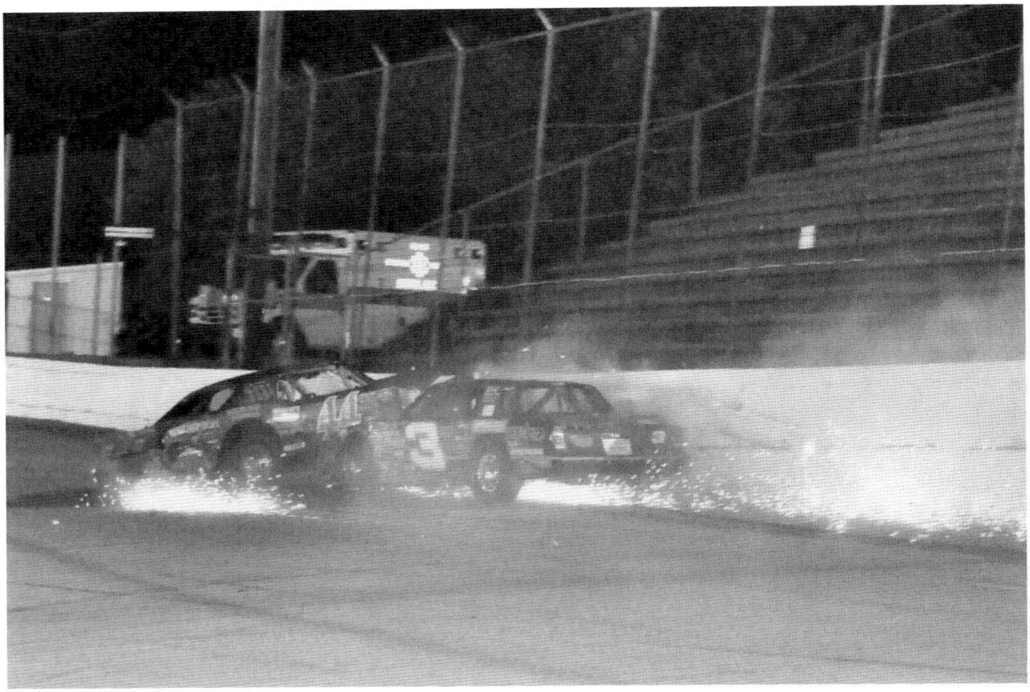

Drivers Greg Grindstaff (No. 3) and Mark Hawkins (No. 44) got together (above) on the final lap of a 30-lap Street Stock feature. The Hawkins car got turned around as they slid along the front stretch wall and was impaled on the concrete barrier outside turn one. The impact destroyed Hawkins's car (below), but he was uninjured. (Both, photograph by Randall Perry.)

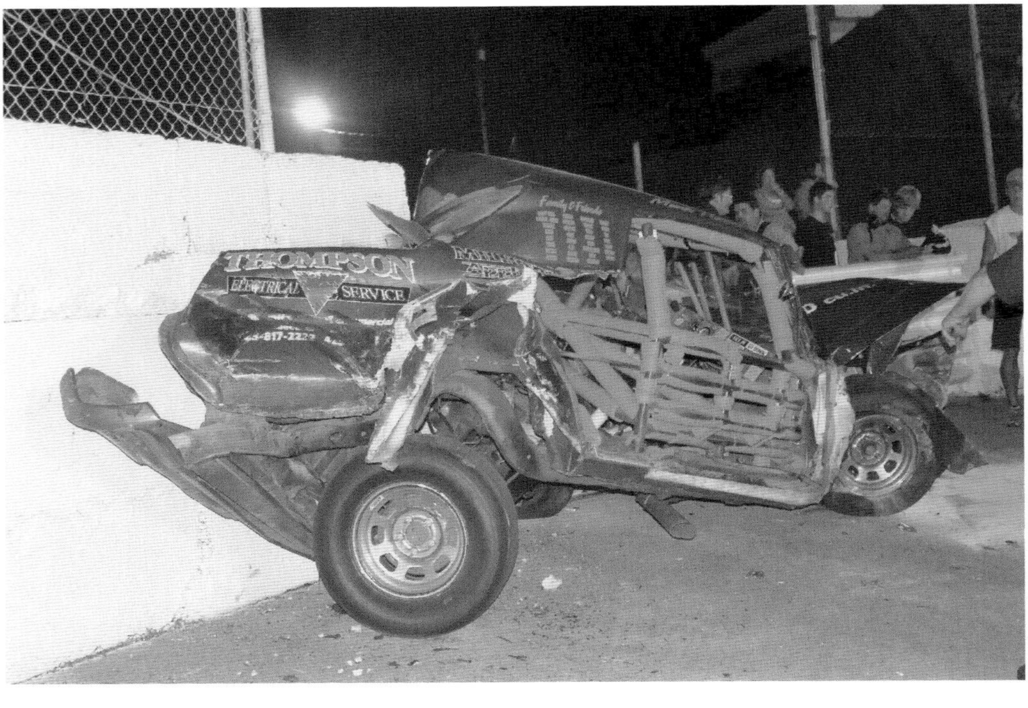

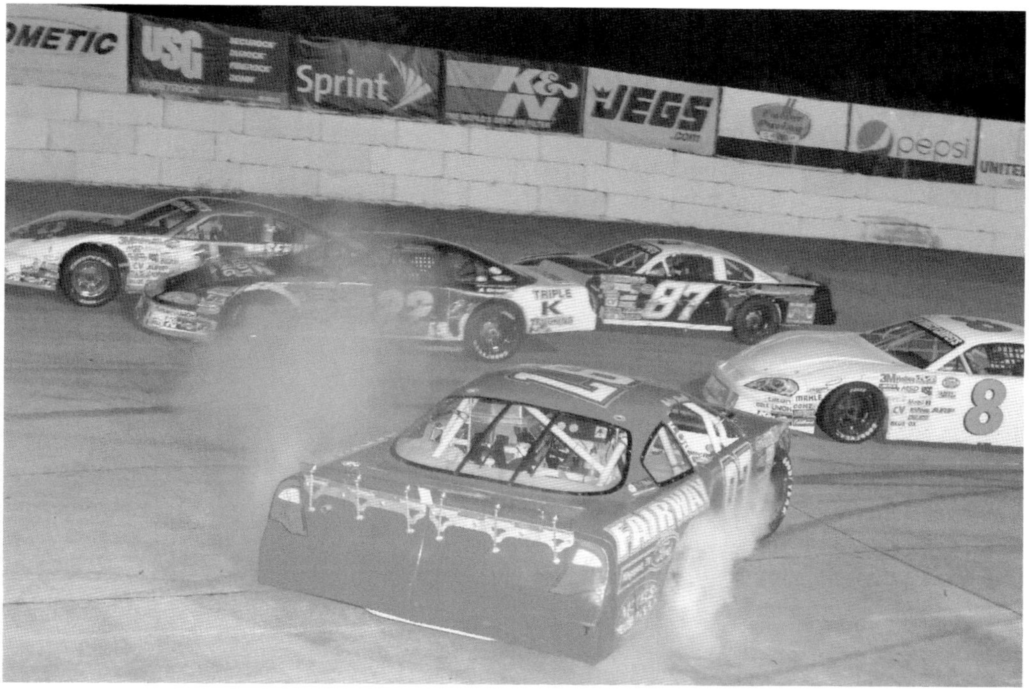

Smoke pours from the rear tires of Zeke Shell's (No. 97) Ford after a spin, as he tries to get turned in the right direction. Among those taking evasive action are Ryan Stiltner (No. 22), Kyle Barnes (No. 15), Hayden Woods (No. 87), and Mike Potter (No. 8). (Photograph by Randall Perry.)

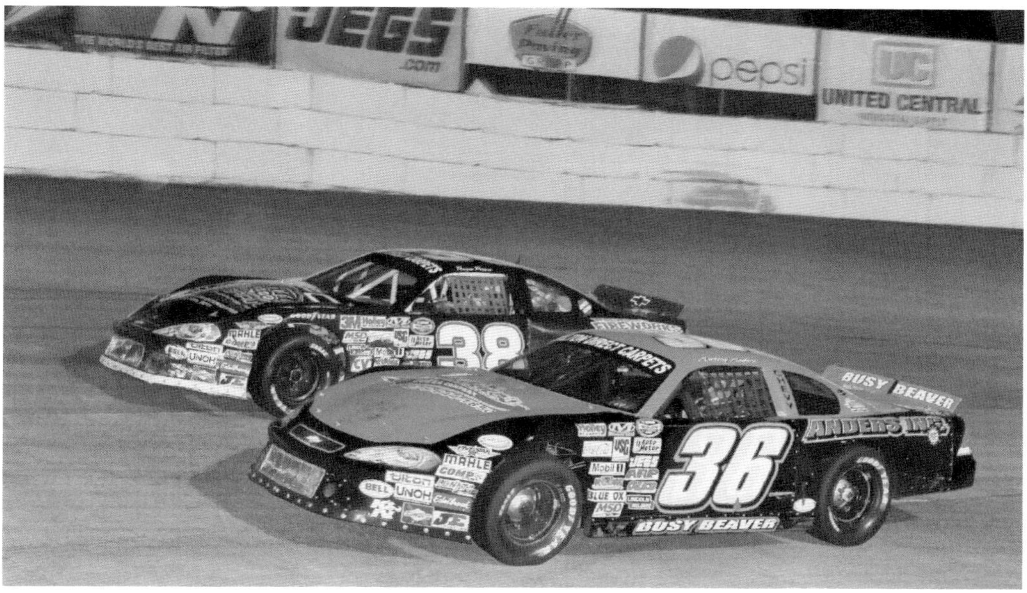

The Late Model Chevrolets of Anthony Anders (No. 36) from South Carolina and Royce Peters (No. 38) of Kingsport race side by side through the tight confines of Kingsport's turns three and four. Both drivers scored top-10 finishes in the track's 2012 points standings. (Photograph by Randall Perry.)

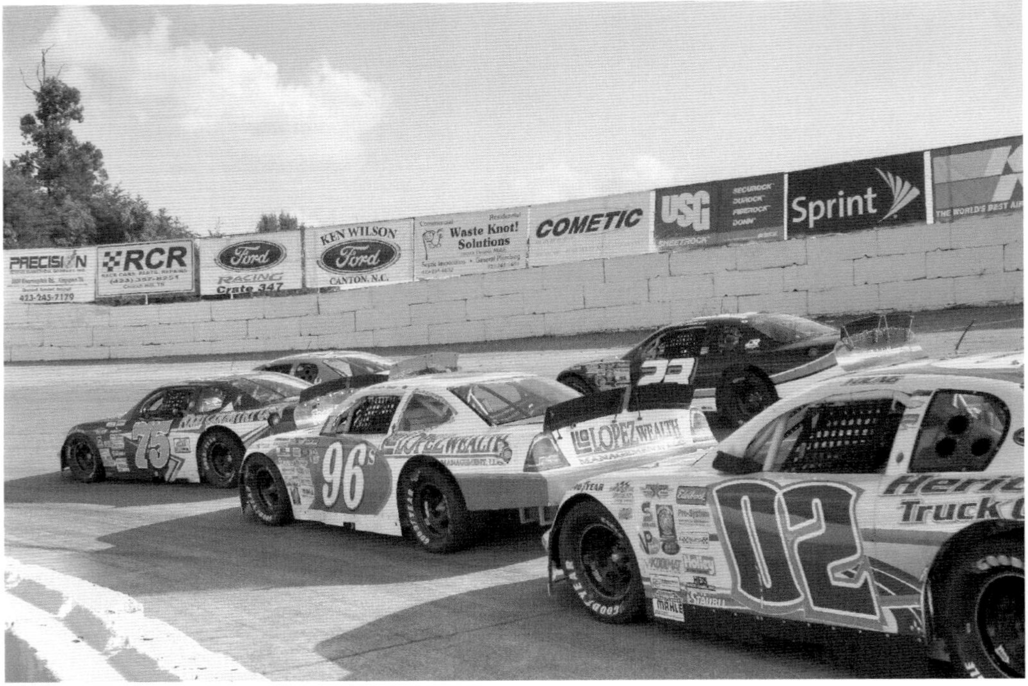

Caleb Holman (No. 75) leads the field through turn two in the Food Country USA 250 for the CARS Pro Cup series. Holman led 60 laps and finished sixth, while Wade Day (No. 96) captured the victory. J.P. Morgan (No. 23) finished second, but he won the encore race in 2013. (Photograph by Randall Perry.)

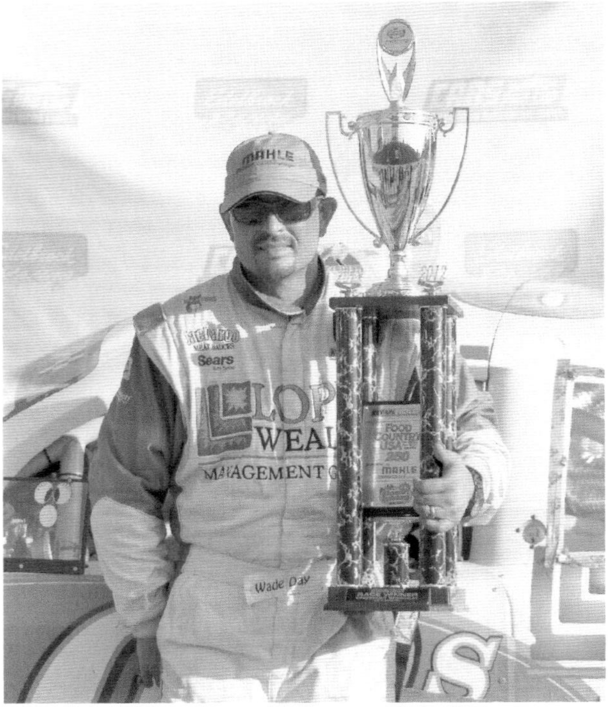

Wade Day displays the trophy for winning the 2012 Food Country USA 250 for the CARS Pro Cup series. A former Kingsport track champion, Day led 187 laps in the field's only Ford entry. (Photograph by Randall Perry.)

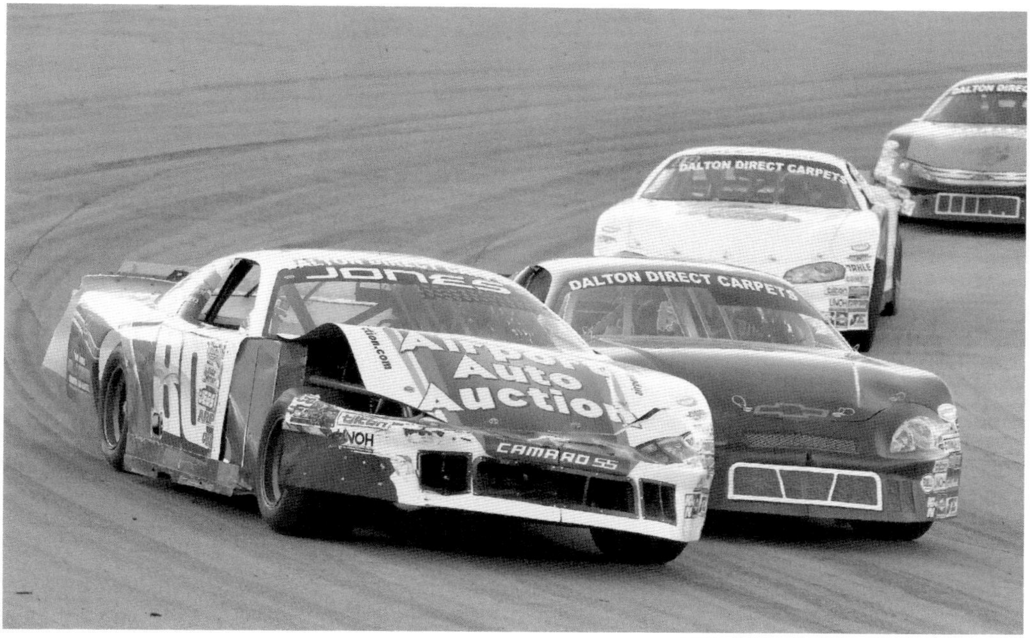

The Chevrolet of Blake Jones (No. 80) displays some typical short-track scars, as contact with another car damaged the right front fender and hood. His crew ripped away the fender and sent him back into battle during 2013 action. (Photograph by Randall Perry.)

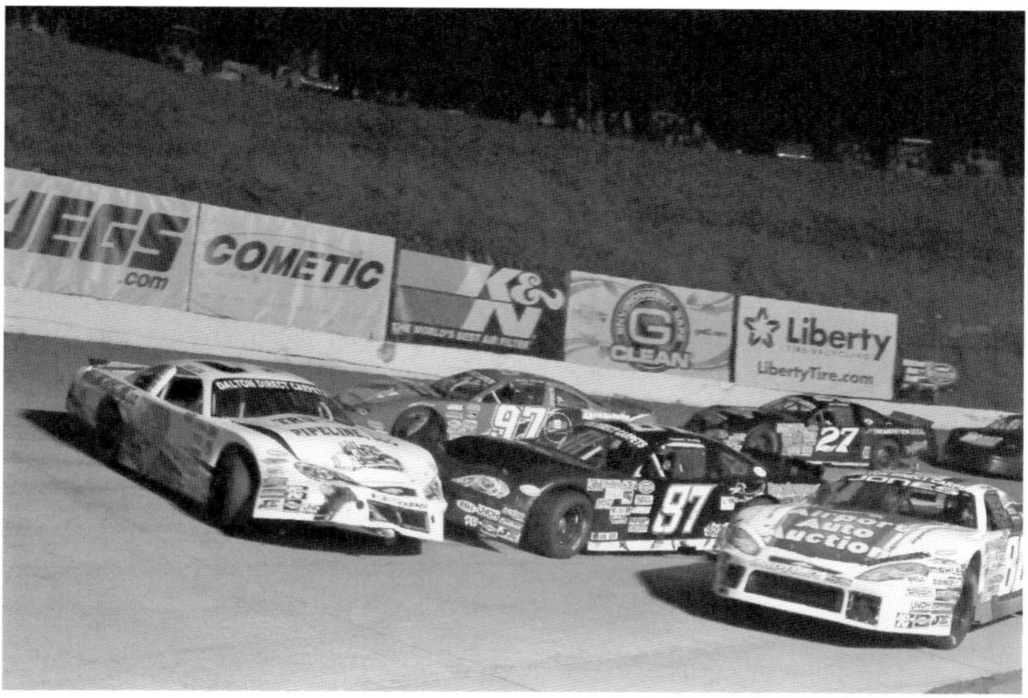

Adam Long (No. 3) gets sideways in front of a pack of cars, forcing others to take evasive action in April 2013. Included in this photograph are Zeke Shell (No. 97), Hayden Woods (No. 87), Blake Jones (No. 80), and Lee Tissot (No. 27). (Photograph by Randall Perry.)

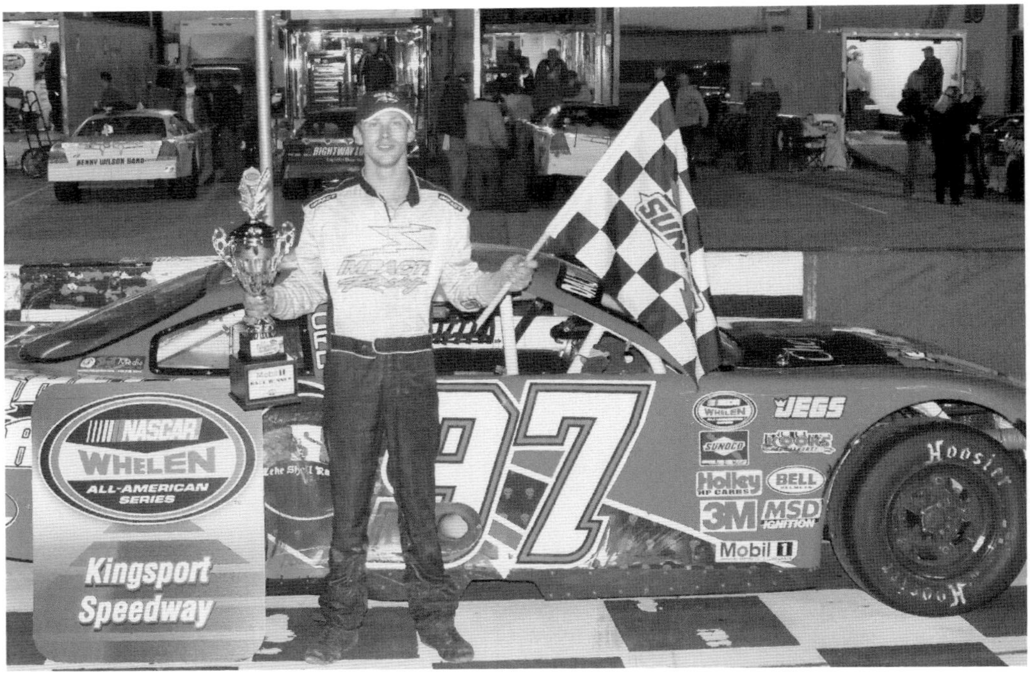

Zeke Shell of Johnson City, Tennessee, celebrates a Late Model victory in the summer of 2013. Shell finished second in the season Late Model standings, with three victories. He was ranked among the top 20 in NASCAR's All-American national points standings. (Photograph by Randall Perry.)

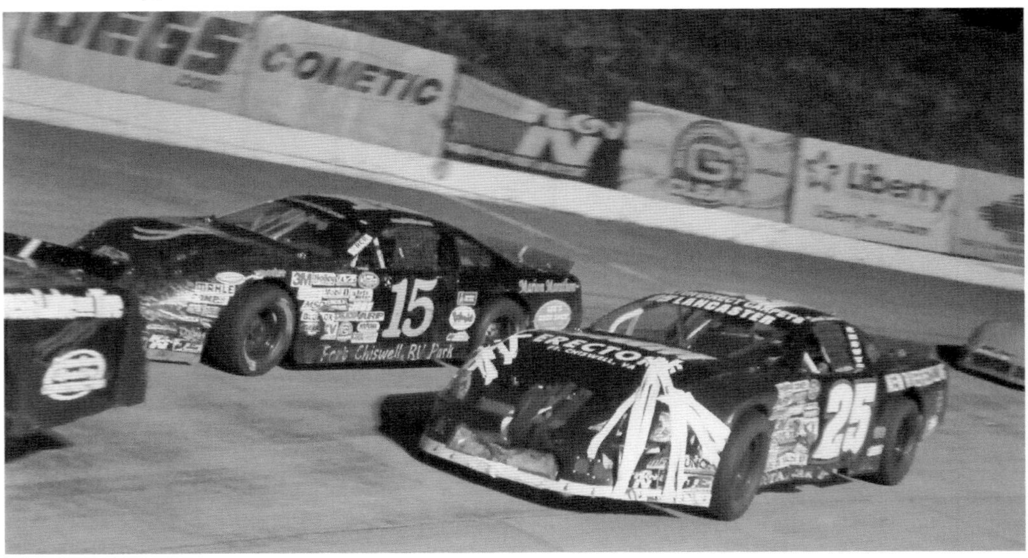

Derrick Lancaster (No. 25) captured a controversial victory in the Friends of Coal 125 race in October 2013. The Virginia driver tangled with Ronnie McCarty on the final lap, and the caution meant officials reverted to the previous lap for the finishing order. Law enforcement broke up the postrace altercation. Here, Lancaster races with Kyle Barnes (No. 15). (Photograph by Randall Perry.)

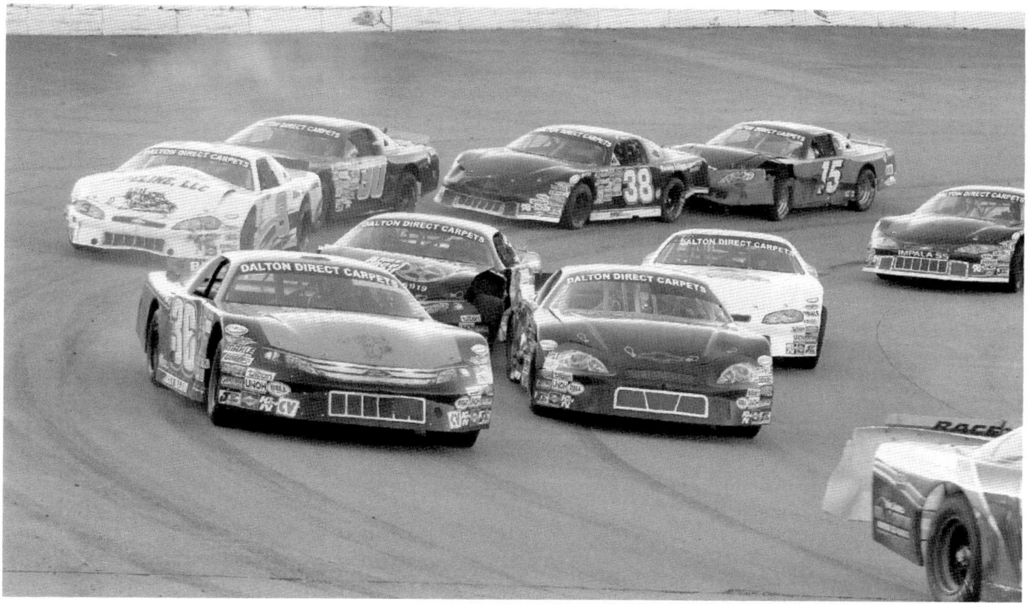

Cars bump and jostle while racing three-wide through the first and second turns at Kingsport Speedway. The old saying "rubbing is racing" often applies at this track. It would be tough to find a car in this photograph without at least some body damage. (Photograph by Randall Perry.)

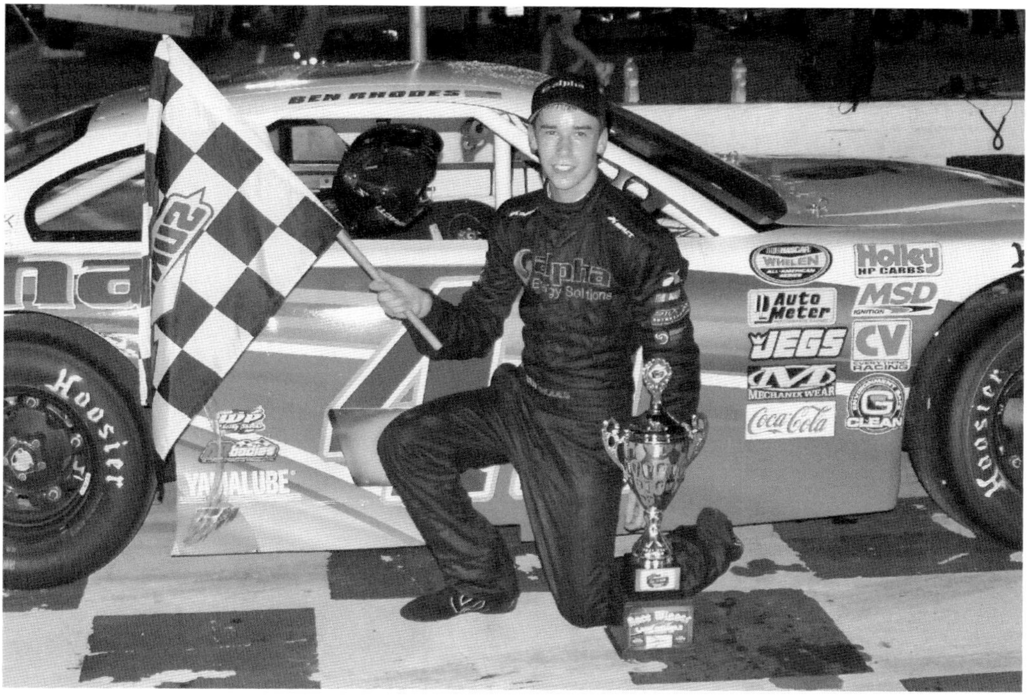

Ben Rhodes of Louisville, Kentucky, was named a member of the NASCAR Next program for rising drivers. He registered his first-ever NASCAR Whelen All-American Late Model victory at Kingsport in August 2013. The teenager has since advanced to compete in other divisions, including the NASCAR truck series. (Photograph by Randall Perry.)

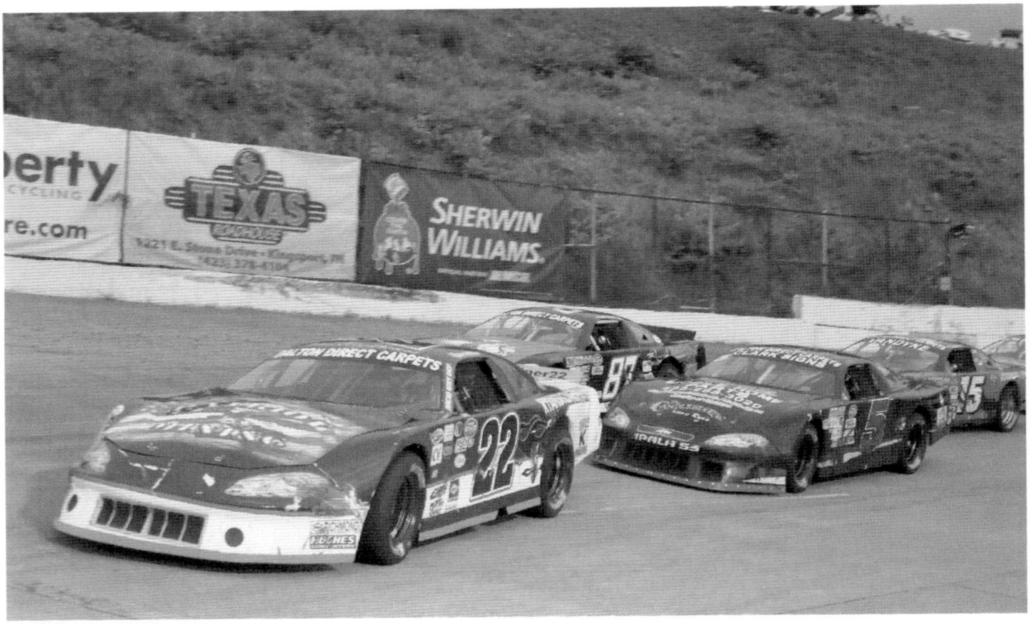

Ryan Stiltner (No. 22) charges off turn four with the late models of Ronnie McCarty (No. 5), Hayden Woods (No. 87), and Kres VanDyke (No. 15) in close pursuit. All have been regulars in recent action at Kingsport. Stiltner is the son of former Kingsport track champion Keith Stiltner. (Photograph by Randall Perry.)

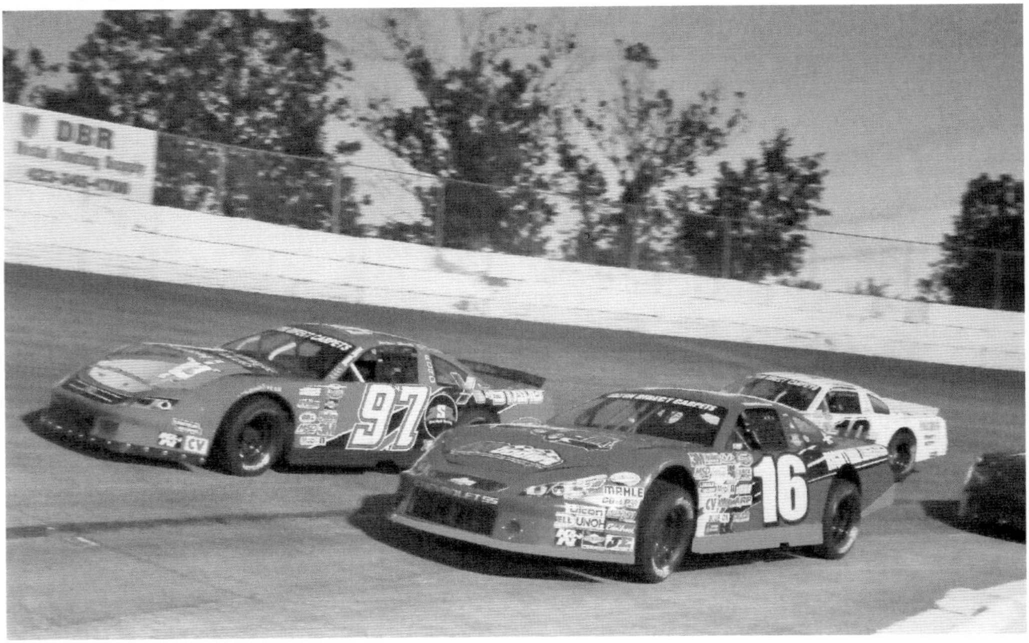

A tight pack races for the top spot during 2013 action at Kingsport Speedway. Zeke Shell (No. 97) runs upstairs, while Daniel Pope (No. 16) takes a lower line through the corners. Pope and Shell battled for the track title, but they finished second and third, respectively. (Photograph by Randall Perry.)

Karen Tunnell was named the manager and promoter of both Kingsport and Lonesome Pine raceways to begin the 2014 season. Tunnell brought years of experience as a race official to the job, embracing the challenge of running two tracks with a combined points program. (Photograph by Randall Perry.)

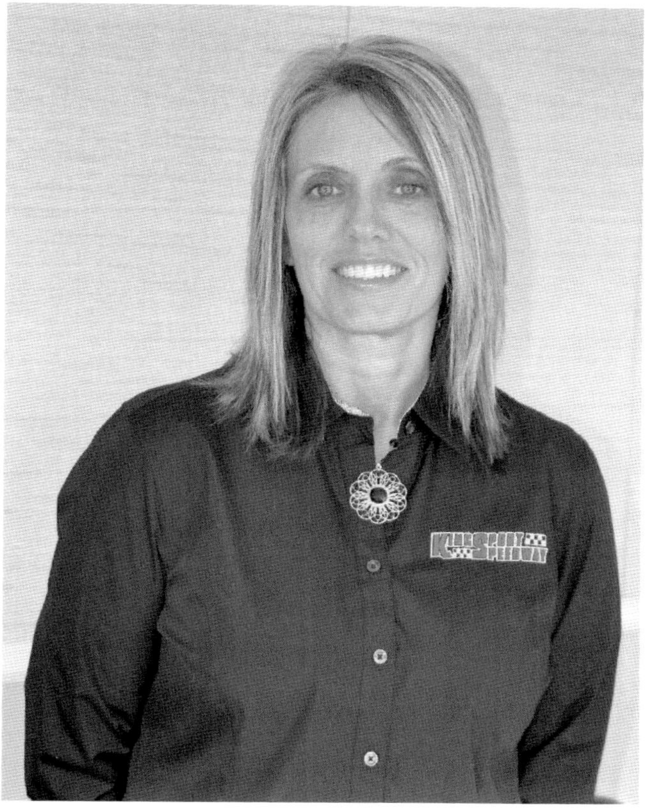

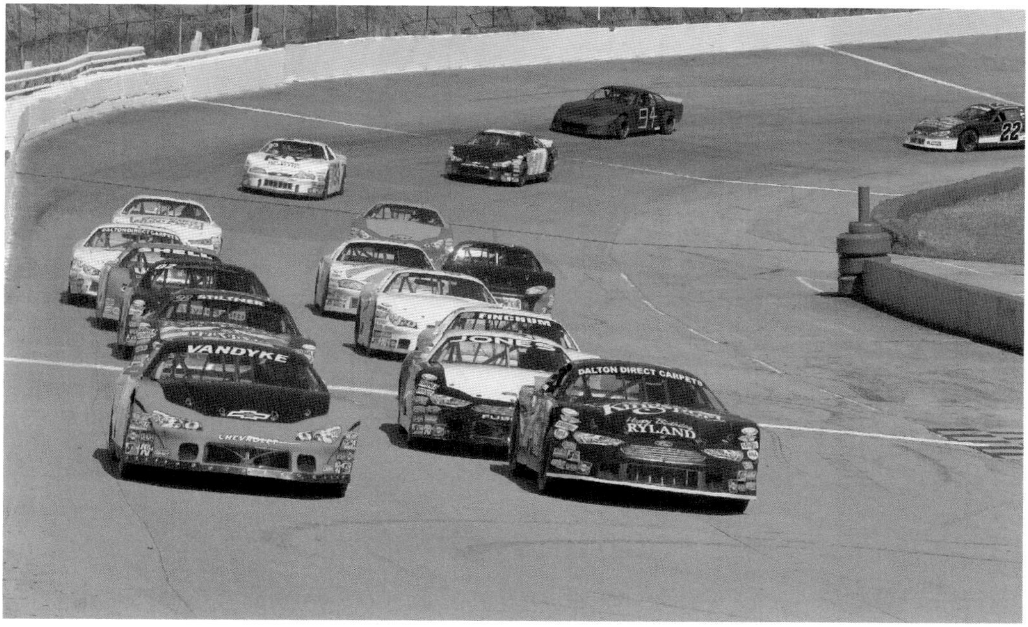

Kres VanDyke (No. 15) and Lee Tissot (No. 7) lead a snarling pack of Late Model drivers across the start-finish line in April 2014. VanDyke went on to claim victory in the 60-lap early-season contest, while Tissot ran a disappointing 11th. (Photograph by Randall Perry.)

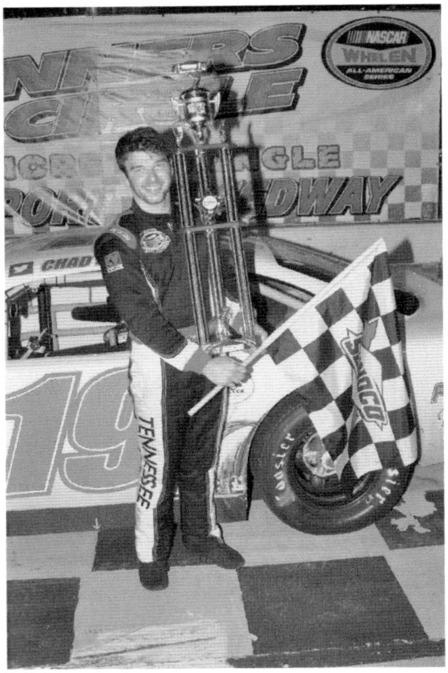

Chad Finchum hoists the trophy after claiming another Kingsport Late Model victory. The Knoxville, Tennessee, driver won a combined 19 races at Kingsport and Lonesome Pine to finish fifth overall in the 2014 NASCAR Whelen All-American national standings. (Photograph by Randall Perry.)

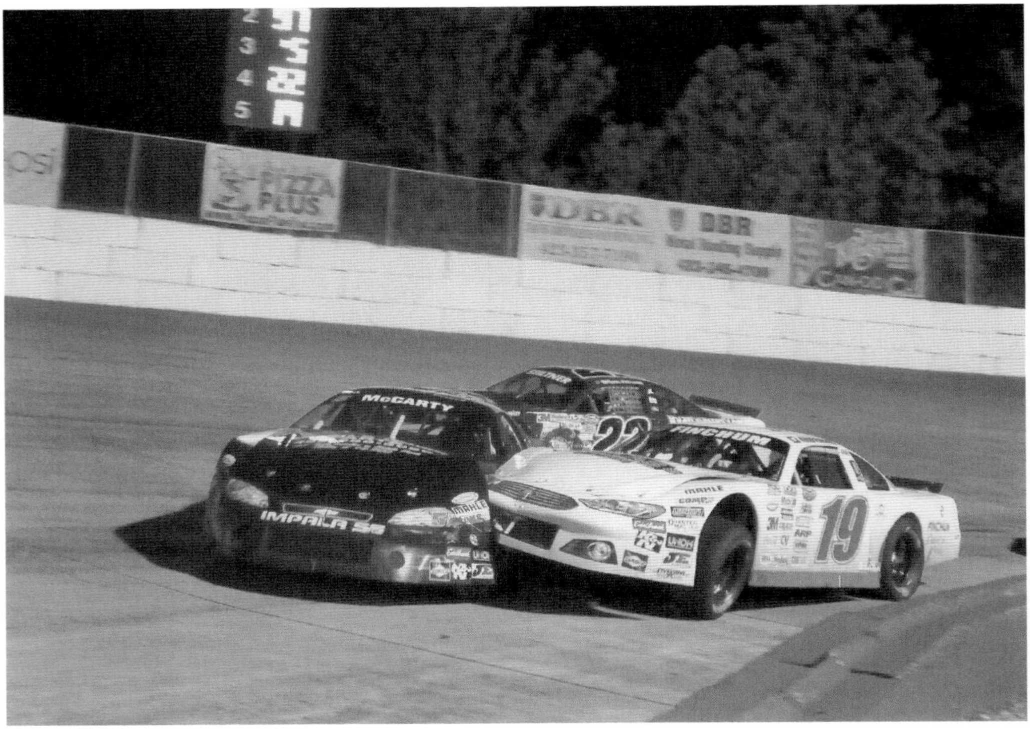

Chad Finchum (No. 19) and Ronnie McCarty (No. 5) get together in the second of two 35-lap Late Model feature races in May 2014. Finchum managed to finish fifth; McCarty was not so fortunate. Finchum won the first race over Kres VanDyke, who came back to win the second contest. (Photograph by Randall Perry.)

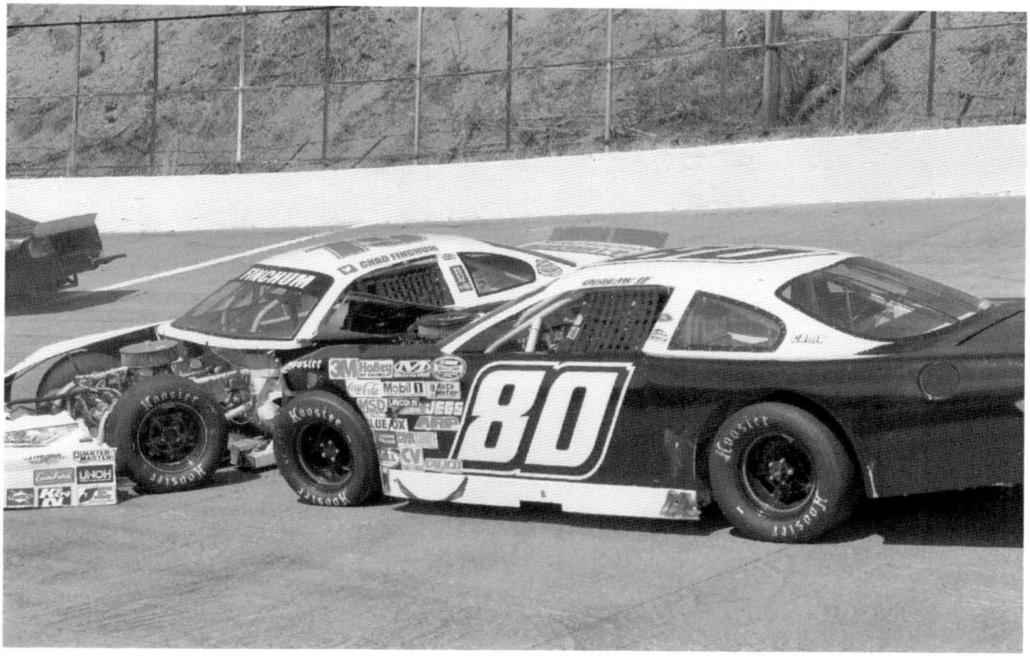

Chad Finchum (No. 19) and Blake Jones (No. 80) got together early in the race in April 2014, and both were knocked from contention that day. Finchum rebounded nicely, with a stellar 19-victory season. (Photograph by Randall Perry.)

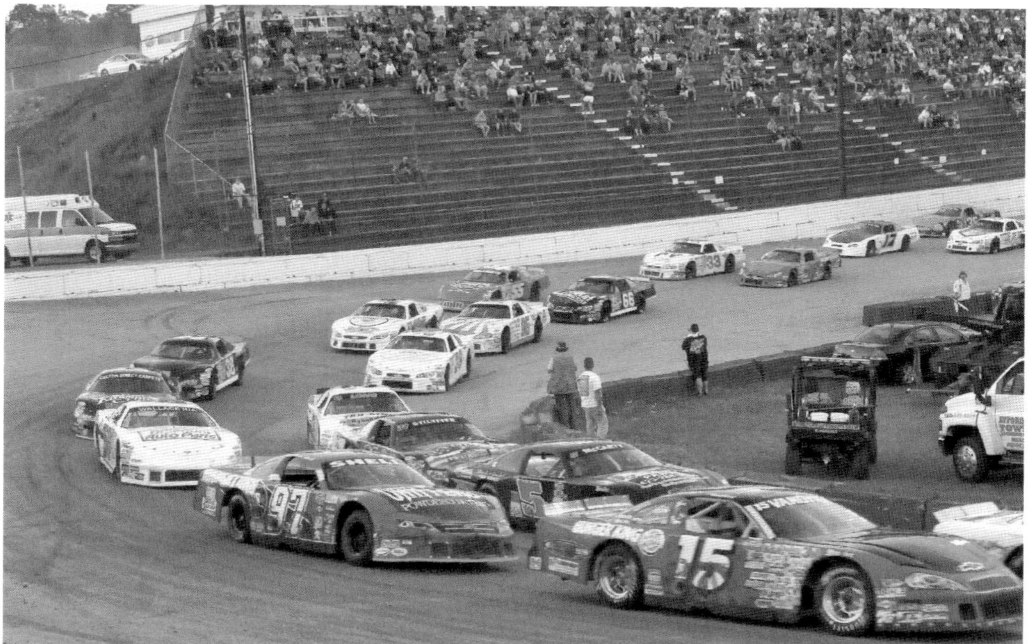

Drivers Kres VanDyke (No. 15), Zeke Shell (No. 97), Ronnie McCarty (No. 5), Ryan Stiltner (No. 22), Adam Long (No. 3) are part of a large pack of cars racing through turns one and two during the 2014 season. (Photograph by Randall Perry.)

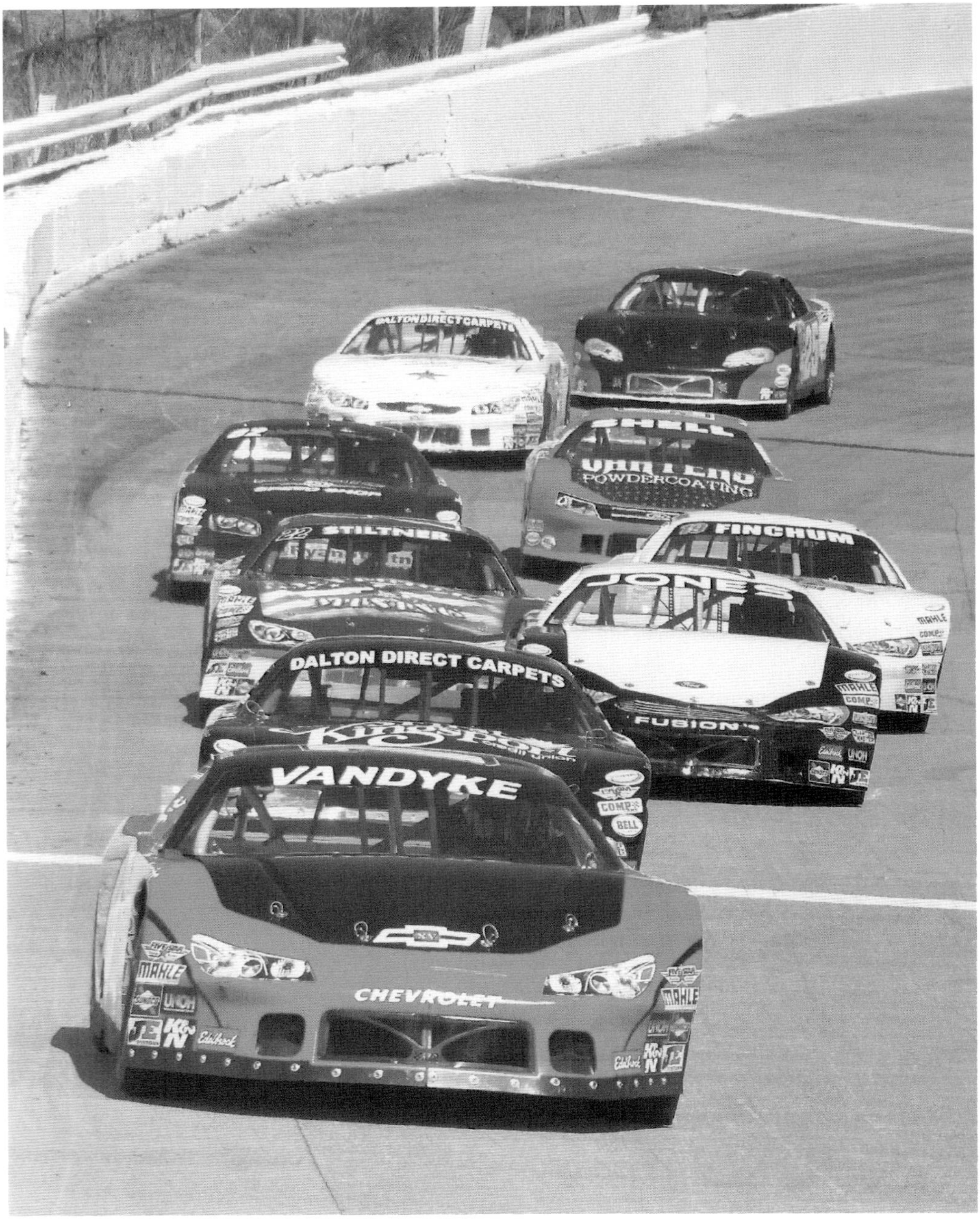

Kres VanDyke shows his back bumper to the field during 2014 NASCAR Late Model stock action at Kingsport. It was a familiar site, as VanDyke captured the Kingsport and Tennessee state championships in his red-and-black Chevrolet. With 10 victories and 37 top-10 finishes in 39 combined starts, he finished seventh in the nation. (Photograph by Randall Perry.)

9

Thrills and Chills

The overwhelming majority of events held during Kingsport Speedway's first 50 years were serious, often hard-fought contests between drivers determined to claim victory.

For competitors, auto racing is an expensive, potentially dangerous avocation, meaning they must risk more than financial investment while hurtling door-to-door into the turns at about 90 miles per hour. Dominance is the goal of many. But, for the majority of spectators, racing is entertainment. They drive to the track and plunk down hard-earned money to spend hours sitting on concrete grandstands, wagering that the program will entertain. Most are willing to tolerate extreme temperatures or racing's age-old nemesis, precipitation, to witness a great show.

Auto racing in the United States largely evolved from primitive fairgrounds tracks originally designed for horses. Sometimes, that fairgrounds element resurfaces at today's more modern speedways, in the form of bonus attractions, such as stunt shows, car-crushing monster trucks, demolition derbies, jet-powered vehicles, and tractor pulls.

Kingsport Speedway has hosted its share of such acts. Legendary drag racer Doug Rose blasted 20-foot flame trails from the afterburner of his jet dragster *Green Mamba*. Randy Warren drove a pickup truck on its left-side tires in the tradition of 1960s stunt shows, while his daughter Stacy crawled out the passenger window and did a full handstand as the truck was moving.

And then there was Benny "the Bomb" Koske, a former aerospace worker. The daredevil crawled inside cars or wooden caskets containing an explosive charge and flipped a switch that blew up his container. He put himself in a wooden coffin when he appeared in Kingsport in 1984. Luckily, Koske walked away. Insane? Perhaps.

More recently, the speedway hosted a Night of Destruction, with everything from daredevil stunts to races featuring old, decommissioned school buses. And the crowds loved it.

Cheap tickets were another fan favorite, and Kingsport Speedway offered a special program for many years. Known as FunFest Goes to the Races, the track hosted the community each summer as part of the Model City's popular community festival.

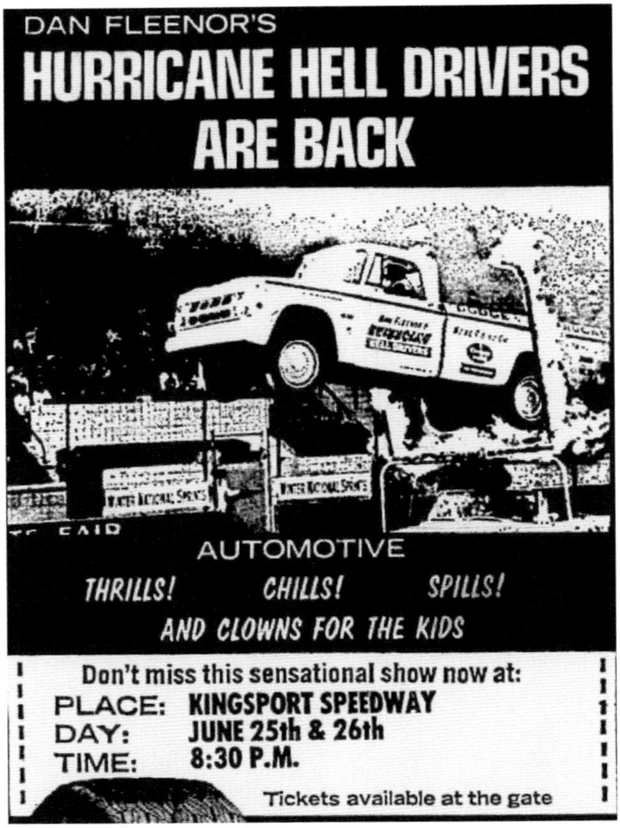

During the 1960s, Dan Fleenor's "Hurricane Hell Drivers" were among the nation's most noted thrill-show acts. They performed at speedways and at county and state fairs, wheeling identically painted vehicles through a series of hair-raising stunts. The show made multiple visits to Kingsport, including in the late 1960s, as shown in this advertisement. (Author's collection.)

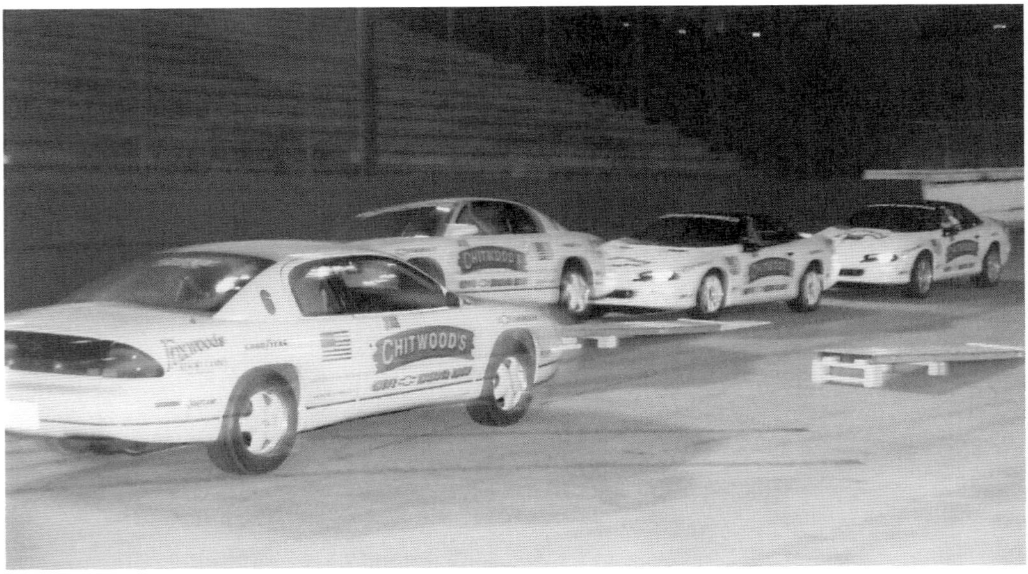

Auto thrill shows remain popular today, as evidenced by this more recent appearance by the Joie Chitwood Thrill Show at Kingsport. The stunts and thrills remain much the same as when Chitwood quit racing open-wheel cars to start a 40-year career in the thrill-show industry. (Photograph by Randall Perry.)

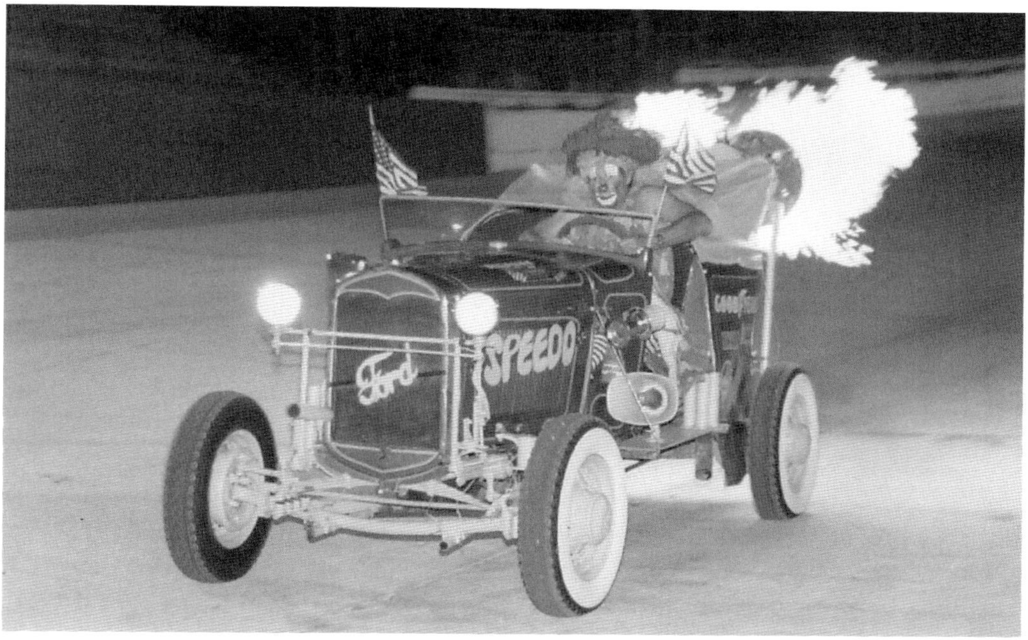

Jet-powered machines are a staple in drag racing, but several have appeared at Kingsport's oval, dating back to Doug Rose and the dragster *Green Mamba* in the 1980s. None are as outrageous as this jet-powered antique Ford piloted by Speedo the clown, who is not wearing any protective safety gear. (Photograph by Randall Perry.)

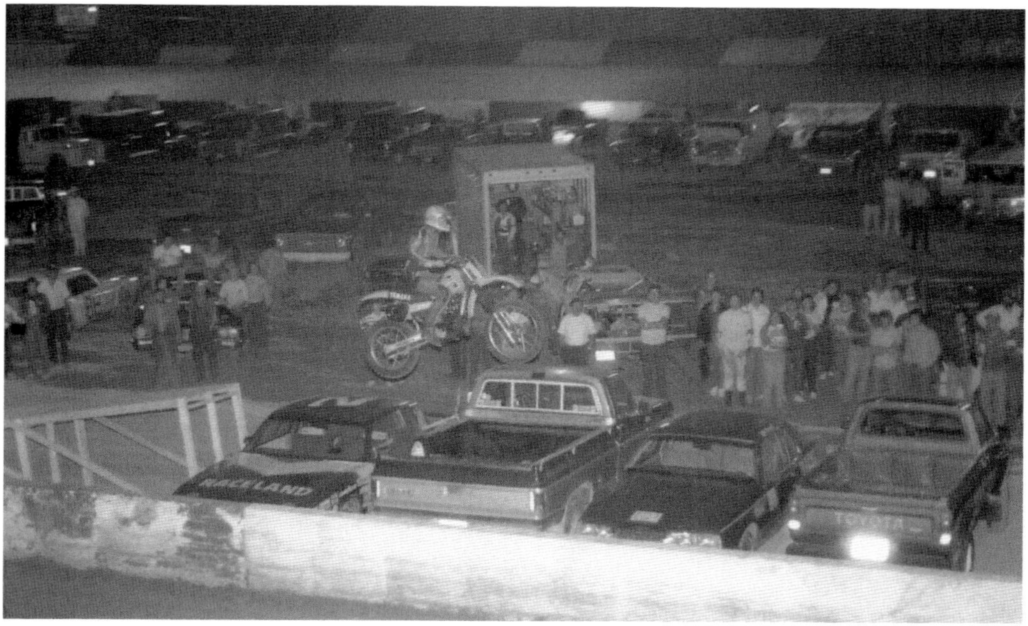

Motorcycle stunts have long been another short-track sideshow standard. When J.D. Stacy made Kingsport the flagship track for his Raceland program in 1984, he brought in stunt rider Gene Ledbetter to jump this lineup of vehicles, including the Raceland pace car. (Photograph by Mike O'Dell.)

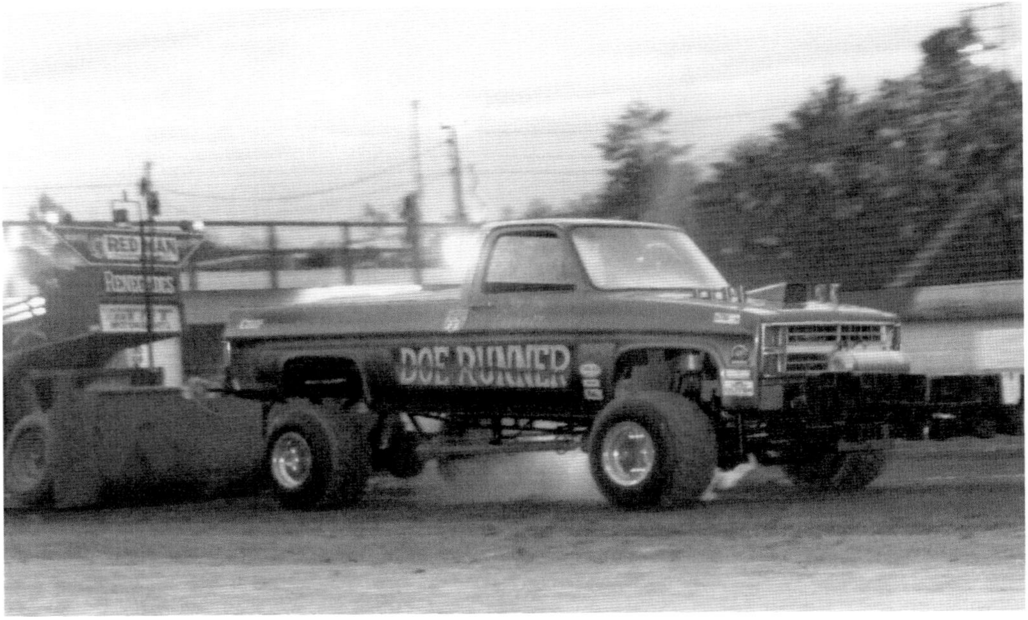

Truck and tractor pulls remain highly popular events and have attracted a variety of national series sponsors and television coverage. Here, the *Doe Runner*, a four-wheel-drive Chevrolet driven by three-time national champion Roy Everett of Georgia, pulls during a 1989 TNT series event in the Kingsport Speedway infield. (Photograph by the author.)

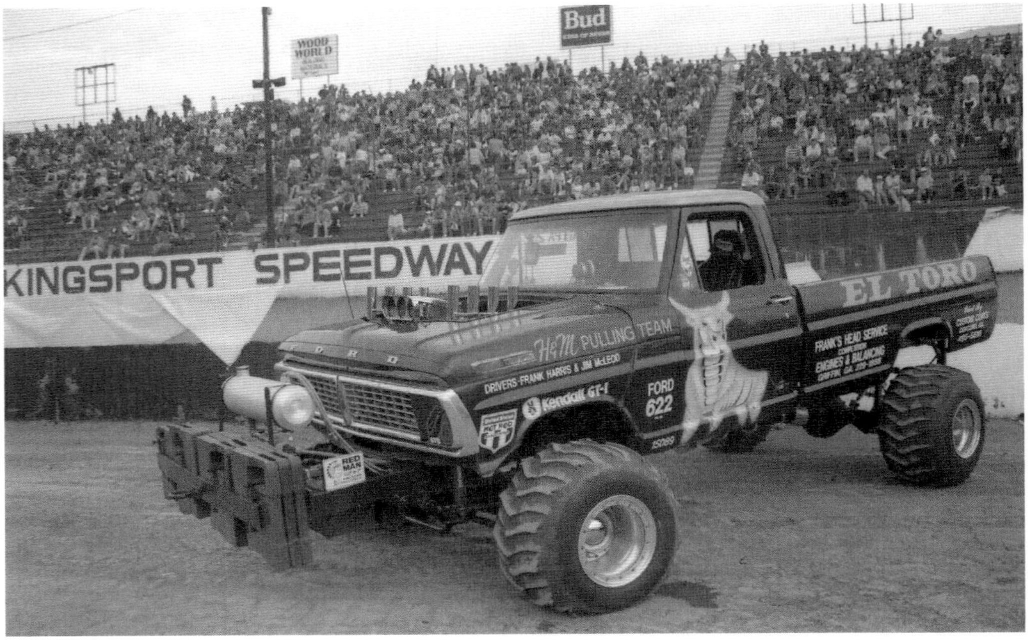

El Toro, a supercharged Ford four-wheel-drive pickup from Georgia, waits its turn to try and pull a weighted sled down a 300-foot-long dirt pulling track in the infield of Kingsport Speedway. A large crowd turned out to watch the competition at the 1989 TNT truck- and tractor-pulling event. (Photograph by the author.)

Young and old alike gravitate toward monster trucks, which combine a toylike appearance with some serious technology, brute horsepower, and crowd-pleasing antics. Here, Jeff Smith, in his Dodge *Rambunctious*, takes aim on a row of cars lined up in Kingsport's infield. (Photograph by Randall Perry.)

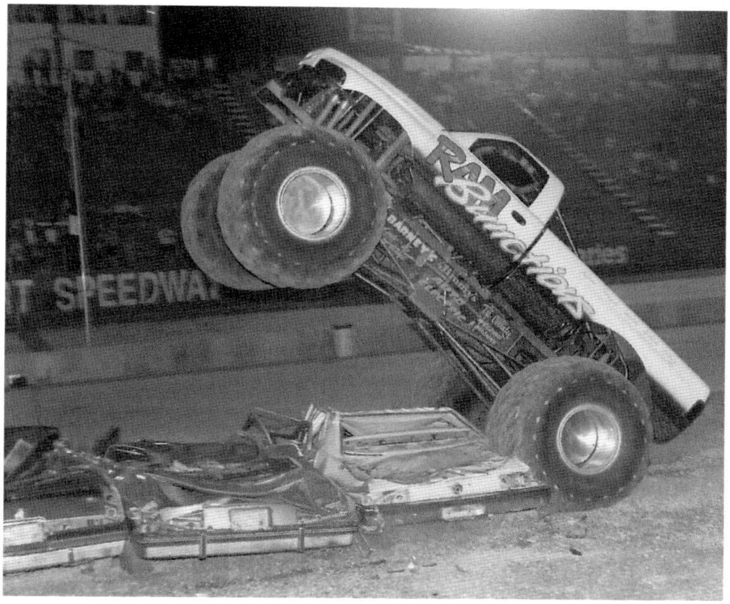

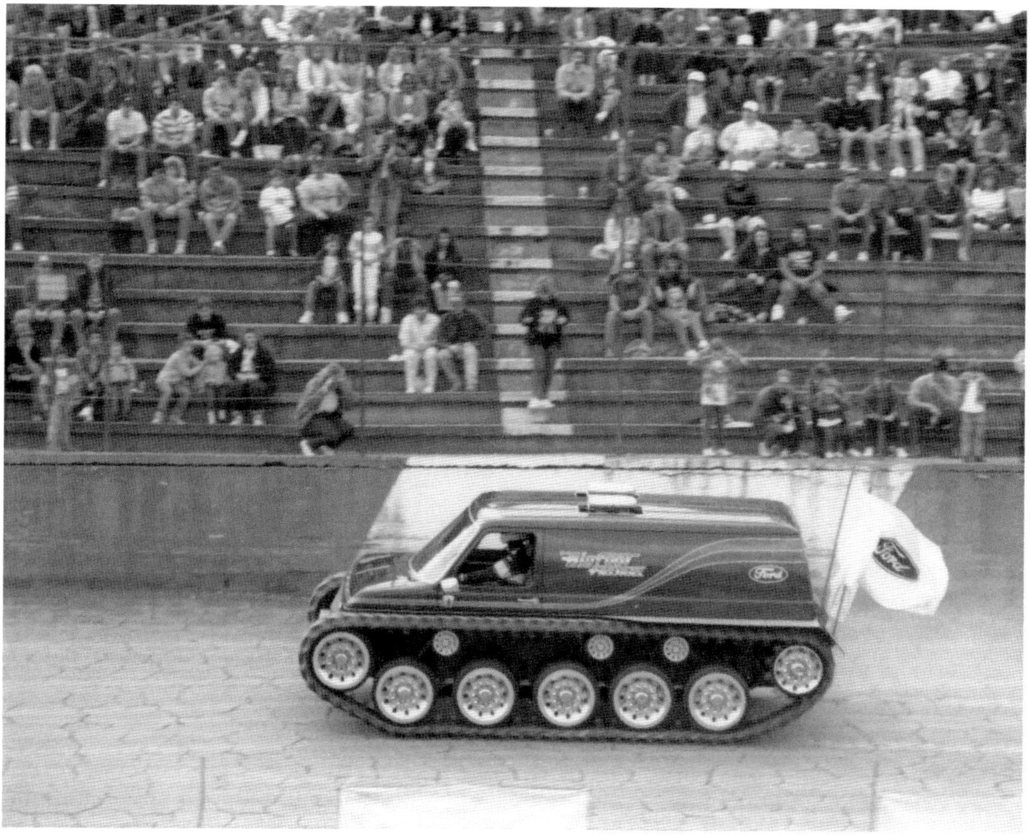

Fans strain to get a closer look at *Bigfoot Fasttrax* during a 1989 truck- and tractor-pull event at Kingsport. The chassis of the modified military personnel carrier featured a fiberglass Ford Aerostar replica body and two supercharged Ford engines. (Photograph by the author.)

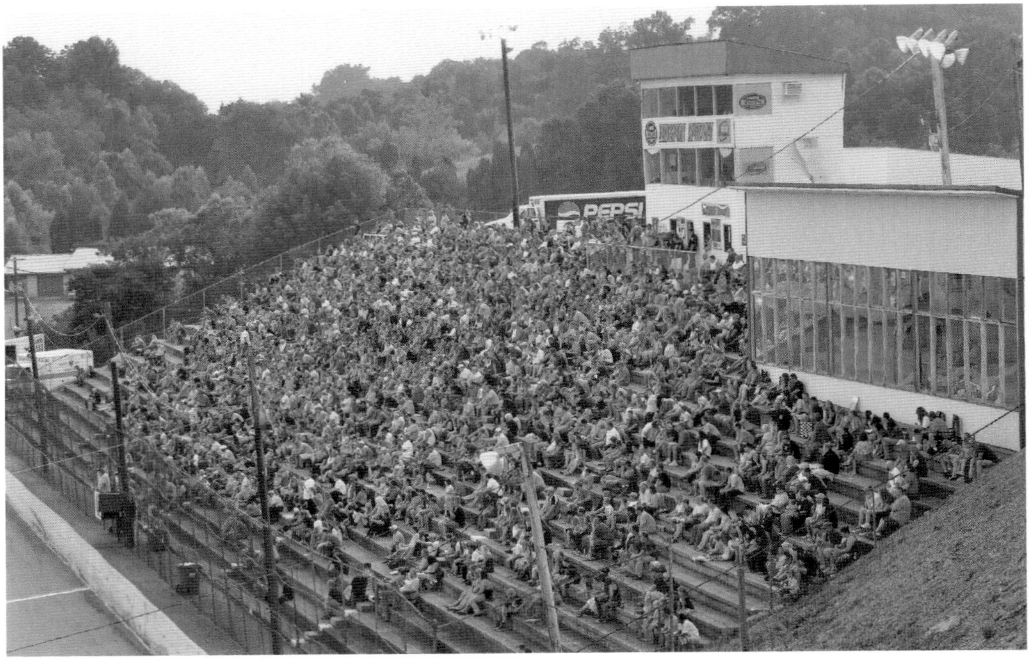

Thrill shows, like the 2013 Night of Destruction, have attracted some of Kingsport Speedway's largest crowds in recent history. The shows offer a wild array of different acts. As the hyperbolic radio commercial says, "We'll sell you the whole seat, but you'll only need the edge." (Photograph by Randall Perry.)

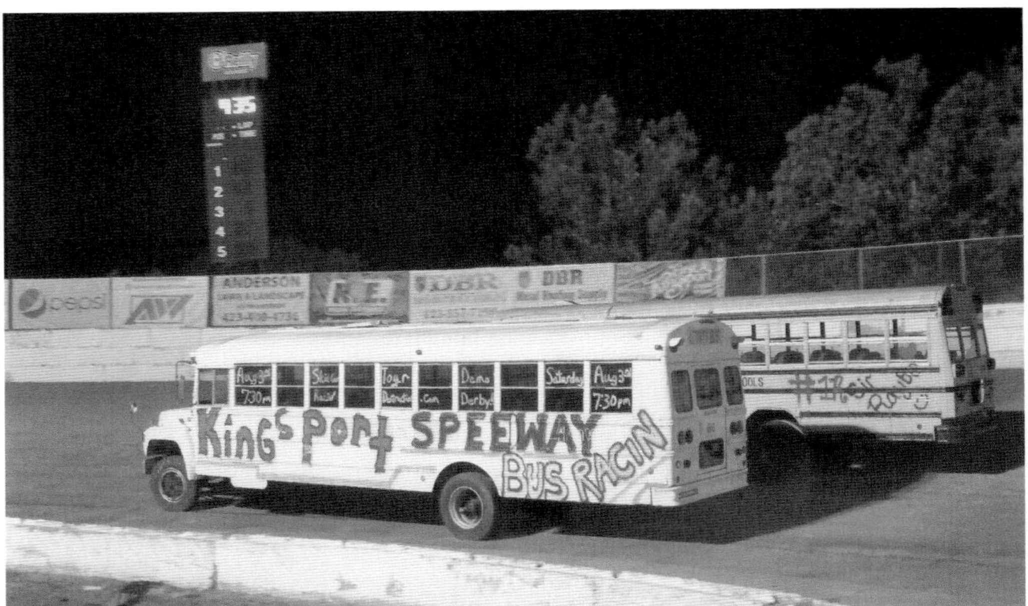

Among the more popular attractions during Kingsport's Night of Destruction were the sheet-metal-bending races featuring decommissioned school buses. No, really. (Photograph by Randall Perry.)

MAJOR TOURING SERIES RACE WINNERS

NASCAR Winston Cup/Grand National

Date	*Race*	*Winner*
May 23, 1971	Kingsport 300	Bobby Isaac
June 26, 1970	Kingsport 300	Richard Petty
June 19, 1969	Kingsport 250	Richard Petty

NASCAR Late Model Sportsman (selected)

Date	Race	Winner
August 8, 1981	Late Model	Jack Ingram
June 21, 1981	Late Model	Jack Ingram
March 28, 1981	Late Model	Tommy Ellis
October 19, 1980	Late Model	Brad Teague
August 9, 1980	Late Model	John A. Utsman
June 29, 1980	Late Model	Jack Ingram
June 1, 1980	Late Model	Geoff Bodine
October 21, 1979	Winston 250	Gene Glover
August 11, 1979	Late Model	Larry Utsman
July 1, 1979	Late Model	Jack Ingram
April 28, 1979	Late Model	Bob Pressley
October 1978	Winston 250	Harry Gant
August 18, 1978	Late Model	Bob Pressley
July 30, 1978	Late Model	Butch Lindley
June 30, 1978	Late Model	Bob Pressley
April 28, 1978	Late Model	Butch Lindley
October 23, 1977	Winston 250	Butch Lindley
August 12, 1977	Hayes Memorial 250	Butch Lindley
July 15, 1977	Light Memorial 200	Harry Gant
May 27, 1977	Miller 250	Harry Gant
April 15, 1977	Winston 250	Tommy Houston
August 27, 1976	Jim Hayes Memorial	Larry Utsman
July 2, 1976	Winston 250	Butch Lindley
March 26, 1976	Falstaff 150	Jack Ingram
September 14, 1974	Winston 200	Jack Ingram
September 1, 1974	Permatex 200	Jimmy Hensley
July 5, 1974	Falstaff 200	Jimmy Hensley
June 7, 1974	Miller 200	Ray Hendrick
March 15, 1974	Kingsport 150	Harry Gant
September 1, 1973	Permatex 300	Morgan Shepherd
September 2, 1972	Permatex 300	Jimmy Hensley
September 12, 1971	Permatex 300	Hank Maxwell
July 4, 1971	Falstaff 300	Harry Gant

NASCAR Grand Touring Series

Date	Race	Winner
April 13, 1969	Model City 500	T.C. Hunt
June 4, 1968	Model City GT 100	Buck Baker

NASCAR Grand American Series

Date	Race	Winner
September 5, 1970	Kingsport 300	Jim Paschal
May 3, 1970	Model City 300	Tiny Lund

NASCAR Modified

Date	Race	Winner
October 21, 1979	Winston 250	Richie Evans
October 28, 1978	Winston 250	Ron Bouchard
October 23, 1977	Winston 250	Ron Bouchard
November 14, 1976	Winston 250	Geoff Bodine

NASCAR All-Pro Series

Date	Race	Winner
August 7, 1999	Don Hill Pontiac 200	Billy Bigley Jr.

NASCAR Dash Series

Date	Race	Winner
April 11, 1997	Fairway Ford 125	Will Hobgood
October 20, 1979	Baby Grand 100	Dean Combs

UARA-Stars

Date	Race	Winner
September 14, 2013	UARA 150	Dillon Bassett
September 14, 2012	UARA 150	Dillon Bassett
May 4, 2012	UARA 150	Coleman Pressley
August 14, 2011	UARA 150	Lee Tissot
April 9, 2011	Courtesy Chevy 150	Brennan Poole
August 2010	Courtesy Chevy 150	Brennan Poole
March 27, 2010	UARA 150	Clint King
November 7, 2009	UARA 150	Brandon McReynolds
August 9, 2002	Sunshine Auto 125	Danny O'Quinn
May 25, 2002	UARA 125	Keith Stiltner
April 6, 2002	UARA 125	Wade Day

ProCup

Date	Race	Winner
August 25, 2013	X-1R 250	J.P. Morgan
May 17, 2013	Mahle 250	Clay Rogers
August 26, 2012	Food Country 250	Wade Day
July 19, 1997	Food City 250	Chad Chaffin

Hav-A-Tampa Dirt Series

Date	Race	Winner
March 25, 1995	Hav-A-Tampa	Bill Frye
August 25, 1994	Night Before Bristol	Scott Bloomquist
May 17, 1992	Hav-A-Tampa	Rex Richey

National Dirt Racing Association

Date	Race	Winner
October 13, 1985	Stroh's Invitational 100	Buck Simmons
March 30, 1985	Ram Tough 100	Freddy Smith
August 19, 1984	Ram Tough 50	Mike Duvall

ABOUT THE AUTHOR

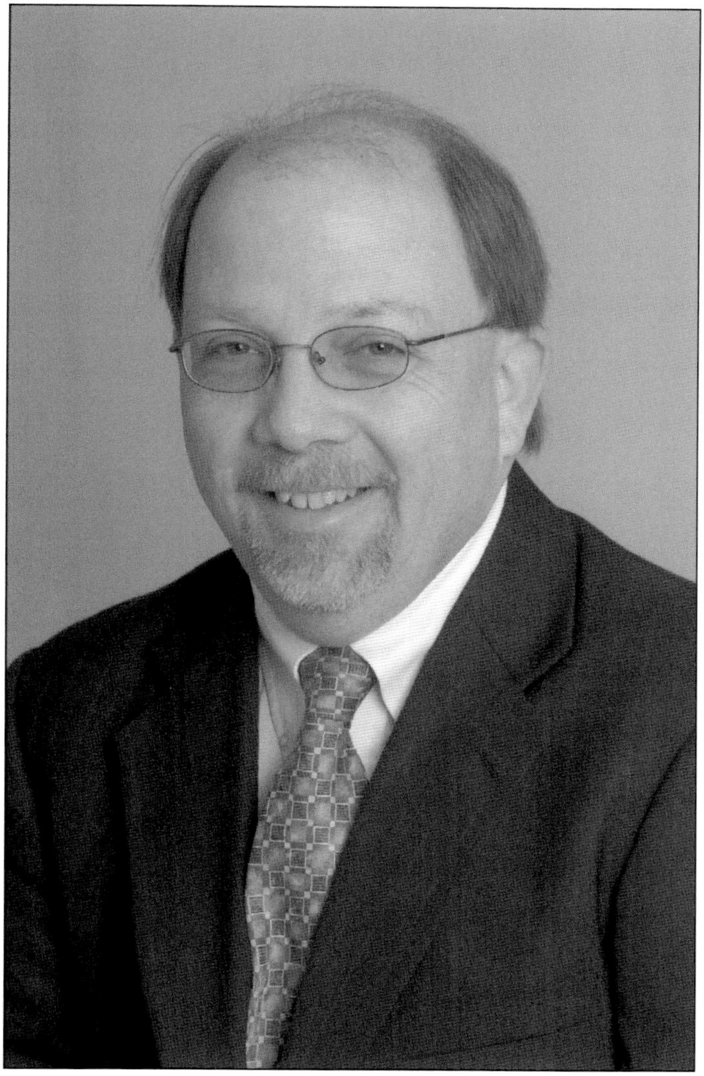

David M. McGee made his first visit to Kingsport Speedway in 1985. He currently serves as the senior public-address announcer at Bristol Motor Speedway and Bristol Dragway and as its unofficial historian. He is also a member of the executive committee of the Kentucky Motorsports Hall of Fame. McGee is the author of other motorsports titles, including *Bristol Motor Speedway* and *Bristol Dragway* (Arcadia Publishing) and *A History of East Tennessee Auto Racing* and *Tales of Bristol Motor Speedway* (History Press). McGee is a resident of Bristol, Tennessee, where he is employed as an award-winning journalist for the *Bristol Herald Courier* in Bristol, Virginia. A Kentucky native with a lifelong passion for motorsports, he holds a degree in journalism from Morehead State University. (Photograph by Earl Newkirk.)